WHAT DO THE STARS SAY ABOUT YOU IN 1995?

Whatever it is you seek—love, adventure, good health, or good fortune—Sydney Omarr has an astonishingly accurate forecast for every aspect of your life. For 18 exciting months from July 1994 to December 1995, you will learn:

- how to make your love connections strong and sexy
- how to fine-tune your life by coordinating your activities with the rhythms of the universe.
- how to use the Saturn sign to master a fear, phobia, or anxiety.
- how to use the moon and planets for prosperity
- how to relieve your stress and live a healthier life

So chart your very own star-studded course now—and make 1995 your best year ever!

SYDNEY OMARR'S DAY-BY-DAY ASTROLOGICAL GUIDE FOR VIRGO IN 1995

SYDNEY OMARR'S 1995 DAY-BY-DAY ASTROLOGICAL GUIDES
18 Months of Daily Horoscopes From
July 1994 to December 1995

Let America's most accurate astrologer show you what the signs of the zodiac and Pluto's welcome transit into Sagittarius will mean for you in 1995! Sydney Omarr gives you invaluable tips on your love life, your career, your health—and your all-round good fortune.

☐ **Capricorn**—December 22–January 19   (181166—$3.99)

☐ **Taurus**—April 20–May 20   (181131—$3.99)

☐ **Virgo**—August 23–September 22   (181123—$3.99)

☐ **Sagittarius**—November 22–December 21   (181239—$3.99)

☐ **Scorpio**—October 23–November 21   (181220—$3.99)

☐ **Aquarius**—January 20–February 18   (181174—$3.99)

☐ **Libra**—September 23–October 22   (181247—$3.99)

☐ **Leo**—July 23–August 22   (181212—$3.99)

☐ **Cancer**—June 21–July 22   (181190—$3.99)

☐ **Gemini**—May 21–June 20   (181158—$3.99)

☐ **Aries**—March 21–April 19   (181204—$3.99)

☐ **Pisces**—February 19–March 20   (181182—$3.99)

SYDNEY OMARR'S

DAY-BY-DAY ASTROLOGICAL GUIDE FOR

VIRGO

August 23–September 22

1995

A SIGNET BOOK

SIGNET
Published by the Penguin Group
Penguin Books USA Inc., 375 Hudson Street,
New York, New York 10014, U.S.A.
Penguin Books Ltd, 27 Wrights Lane,
London W8 5TZ, England
Penguin Books Australia Ltd, Ringwood,
Victoria, Australia
Penguin Books Canada Ltd, 10 Alcorn Avenue,
Toronto, Ontario, Canada M4V 3B2
Penguin Books (N.Z.) Ltd, 182–190 Wairau Road,
Auckland 10, New Zealand

Penguin Books Ltd, Registered Offices:
Harmondsworth, Middlesex, England

First published by Signet, an imprint of Dutton Signet,
a division of Penguin Books USA Inc.

First Printing, July, 1994
10 9 8 7 6 5 4 3 2 1

Sydney Omarr is syndicated worldwide by
Los Angeles Times Syndicate.

REGISTERED TRADEMARK—MARCA REGISTRADA

Printed in the United States of America

Contents

INTRODUCTION

Setting the Stage
for the New Century

There's a new feeling of anticipation in the air as we go to press. There's a new century ahead and we're rushing forward to meet it! Headlines in the business news at this writing tell the story: "American Rush to Funds That Invest Abroad" and "Bell Atlantic Takes a Big Step into Mexico." Globalism is here, marking the next step in our evolution as the year 2000 approaches. There is uncharted territory ahead, full of new kinds of experiences, thanks to the mushrooming progress of high technology. There are sure to be new people in our lives, perhaps introduced over a computer screen. In this year's atmosphere, when everyone's more optimistic, more in the mood for risk taking, there are fortunes to be made as well as potential disasters for the overly optimistic.

We're here to help you chart the future and make your dreams happen. Astrology can provide you with insight into the latest trends, help you know where the action is and how to take advantage of it. This book is designed to help you ride the crest of '95 and develop ideas that take full advantage of this year's potential by moving in harmony with the cosmic cycles. We'll tell you what's "in" this year, from what you'll be wearing to where the hot jobs are. We'll help you set up your daily agenda so you'll be doing the right thing at the right time.

The most valuable knowledge of all is self-knowledge, and here astrology has much to offer you. We take you through your sun sign and beyond, into the territory of eight other planets, to help you better know yourself and how you get along with others. Remember, astrology was one of the first techniques to give psychological insights, and it's still one of the best.

We'll give you basic information, so you'll know what astrology is all about. We'll tell you everything you need to know about your sun sign. And what's more, you can look up all your planets and find out how each contributes to your total personality. If you're interested in going deeper into astrology, there's a resource list where you can find computer programs, clubs, tapes, or classes to expand your knowledge and connect with fellow astrology buffs.

Many readers are fascinated by astrology's insights into their love lives. Sometimes the one you love is not the sign you thought you were supposed to get along best with. The fact is, our hearts don't always read horoscopes. Through our "love games," you might discover the sign you're *really* attracted to—it might come as a surprise! You'll find out how a tiny planet on the edge of the solar system can change our lifestyle and how it will color the next century.

The year 1995 marks a major shift in emphasis from the materialistic, sex-and-power issues of the eighties and early nineties to a higher vision of world unity. As the groundwork is laid for the new century, we'll be reborn on a new spiritual level, brought about by the movement of Pluto from Scorpio, where it has been transiting for the last ten years, into Sagittarius. You'll be able to understand this main event of 1995 and where it will affect your life, for we've devoted two chapters to this powerhouse planet.

Your daily forecasts will guide you with wise advice, lucky numbers and moon-sign positions, so you can plan your activities in harmony with the lunar and numeric cycles.

Let this guide help you set your personal stage for the next century and make 1995 the happiest, most productive, successful year ever—in both your personal and professional lives!

CHAPTER 1

What's "In" This Year

The year 1995 is sure to be full of breakthroughs. To help you plan ahead, here are some predictions about where we're heading and what we'll be doing and wearing in '95. These ideas are based on the movement of the distant, slow-moving planets, Uranus and Pluto, into different signs. When this happens, there is a major shift in mass consciousness that shows up throughout our lives. In April, Uranus, the planet of sudden changes, electricity, and high technology, moves into Aquarius, the sign it rules, marking a big push forward in technology. Though we have covered Pluto's move into Sagittarius elsewhere in the book, we'll also be considering some more specific ways it will influence our daily lives in this chapter. Jupiter's move into Sagittarius, the sign it rules, is another powerful factor that reinforces expansive new directions in Jupiter-ruled areas.

What You'll Be Wearing

Throw out those black clothes and buy some clothes in bright colors, especially the Sagittarius-influenced colors: purple, turquoise, and orange.

Clothes will have a strong ethnic look influenced by exotic cultures, especially those with a strong religious tradition. Fashion should also have the flavors of Spain and Latin America. Clothing styles at this writing are beginning to show a more monastic, religious look. This will increase; we may all be wearing updated versions of monk's garb or ecclesiastical robes.

Outdoor hunting, fishing, and forest gear is very important this year. We should be deeply into the environmentally conscious trend, with the use of natural fabrics and with motifs that proclaim ecology consciousness. We may be buying these in ecological themed stores and washing them in environmentally conscious laundromats.

Other inspirations could be the Renaissance look, inspired by fashions of the early sixteenth century. Horse themes will abound in prints and equestrian hunt-club looks.

Clothes and clothing advertisements will trade the current sexual emphasis for a more spiritual, visionary approach.

Look for revolutionary high-tech ways of selling clothes by television, CD, or computer mail. Home shopping networks will become more sophisticated. If you want to buy an Italian suit, for instance, you might be able to view the store's merchandise on your computer screen and place an order by fax. The merchandise would then arrive the next day by high-speed mail.

What Music You'll Be Playing

Music will be more cross-culture oriented. At this writing, Paul Simon and Sting have got the right message. Blends of many cultures will influence the arts, which will become a true melting pot. At the same time, many cultures will be trying to maintain the purity of their artistic tradition.

Look for new kinds of music that is more spiritually uplifting, if not actually promoting a specific religious message. The sexual content of the early nineties Pluto-in-Scorpio period should be deemphasized as we begin to look for a higher meaning in life.

The New Games Will Serve Many Purposes

Computer games will become more sophisticated and used as a means of teaching or preaching. Learning through creative play will become more important, as will games and recreational activities that bring people and families together. In this area, there will be many new multipurpose toys, which have an extra message besides that of play.

Portability Is a Key Word

"You *can* take it with you" is the motto this year, as Pluto and Jupiter in Sagittarius have us all up and running! Everything will be on wheels. You'll be able to pack up your office in a suitcase and roll it anywhere you like, with ever-smaller personal computers, fax modems, printers, and portable phones.

Global Communication Gets Easier

Thanks to computerized communication, via E-mail and computer bulletin boards, you'll be able to talk to someone in Australia or China more easily and inexpensively than ever. Perhaps there will be a computer that instantly translates your message into any language you wish.

With so much shopping by mail, home-delivery services will be expanded and central mail-processing systems like Fedex should thrive, becoming much more sophisticated.

What You'll Be Reading and How

Publishing, which is ruled by both Sagittarius and Jupiter, is in for a rapid sea change. Books will be visualized on computers or video disks; magazines will come in CD-ROM versions. Soon we'll be able to tap into a library anywhere in the world and log in the latest magazines on our home PCs. Imagine dialing a number and having your favorite magazine appear on your TV or computer screen!

Desktop publishing will make it possible for many new players to get into the publishing field. How about writing that novel on your computer and selling it via a worldwide computer bulletin board system instead of a bookstore?

Along with a new philosophical and spiritual emphasis in the kinds of books you'll be reading, look for new interpretations of ancient manuscripts. This is also happening in astrology, as scholars are reinterpreting many ancient writings in a more astrology-friendly light.

What You'll Be Driving

The year 1995 marks the beginning of an era of incredible global mobility. While some may choose to stay home and log onto a world communication network, others may investigate the new possibilities in long-distance travel, such as high-speed trains and planes, solar-powered vehicles, and many high-tech advances in automobiles

Individual mobility also takes new leaps. Possibly, the current trend in rollerblading is only the beginning of a trend toward individual movement that is fast and fun. High-speed water transport is another way to get where you're going in record time.

What You'll Be Doing

There's a good possibility that many of us will be going back to school, either to expand our personal interests or to keep up with the new technology. Both Pluto and Jupiter in Sagittarius, which rules higher education, will make this a prime area for creative development and profitable investment. Being an intellectual, a philosopher, or a theologian will be "in" this year, as the life of the higher mind is accented.

Studying via videotape, tapping into libraries with a computer, accessing many teachers easily on electronic bulletin boards open up many educational options to a wide market. It will be easier to learn than ever.

Where You'll Be Going

The trend toward more ecologically oriented vacations and resorts designed to enhance the environment will grow. So will action-oriented vacation places, which offer either physical diversion or a chance to improve mental skills. Spiritual retreats to ashram-like resorts and vacations with a religious emphasis, such as pilgrimages to sacred places, are hot now.

Since Sagittarius is the sign of the gambler, this too, is

an area of expansion, especially in underdeveloped countries and on Native American reservations.

Sagittarius-influenced places should be where the action is: Latin America, Madagascar, Singapore, Czechoslovakia, Spain, Hungary, Moravia, Australia. Within countries, important areas are Tuscany and Naples in Italy, Provence and Narbonne in France, Toronto in Canada, Nottingham and Sheffield in England, Cologne and Stuttgart in Germany. In the United States, there's Toledo, Seattle, Pennsylvania, the Mississippi River, and New Jersey.

Your Financial Life

When Jupiter, the sign of expansion, is strong in the sign of bankers, this should be prime time for investments. There should be a much more favorable atmosphere for taking risks. The danger is in overoptimism. However, after the past few years, this time should definitely be an upswing.

Your Love Life

Interracial, cross-cultural romance could be the new trend, as long-distance communications turn to matters of love and romance. There should be many new ways to meet people, as the "personals" expand to accessing worldwide databases of eligibles. You may be able to review photos or videos of potential romances, meet and network through computer or video parties, or meet each other over a video phone.

After the telephone sex of the Pluto in Scorpio period, it's possible that lovemaking will enter the high-tech realm of virtual reality. You may find yourself falling in love with a computer-designed mate.

Hot Careers

The sky's the limit in publishing now, especially for those with high-tech knowledge. Higher education, as well as all areas of the travel business, publicity, and advertising, should present new options.

Religion will be redefined, as more people seek out the spiritual life in new ways. Churches could be revitalized as forces in the community and as educational and recreational institutions. This should open up many new kinds of careers within the context of church or spiritual life.

The sign of the Centaur, Sagittarius has always been associated with hunting, hunters, and archery. It's anyone's guess how these might provide career opportunities now.

Banks and banking, the legal and judicial profession, and any professions involving foreign trade, such as the import–export business, should present many new kinds of opportunities. Look for new high-tech areas of these businesses for the best way to get in on the ground floor.

Sagittarius Personalities in the News

New Sagittarius stars will be coming to center stage, and some old favorites should be still in the news:

On TV, there's Phil Donahue, William F. Buckley, Lesley Stahl, Don Johnson, Susan Dey, Donna Mills, Robin Givens, Charlene Tilton, Richard Pryor, Morgan Brittany.

In film, there's Steven Speilberg, Woody Allen, Kim Basinger, Jeff and Beau Bridges, Liv Ullman, Jennifer Beals, Teri Garr, Tim Conway.

In music, there's Bette Midler, Tina Turner, Frank Sinatra, Sinead O'Connor, Dionne Warwick, Beethoven.

In sports, there's Chris Evert, Cathy Rigby, Suzy Chaffee, Katarina Witt.

In fashion, there's Gianni Versace and Thierry Mugler.

Mega-celebrities: J.F.K. Jr., Darryl Hannah, Caroline Kennedy Schlossberg, Jane Fonda, Tom Hayden, Strom Thurmond.

CHAPTER 2

The Big Switch—Pluto, the Power Planet, Enters Sagittarius

1995 is sure to be a year of changes, from Teenage Mutant Ninja Turtles to religious cartoons, from dirt bikes to the World Car, from movies about Dracula to those about angelic visitations. These are only a few possible manifestations of a powerful shift in energy that marks a turning point in the decade and points us toward the coming millenium.

We're talking about the power of Pluto. This tiny planet orbiting on the farthest reaches of our solar system moves into Sagittarius on January 17 until April 21, then retrogrades back into Scorpio to tie up loose ends and take care of unfinished business before it finally moves onward to Sagittarius for good on November 10. Those who are new to astrology may well wonder how a planet so far away that it has never been accurately mapped can affect our daily lives. Pluto is the mystery planet of the zodiac, one that can't be seen, but makes a powerful impact on mass consciousness.

We'll sense Pluto power in a subtle shift in the atmosphere. Things may seem to be looking up, after the chaos and confusion of the early nineties. Now we may feel it's safe to take more risks, as if a heavy cloud has lifted. Will the second half of this decade be the "Gay Nineties" of the twentieth century? Perhaps. There will definitely be a more optimistic feeling in the air.

Yet Pluto power is as shrouded in mystery as the planet itself. We're never quite sure what is in store. This is the planet of extremes, discovered at the same time as atomic energy, as the growth of extreme political movements and the rise of mass media. Astrologers associate Pluto with intense forces that lie dormant within collective systems and burst forth, like the invisible power of the atom—or like the planet's namesake, the legendary god of the underworld, who opened the earth and kidnapped the innocent maiden Persephone, precipitating a drama that resulted in the creation of the seasons. With Pluto, our lives are forced to evolve in important ways.

Discovered in 1930, Pluto has never been explored by a satellite like other planets. Scientists guess that it is about four thousand miles in diameter. We do know that Pluto has a large moon, almost a twin planet, and a very eccentric elliptical orbit, which means it spends a varying amount of time in each sign, as little as eleven years or as long as thirty-one years. It takes about 248 years to travel through the entire zodiac. Astrologers decided that Pluto had certain qualities, based on observation of its effects in horoscopes and on what was happening at the time of the planet's discovery. Therefore, some of the most important characteristics of Pluto are power, elimination, mass movements, collective phenomena, the media, mob psychology, atomic energy, sexuality, healing, recycling, the occult, and needs for control.

We've been feeling Pluto power throughout our lives on a personal and collective level, especially during the past eleven years, when Pluto has been traveling through Scorpio, the sign it rules. Like the underworld of the mythical god Pluto, this planet inspires fear of the unknown. Perhaps that is why, during this time, there was so much fascination with vampires (*Dracula*), the more sinister side of the occult (*Kiss of the Beast*), violent aberrations (*Silence of the Lambs*), or underworld organizations like the Mafia. But the purpose of Pluto is to transform in order to transcend. Just as in the transcendance of death there is immortality, Pluto forces one to evolve to the next stage by confronting the lessons of the sign it is passing through.

As Pluto slowly moves through a single zodiac sign, important transformational changes take place that impact the whole generation born during that time. Since 1984, Scorpio-type influences were all over our mass consciousness. In order to understand how Pluto works, let's look at the past dozen years.

In Scorpio, we see Pluto at its most potent. Scorpio is

the sign of sex, and nobody can deny that our lives were saturated with a hypersexual charge—from blatant sexuality in advertisements, to suggestive clothing (in the Scorpio noncolor, black), to S&M themes in fashion, to telephone sex, to readily available adults-only videos, to the proliferation of sexually oriented adult-entertainment clubs.

At the same time, there was the Plutonian emphasis on life or death—abortion issues, suicide, mercy killing, AIDS, and new strains of sexually transmitted diseases. The irony is that, at the same time as we were bombarded with all kinds of sexual titillation, we were also told that sex is dangerous—we must have "safe sex." Sexual issues were hot topics politically, as abortion attitudes and candidates' sex lives made headlines. Rape, sexual harassment, child sexual abuse, and incest made the rounds of media talk shows and tabloids, as deep secrets were exposed and publicly analyzed.

On another note, Pluto in Scorpio brought Scorpio media celebrities to prominence: Roseanne Arnold, Demi Moore, Whoopi Goldberg, Julia Roberts, Goldie Hawn, Jodie Foster, Dan Rather, and Kevin Kline, to name a few. These people transformed our ideas about what is acceptable in our mass media—whether it's a pregnant nude, a fat bluntly sexual comedienne, the first black woman to receive an Academy Award, or the female producer–star who calls the shots with studio honchos. Other stars with strong Pluto influences in their horoscope, such as Madonna and Michael Jackson, pushed the limits of what is acceptable behavior on and off screen.

In retrospect, it might be useful to examine what some of the events of this Pluto in Scorpio transit accomplished. For better or for worse, we're freer than we were at the beginning of the eighties. The AIDS epidemic forced us to confront our attitudes toward death and toward those with different sexual orientation, resulting in a new tolerance and understanding. When many prominent personalities, such as Arthur Ashe, Rudolf Nureyev, Rock Hudson, and Halston, died, everyone was touched. Transvestite trends like "voguing" and exposure in plays like *M. Butterfly* or in films like *The Crying Game* opened up more formerly hidden areas and moved American culture to new levels of acceptance.

We also had our own personal life-or-death issues

aroused with the transformation of the insurance and health-care industries. Many of us were involved in self-transformation via the New Age and human potential movements. Plastic surgery became more prevalent as celebrities resculpted bodies with liposuction, inflated lips, and lifted faces. Body building became another way to take control of our looks and transform them, as muscle-bound heroes in life-or-death action dramas like *The Terminator* and *Die Hard* became male ideals.

Power became a key word at this time, becoming an adjective to describe meals, as in "power lunches" or exercise, as in "power aerobics," computers, such as the Macintosh PowerBook or in the titles of omnipresent self-help books. The news stories headlined those who manipulated others to get power, such as David Koresh and the Branch Davidian cult or, more positively, corporate takeovers and leveraged buyouts that transformed or eliminated entire industries.

On the other hand, there were many teachers who were dedicated to empowering others, helping people free themselves from their own limitations so they can progress in their own development. And there were endless talk shows, where people who had experienced different forms of abuse or limitation shared their experiences with the public.

At this writing, as Pluto is winding up its stay in Scorpio, we are already seeing harbingers of change. The focus is gradually shifting to Sagittarius-ruled topics and trends in the mass culture. A fire sign, Sagittarius is ruled by Jupiter, the planet of expansion and optimism, which sounds like very good news. After a decade of black clothes and sexual allusions everywhere, we can expect the happier, brighter influence of Sagittarius. This will be amplified the first year, brought in with trumpets, when Jupiter joins Pluto in Sagittarius as well. (Coincidentally, 1995 is the year that the satellite Galileo is scheduled to rendezvous with Jupiter.) Perhaps, with this expansive shift in energy, cures will be found for the sexually transmitted diseases that have plagued us over the last decade.

Sagittarius is a sign concerned with the big picture and with how everything relates to everything else. It is the sign of wisdom, of philosophers, educators, teachers, priests, and gurus.

Sagittarius is connected to expansion through transportation. That means all kinds of new forms of transportation are possible—high-speed trains, automobiles powered by a new kind of fuel, different forms of air travel. Some astrologers are predicting more space travel (and possibly space visitors). Already, Ford is announcing a high-tech "World Car," which will be built and sold in the same form all over the world. An expensive and risky effort, this uniform global design is sure to characterize new marketing ventures in the late nineties, when open world trade will allow more contact between cultures than ever before. Historically, this was the time when Venice rose to world power, expanding its territory throughout the Mediterranean. In the 1750s, England became a major world power, gaining territory after winning the French and Indian War and establishing itself as a major force in India. In the thirteenth century, the Mongol empire, the largest in history, was at its height, spanning from the Siberian steppes to the Danube and the Arabian Sea. With the current world trade talks forging new relationships between governments, the result is sure to be an entirely different kind of international trade that transcends each country's individual concerns and ethnic biases.

Pluto pushes to extremes, so we'll see the extreme form of Sagittarius-ruled things. This sign is connected to higher education, philosophy, religion, and expansive thinking in general, and should be good for universities. We'll be much more concerned with the quality of education overall, and with educating our children to have higher aims and ideals. The mid-eighteenth century, a previous Pluto-in-Sagittarius time, was one of the great times for philosophy, when great philosophers challenged the prevailing religions and created the humanistic movements of the period. This was the time of Diderot, Rousseau, Hume, Voltaire, and the Encyclopedists, who foreshadowed the French Revolution. At an earlier time, the philosopher Thomas Aquinas attempted to reconcile reason with revelation in the mid-thirteenth century.

Religion is also Sagittarius territory, and with the planet of extremes activating religious and metaphysical issues, it's anyone's guess how this energy will manifest. Already we are experiencing edicts from the pope against sexual permissiveness, calling for a "higher vision," a new morality to guide youngsters who are without values. We will probably get the extremes of either side, with conservatives becoming more dogmatic and liberal metaphysical leaders also asserting themselves. Through the many spiritual and philosophical confrontations, we in the West must learn to deal with spiritual challenges as well as material ones. At this time, the West is apprehensive about dealing with the more spiritually oriented Islamic cultures, which should bring some interesting developments as this transit moves on. In previous years, Pluto in Sagittarius was the time of the Spanish Inquisition (early 1500s) and the Protestant Reformation.

In America, religious conservatives have been addressing Scorpio issues like abortion and homosexuality for the last decade. Now this sector of the Right is reaching out into education and other social arenas. The influence of religion on education and vice versa is sure to be a much-debated topic. So will the creation of values and ideals in our children, and motivating them to prepare for higher education.

Sagittarius influences several countries, and it is amazing how many are in the news at this writing, either as scenes of controversy (Dalmatia, Czechoslovakia, Hungary, Arabia), or as up-and-coming places (Australia, Chile, Provence in France, Spain, Singapore). With Hong Kong changing hands, it is possible that the headquarters of Far Eastern trade will now move to Singapore.

Sagittarius is the sign of optimism and risk taking. Expect a surge in gambling casinos, lotteries, and chance-taking ventures. The downside of this is that we must guard against overspending and too much risk taking without any practical grounding. It is very important that we understand how to manage money so it can do the most good.

This is one of the most animal-loving signs of the zodiac, so Pluto here should push our concern for animals to the limits. Expect animal-rights activism to hit a new high. Sports involving animals, especially horses, like racing, polo, horse shows, jumping, and rodeos should be super-popular.

As a sign that represents hunters, Sagittarius has an affinity for Native Americans. As we go to press, there is discussion about whether Native Americans should operate gambling casinos (also Sagittarius-ruled) on their reservations.

In the media, "global" is the key word, as networks go

worldwide via satellite. Expect more programming from foreign countries, with subtitles, and more CNN-type stations that give intensive round-the-globe reporting. Shopping via television will extend to worldwide shopping. You might be able to buy a suit made in Hong Kong or glassware directly from Italy via your television shopping channel. American television is already reaching out to viewers in different countries, especially with MTV Latino (Sagittarius rules Spain and strongly influences most Latin countries), its new Latin American TV network that will include twenty countries in the Caribbean and South America.

Sagittarius rules publishing, so it's no surprise that the very first book was printed in China in 576 A.D. under Pluto in Sagittarius. It's fascinating to speculate about how Pluto will transform the publishing business beyond recognition in the next twelve years. Perhaps future readers will buy this book on computer disk, complete with astrology programs to calculate their own charts. The whole field of desktop publishing has many ramifications for the publishing industry, as more players will be entering the industry and publishing on a smaller scale. At the same time, the way books are being sold is changing, with block-long book markets, cafes, and celebrity autograph signings revising our ideas of what a bookstore can and should be. Perhaps the bookstore–coffee house will become a new center of intellectual and philosophical discussion.

Will the printed word be conveyed by paper, by computer screen, by voice, or by "virtual reality," where you'll experience the contents via electronic simulation of reality? One thing's for sure—after this transit, publishing will take off in some exciting new directions.

On a deeper, evolutionary level, this is a time when those who have strongly held, inflexible beliefs and principles may realize that there are many different points of view that are equally valid. Over the past few years, there has been much dissolution of the boundaries between cultures, and now the actual cross-contact will begin, thanks to global media and new trade agreements. It is those cultures which are firmly grounded in traditional beliefs who will feel the transformational impact of other points of view, because it will be very difficult to remain isolated. The religious extremes that have caused wars in Czechoslovakia, the Middle East, and Ireland will no longer be able to operate as before. Thanks to the new global society, there will be much more exposure to other cultures, and mutual exchange of ideas and beliefs. And through these exchanges, we should be able to arrive at a more universal understanding and tolerance of each other's version of truth.

True, there will be many who will not want to risk their safe, established belief systems, or who will fiercely resist any challenges, as happened during the Spanish Inquisition. But the most positive way to use this transit is through an attitude of mutual sharing, realizing that differing belief systems have valuable insights to why we are here. By exposure to many diverse points of view through the new globalism of Pluto in Sagittarius, we should have a much better understanding of who we are as a world culture and what our higher purpose might be.

For each one of us, Pluto's passage through this sign of truth and high moral vision should bring us many experiences, though a clash of cultures, through philosophical discussions, and through unprecedented exposure to the rest of the world, which will force us to examine our own point of view. And by confronting our own belief systems, we should come closer to discovering an authentic individual personal truth for ourselves. Many of us will be shaken up and transformed; however, in doing so, we may also have a true experience of a higher power.

CHAPTER 3

Where's Pluto in Your Life?

With Pluto making the most waves this year, you'll want to know how it will affect your personal life and what kinds of happenings to expect. You don't need an astrologer to do this; you can make a very good estimate yourself, and learn some more about astrology while doing it. The object of this exercise will be to find the Sagittarius area of your astrological chart, which is where Pluto will be passing through.

First, you must find out your time of birth, preferably from your birth certificate or hospital records. Then, look up your rising sign in the chapter in this book.

Now you're ready to make an estimated astrological chart. We'll keep it as easy as possible. Draw a circle and divide it into twelve equal segments, like a clock. Write your rising sign down at the nine o'clock position, then list the other signs in sequence on each spoke of the wheel, working counterclockwise around the circle. For example, if you have Leo rising, then Virgo would be on the eight o'clock spoke, Libra on the seven o'clock spoke, Scorpio on the six o'clock spoke, Sagittarius on the five o'clock spoke, and so on around the wheel.

When you've completed your wheel, you'll have a rough approximation of the outline of your horoscope chart. It will not be exact, because there are many different systems of dividing the wheel, based on the precise moment of your birth. Each chart is a unique portrait of a moment in time, after all. However, this chart can be quite useful in helping you determine what Pluto is plotting in your life.

Each segment of the wheel, in astrology language, is called a "house" and represents an area of your life. The spokes are called "cusps" and the sign on the cusp is the one that influences happenings in that house. Each house is numbered, starting with the rising sign, which governs the first house, then working downward, counterclockwise around the wheel. Again, assuming Leo is the rising sign, the second house would have Virgo on the cusp, the third would be Libra, and so on. Sagittarius, our key house this year, would be on the 5th-house cusp. So our Leo-rising reader would have major emphasis on the 5th-house matters this year.

To make life even easier for you, here's a list of rising signs and their Sagittarius houses:

Aries rising—ninth house
Taurus rising—eighth house
Gemini rising—seventh house
Cancer rising—sixth house
Leo rising—fifth house
Virgo rising—fourth house
Libra rising—third house
Scorpio rising—second house
Sagittarius rising—first house
Capricorn rising—twelfth house
Aquarius rising—eleventh house
Pisces rising—tenth house

Pluto is a transformative planet; therefore, the events in your life that it activates are designed to bring up beliefs or circumstances that have been holding you back or limiting you in some way, and either resolve or eliminate these issues. You change with Pluto in such a way that there's no going back. However, the point is to help you evolve, to bring up those deep, hidden areas from Pluto's underworld "cave" for reexamination, and to eliminate or change them if necessary. Look upon this time of soul searching as a process that has been made necessary by the course of your life, not something that just happened out of the blue. It was precipitated by your previous attitudes and patterns. So rather than resist the elimination of old, outmoded patterns or cling to what has provided you with security, your best strategy is to examine why you are being asked to make this transformation. What deep, underlying concepts of reality are you required to change? What is getting in the way of becoming all you are meant to be?

As we've mentioned before, each house represents an area of your life. The following interpretations should help you determine where Pluto may transform your personal experience in the coming years. Keep in mind that Pluto works slowly, therefore the actual transformation may not be apparent for several years.

Another point to remember, since the houses in your chart usually occur later in the sign (rather than beginning at the actual first degree of the sign), is that Pluto is now traveling through the house *before* the one with the Sagittarius cusp. For instance, if Sagittarius is on your fifth-house cusp, it will be some time before Pluto actually travels over that cusp—at the moment, it is still in the fourth house. However, because the Sagittarius house will be transformed next, you should consider the changes that have happened over the past twelve years in the Scorpio area of your life, for a preview of what Pluto can do in the following house.

Pluto in the First House

This is a time when you make a break from the past. Whatever has been holding you back, whatever is outworn, outmoded, or outgrown, has to go. This powerful transit begins a new cycle in your evolution that involves a transformation in your outward identity, a challenge to add new dimensions to your personality. Often there is an actual physical transformation—you will look different to others. This could come from a conscious decision to change your appearance via plastic surgery or body building. Or you may suddenly look older, lose your hair, put on or lose weight. Some may go through a physical transition, such as menopause or pregnancy, or experience an illness that gives you a sense of your own mortality. Life-or-death questions about how you're going to survive in the future are possible.

In this house, Pluto will bring up the kind of situations that challenge your independence. For instance, you might break off relationships that are too confining, or become more assertive because of the new confidence gained from deep psychological or spiritual work.

Pluto in the Second House

Your sense of values and material resources now feel the transforming touch of Pluto. You'll ask yourself what is really important in life and why. There may be an increase or decrease in your material resources. You may decide to change the way you earn your living if your job is not truly meaningful to you. If your work is simply providing you with security, you may either be forced to change it or you may have a strong compulsion to do what you really want to do. If you are not using your own personal resources, you may find new ways to do so that will change your life in some way. Many of you will sell off property or possessions that have been weighing you down. Others will change how you handle finances or discover hidden sources of income.

Pluto in the Third House

Why do you think like you do? This process will transform the way you think, communicate, reach out to others. There could be a big difference in your perceptions of the world around you and the people in it. You may question and change some of the opinions and assumptions you've held for years. You may find yourself attacking others' ideas. Or, instead of agreeing with you, those who enter your life now could oppose your ideas. The challenge is to find out where you're coming from, bring in new information, and find out what has caused you to hold your strongest beliefs. Since your desire now is for deep knowledge, this is an excellent time for intensive study that will alter your perspective. Relatives and happenings on the local scene may have a very strong influence now.

Pluto in the Fourth House

This is your center, the place you call home, your deep sense of security and your ideas of family. Are you "at home" where you are? If you are too dependent, Pluto's transit can create some very uncomfortable times. However, through the experience of examining what makes you feel emotionally secure, and overcoming dependencies that have been holding you back, you'll emerge a much more productive individual. It is also a time to examine fears of abandonment and intimate family relationships, especially with your mother.

Pluto in the Fifth House

This is the time to ask if you're truly expressing yourself creatively. How are you giving of yourself to others? Here Pluto enforces the transformation of one's creative potential and self-expression. Many will do this through having a child or relating to a child in some way, or bringing out the creative "child within." If you already have children, your relationship with them could be transformed as deep feelings emerge.

Pluto can also transform the way you get recognition. Do others in your life give you the love and attention that encourages you to express yourself? If not, you may look for love elsewhere through an intense love affair, where you get swept away by romantic feelings, or you may have a series of affairs to provide you with all the attention you crave.

Pluto in the Sixth House

Does your life work? Or do you need to create new systems that support your ideas and can make them happen? If you're unfocused, with your energies scattered and your life cluttered, Pluto will make this clear to you. This transit brings much self-scrutiny and self-criticism. You may feel compelled to perfect your skills and techniques, to reorganize your life. Any areas that are out of control will be manifested. Health or diet issues become priorities, and any kind of self-indulgence or physical abuse over the years could surface as illness now. But this is an excellent opportunity to make changes that revitalize your body and create a healthier lifestyle for the future.

Pluto in the Seventh House

Is the one you love really holding you back? Now is when you'll find out. Here Pluto transforms close relationships, partnerships, and commitments you make to others. You'll feel the need to create a new way of being together with someone, a way that allows you both to grow. This is your chance to resolve issues that have been limiting the relationship, or if they can't be resolved, to break up. But, rather than taking sudden action, it is important to examine the deeper reasons why the relationship isn't working out, so both partners can understand that it has completed its mission in your lives and move on with no recriminations.

Pluto in the Eighth House

This is the power house, where you examine what you must give up to achieve a higher goal. Pluto here transforms how you exercise power over others. This is sure to be a very charismatic time, when you examine your own relationship to both internal and external power. It is a time when you empower yourself by facing your fears, risking insecurity, and moving forward. You may also feel powerless, at times, in the grip of forces you can't control. Since this is the house of strong sexual urges and mergers, you may find yourself in a relationship that's "bigger than both of us." On a material level, you'll transform the way you handle the powers that be: the IRS, banks, debts, credit cards.

Pluto in the Ninth House

Here is where you'll be confronting the limits in the systems you believe in. And, since this is the natural Sagittarius-ruled house, this should be a *very* powerful year, with both Pluto and Jupiter activating this area. You may feel compelled to free yourself from any obligations that keep you from expanding now. You'll be required to be on the move, stretching your limits and transforming your concept of reality through exposure to new ideas and interacting with people from many different cultures, with teachers or with religious leaders. As a result, you may change your direction in life or literally move to another location. The big question will be: What is truth for you? When you find out, you may become a teacher who shows others the way.

Pluto in the Tenth House

What does success mean to you? Is your choice career giving you the chance to express who you are and what you believe? Are you being true to yourself in the way you influence others? For those who are not happy with their position either on the job or in some other public capacity, Pluto here could transform your career or the way you take power in society. You might enter public life, become a boss, or restructure your career so that it is more relevant to your inner needs. If you've been a private "inside" person, you may surprise others by taking a more visible role in the outside world. Or you may quit a job or end a relationship that is keeping you from pursuing new goals you have set for yourself.

Pluto in the Eleventh House

Pluto here transforms how you deal with society at large. Who you identify with and why, or where you feel you belong are the deep issues that arise. You might transform your life by working with groups in some way. You may become more socially active or involved with clubs, teams, or professional organizations. You may question why you are so invested in a particular group, or in such an active social life, and you may change the groups you belong to. You may acquire a new political interest. Or you may sever long-standing associations with groups which are no longer relevant to your goals or beliefs.

Pluto in the Twelfth House

The last house of the zodiac is the place of spiritual consciousness, where you are inspired and where you have the most potential for divine illumination. It's also the place where you get "high" via natural or potentially abusive substances. In this house, you have no brakes or structures to keep you from enlightenment or chaos. (That's why it's often called "the house of self-undoing.") Institutions, which are ruled by this house, are places where you go when you are helpless and must be protected or isolated from the outside world, such as convents, hospitals, or prisons. However, when Pluto passes through this place of transformational insights, it's a wonderful time to do deep psychological or spiritual work. You may find that you need more time alone than usual and have more vivid dreams. Now you can tap the collective unconscious and effect a powerful transformation on others with the creative work you do. Some of our most transformative artists (Madonna and Michael Jackson, for instance) were born with this Pluto position.

CHAPTER 4

Introduction to Astrology— Questions and Answers

Even though astrology is a very precise art, the basic principles are not that difficult to learn. And once you know the basics, you can begin to penetrate beyond your sun sign into the realm of influence of the other planets. You'll find that the more you know, the more you'll want to explore further! Here are the questions most beginning astrology students ask.

- **What is a sign and how is it different from a constellation?**

A sign is actually a thirty-degree division of a circular belt of sky called the zodiac, which means "circle of animals" in Greek. The zodiac corresponds to the apparent path of the sun, moon, and planets around the earth. Of course, we know that the earth and other planets orbit around the sun, but astrology takes the planet where we are located as a reference point.

Originally, each division was marked by a constellation, most of which were named after animals (the lion, bull, goat, ram) or sea creatures (fishes, crab), but as the earth's axis changed over thousands of years, so did the stellar signposts. However, the thirty-degree signs retained the names and symbolism of their original markers. In other words, a sign is always the same thirty-degree segment of the zodiac, but the original constellations have moved with time.

As the sun, moon, and planets appear to move (from our observation here on earth) around the zodiac, they pass through each sign. A person born while the sun is passing

31

through a sign is said to be a member of that sign. An Aries, for instance, was born while the sun was passing through the Aries portion of the zodiac.

- **I've heard that Pisces is a water sign, Aquarius is an air sign, and so on. What does that mean and how were these definitions determined?**

It's important to remember that the definitions of the signs were not determined by guesswork or chosen at random. They evolved systematically from several components that interrelate. These four different criteria are a sign's element, its quality, its polarity or sex, and its order on the zodiac belt. These all work together to tell us what the sign is like and how it behaves.

The system is magically mathematical: The number twelve—as in the twelve signs of the zodiac—is divisible by four, by three, and by two. Perhaps it is no coincidence that there are four elements, three qualities, and two polarities. These follow each other in sequence around the zodiac, starting with Aries.

The four elements (earth, air, fire, and water) are the building blocks of astrology. The use of an element to describe a sign probably dates from man's first attempts to categorize what and who he saw in the world. In ancient times, it was believed that all things were composed of combinations of earth, air, fire, and water. This included the human character, which was fiery/choleric, earthy/melancholy, airy/sanguine, or watery/phlegmatic. The elements also correspond to our emotional (water), physical (earth), mental (air), and spiritual (fire) natures. The energies of each of the elements were then observed to relate to the time of year when the sun was passing through a certain segment of the zodiac.

The fire signs—Aries, Leo, and Sagittarius—embody the characteristics of that element. Optimism, warmth, hot tempers, enthusiasm, and spirit are typical of these signs. Taurus, Virgo, and Capricorn are earthy—more grounded, physical, materialistic, organized, and deliberate than fire people. Air signs—Gemini, Libra, and Aquarius—are mentally oriented communicators. Water signs—Cancer, Scorpio, and Pisces—are emotional, creative, and caring.

Think of what each element does to the others: water puts out fire or evaporates with heat. Air fans the flames or blows them out. Earth smothers fire, drifts and erodes with too much wind, becomes mud or fertile soil with water. Those are often perfect analogies for the relationships between signs of these elements! This astro-chemistry was one of the first ways man described his relationships. Fortunately, no one is entirely air or fire. We all have a bit, or a lot, of each element in our horoscopes; this unique mix defines each astrological personality.

Within each element, there are three qualities, which describe how the sign behaves, how it works. Cardinal signs are the activists, the go-getters. These signs—Aries, Cancer, Libra, and Capricorn—begin each season. Fixed signs are the builders that happen in the middle of the season. You'll find that Taurus, Leo, Scorpio, and Aquarius are gifted with focused concentration, stubbornness, and stamina. Mutable signs—Gemini, Virgo, Sagittarius, and Pisces—are catalysts for change at the end of each season; these are flexible, adaptable, mobile signs.

The polarity of a sign is it's positive or negative "charge." It can be masculine, active, positive, or yang like the air and fire signs. Or it can be feminine, reactive, negative, or yin like the water and earth signs. The polarities of each sign alternate around the zodiac, like a giant battery.

Finally, we consider the sign's place in the order of the zodiac. This is vital to the balance of all the forces and the transmission of energy moving through the signs. Notice that each sign is quite different from its neighbors on either side. Yet each seems to grow out of its predecessor like links in a chain and transmits a synthesis of energy gathered along the chain to the following sign, beginning with the fire-powered active positive charge of Aries. Keep this in mind as you read through the descriptions.

ARIES: Fire element, cardinal quality, masculine polarity, first sign

Aries, the harbinger of spring, starts off the zodiac with a powerful charge. This is the youngest sign, the perennial baby, focused on the ego. Aries rushes forward, impatiently, always wanting to be first. This sign is active and assertive in everything it does.

TAURUS: Earth element, fixed quality, feminine polarity, second sign

Taurus is a growing period, a time to acclimate to the physical world and to explore the territory nearby. Taurus distinguishes between what's mine and what belongs to others. It is a sign that nurtures, that slows down and builds step by step after a fast start.

**GEMINI: Air sign, mutable quality,
masculine polarity, third sign**

The third sign, Gemini, is ready to reach out actively to others, to communicate. This is an assertive, changeable, sociable sign that gathers information and breaks new ground.

**CANCER: Water sign, cardinal quality,
feminine polarity, fourth sign**

After reaching out to others, comes an emotionally active sign with the feminine drive to nurture and bear fruit. Cancer, the first water sign, uses the emotions, and the first use of emotions is to nurture, protect, and mother others during the initial growing period of summer.

**LEO: Fire sign, fixed quality,
masculine polarity, fifth sign**

After nurturing others, it is time to lead them into the world in the masculine sense. Leo is a sign to lean on, a bright and steady energy that asserts itself, builds strength and self-confidence.

**VIRGO: Earth sign, mutable quality,
feminine polarity, sixth sign**

Time to stop, analyze. After the confident surge of Leo comes the practical down-to-earth Virgo, that makes sure everything is working well. It serves others by analyzing, teaching, criticizing, and improving what has been done.

**LIBRA: Air sign, cardinal quality,
masculine polarity, seventh sign**

An active mental sign, Libra constantly weighs and balances objectively; sees both sides of the question; and asserts itself to maintain equilibrium and ideals of justice, balance, beauty.

**SCORPIO: Water sign, fixed quality,
feminine polarity, eighth sign**

Coming after the mentally active Libra, we have the decisive, fixed sign of emotional extremes, of commitment. Scorpio is the proverbial still-waters-run-deep sign. It penetrates to the core, tends to be all or nothing. In this sign is the intense desire to procreate, the fascination with control and power.

**SAGITTARIUS: Fire sign, mutable quality,
masculine polarity, ninth sign**

Here is a catalyst for growth, expansion, and change. This sign manifests fire's quest for spiritual development. This is a restless sign—a traveler always on the go who expands by relating to others and prepares the way for our relating to the world.

**CAPRICORN: Earth sign, cardinal quality,
feminine polarity, tenth sign**

Now it is time to move into the world, to organize so we can function on a large scale, to organize. Capricorn is a dutiful sign that is conscious of the expectations of others, of one's status in the scheme of things.

**AQUARIUS: Air sign, fixed quality,
masculine polarity, eleventh sign**

This mental sign is concerned with the correct social values, actively promoting the welfare of groups, discovering new inventions. It comes during the quiet time of winter, the right time for concentrated objective scientific thought, mass communication, planning for the future.

PISCES: Water sign, mutable quality, feminine polarity, twelfth sign

This sign's constantly changing emotions reflect the knowledge obtained in the trip through the other signs and prepare for the rebirth of spring in Aries. This sensitive sign must digest the impressions gathered; it's a creative time of dreams, and a time of contributing to others through service and caring.

• **Besides my "sun sign," how many other signs do I have?**

In compiling your astrological database, we consider eight planets, besides the moon and sun. Some astrologers also use asteroids, the moon's nodes, and certain sensitive points of the zodiac. The phrase "as above, so below" is often used to describe a chart as a microcosm of the universe. The three closest planets to the earth—Mercury, Mars, Venus, and the moon—affect your personal character. The next-farthest out—Jupiter and Saturn—affect influences from others, turning points and outside events, and significant cycles in your life. As we get farther out, the slower-moving planets—Uranus, Neptune, and Pluto—deal with mass trends that effect your whole generation. The zodiac, with its constellations of stars, represents the universal influences.

In the western systems of astrology, we confine our charts to the planets and stars within the zodiac. We would not consider the influence of the Big Dipper or Orion or black holes and supernovas.

The sign the planet is passing through at the time of your birth and that sign's location in the sky determine the way the planet will manifest itself in your life. For instance Mars in aggressive, impatient Aries will show a completely different energy than Mars in dreamy, creative Pisces.

The planets' influence in your horoscope is intensified if they are close together, or affecting another planet, which is called an "aspect." This term refers to a distance between two forces within the 360 degrees of the zodiac circle. Some aspects, such as the "trine" (120 degrees apart) and the "sextile" (60 degrees apart) are considered easy and harmonious. Others, such as the "square" (90 degrees) and the "opposition" (180 degrees) are tense, causing friction and conflict or, more positively, challenges.

Two or more planets traveling close together in the same sign (within ten degrees of each other) is called a "conjunction." Depending on the planets, the conjunction can be difficult or very beneficial. The sun works well with Mercury, Venus, and Jupiter. Mars, Uranus, and Saturn are best left alone. A conjunction will give much more importance to the sign it inhabits. When there are several planets crowding one sign, the activities of that area will dominate the horoscope.

• **What is a "ruling planet?"**
Each sign of the zodiac has a planet that corresponds to its energies. Mars rules the firey, assertive Aries. The sensual beauty and comfort-loving aspect of Venus rules Taurus, while the more idealistic side rules Libra. The quick-moving Mercury rules both Gemini and Virgo, showing its mental agility in Gemini and its critical, analytical side in Virgo. Emotional Cancer is ruled by the moon, while outgoing Leo is ruled by the sun. Scorpio was originally given Mars, but when Pluto was discovered in this century, its powerful magnetic energies were deemed more suitable to Scorpio. Disciplined Capricorn is ruled by Saturn. Expansive Sagittarius is ruled by Jupiter, unpredictable Aquarius by Uranus, and creative, impressionable Pisces by Neptune.

CHAPTER 5

Your Success Profile—
Astrological Self-Help to Tap
Your Potential

If you've ever wondered whether you're on the right track
with your life, if you're making the most of what you've
got, if you have undiscovered capabilities just waiting to
make your fortune, look no further. If you're thinking
about changing directions, trying on a new career for size,
here is a clear road map. Does this sound like a mailer for
one of the popular self-help courses? In a way, it does. The
fact is, that for centuries astrology has been used to help
people discover themselves and make important decisions.
And it's still one of the best ways to learn more about
yourself and what you can do best.

To know yourself astrologically, however, you must go
beyond your sun sign to examine a complete profile of your
personality, including all the planets in their positions at
the moment you were born. Besides the sun, there are nine
other planets (in astrology, by the way, the sun and moon
are usually referred to as planets) that work together to
create the unique astrological personality that is yours
alone. Each planet has a role to play in your total portrait
and each is a great source of information for getting to
know yourself. So if you've been just sticking with your sun
sign, come along with us in this chapter and find out how
much more there is to your astrological portrait.

For those of you who feel you're not typical of your sun
sign, this chapter may show you why. Having several planets in another sign can color your personality strongly with
that sign's characteristics. For instance, a Leo sun sign with

Venus, Mercury, and the moon in Virgo will come across as a much more conservative person than the Leo sun person who has Venus, Jupiter, and Mercury also placed in Leo.

And while you're studying the planets, you can use the charts in Chapter 7—"Look Up Your Planets," to get to know your friends, coworkers, loved ones, and that fascinating person who might be your soulmate.

The Sun: Your Confidence and Sense of Self

The sign of the sun when you were born is always given most importance. This is the sign that's center stage. It is the showoff sign that is the major indicator of your personality, your confidence, and your general sense of who you are. You can find out all about your sun sign in detail from the individual chapters at the end of the book. Astrologers focus on the sun sign in general books like these because the qualities of the sun are the most typical of people who were born when the sun was passing through a given sign. This is the common denominator. You may share other planets with someone, but it's your sun sign that will color your outward personality most strongly.

The Moon: What Do You Need?

Your moon sign reflects your subconscious needs and longings, as well as the kind of mothering and childhood conditioning you had. Your moon sign will tell you what you need to be emotionally happy (rather than what attracts you, which is Venus's territory).

Since accurate moon tables are too extensive to include in this book, we suggest you consult an astrologer or have a computer chart made to determine your correct moon sign.

MOON IN ARIES. Emotionally, you are independent and ardent. You are fulfilled by meeting challenges, overcoming obstacles, being "first." You have exceptional courage. You love the challenge of an emotional pursuit, and difficult situations in love only intensify your excitement. As the legendary film star Bette Davis, an archetypical Aries, once asked, "If it's too easy, where's the challenge?" But the catch-22 is that after you attain your goal to conquer whatever or whomever you're pursuing, your ardor is likely to cool down rapidly. To avoid continuous treat-'em-rough situations, work on developing patience and tolerance.

MOON IN TAURUS. Solid, secure, comfortable situations and relationships are fulfilling to you. You need plenty of open displays of affection, lots of hugs and touching. You'll also gravitate to those who provide you with material comforts as well as sensual pleasures. Your emotions are steady and nurturing in this strong moon sign, but could lean toward stubbornness when pushed. You could miss out on some of life's excitement by sticking to the safe, straight and narrow road.

MOON IN GEMINI. You need constant emotional stimulation and enjoy an outgoing, diversified lifestyle. You could have difficulty with commitment, and therefore may marry more than once or have a love life of changing partners. An outgoing, interesting, talented partner could merit your attention, however. You could spread yourself too thin to accomplish major goals, but watch a tendency to be emotionally fragmented. Find a creative way to express the range of your feelings, possibly through developing writing, speaking, or other communicative talents.

MOON IN CANCER. This is the most powerful moon position, one that can seem even stronger than the sun in the horoscope. You are the zodiac nurturer who needs to be needed. You have an excellent memory and an intuitive understanding of the needs of others. You are happiest at home and may work in a home office or turn your corner of the company into a home away from home. Work that supplies food and shelter, nurtures children, or involves occult studies and psychology could take advantage of this lunar position.

MOON IN LEO. You need to be treated like royalty! Strong support, loyalty, and loud applause win your heart. You rule over your territory and resent anyone who intrudes on your turf. Your attraction to the finer things in people and in your lifestyle could give you a snobbish outlook. But basically you have a warm, passionate, loyal, and emotional nature that gives generously to those you deem worthy. Children and leadership roles that express your creativity can bring you great satisfaction.

MOON IN VIRGO. This moon often draws you to situations where you play the role of healer, teacher, or critic. You may find it difficult to accept others as they are or enjoy what you have. Because you must analyze before you can give emotionally, the Virgo moon can seem hard on others and equally tough on yourself. Be aware that you may have impossible standards, and take it easier on others. A little tolerance goes a long way, and so does a bit of humor!

MOON IN LIBRA. Your emotional role is partnership oriented—you won't live or work alone for long! You may find it difficult to do things alone. You need the emotional balance of a strong "other." You thrive in an elegant, harmonious atmosphere, where you get attention and flattery. This moon needs to keep it light. Heavy emotions cause your Libran moon's scales to swing precariously. So does an overly possessive or demanding partner, so choose well. The right partner can make all the difference for the better in your life.

MOON IN SCORPIO. The moon is not totally comfortable in intense Scorpio, which is emotionally drawn to extremes and can be obsessive, suspicious, and jealous. You take disappointments very hard and are often drawn to issues of power and control. It's important to learn when to tone down those all-or-nothing feelings. Finding a healthy outlet in meaningful work could diffuse your intense needs. Medicine, occult work, police work, or psychology are good possibilities.

MOON IN SAGITTARIUS. This moon needs freedom—you can't stand to be possessed by anyone. You have emotional wanderlust and may need a constant dose of mental and spiritual stimulation. But you cope with the fluctuations of life with good humor and a spirit of adventure. You may find great satisfaction in exotic situations, foreign travels, philosophical and spiritual studies, rather than in intense one-on-one relationships.

MOON IN CAPRICORN. Here, the moon is cool and calculating—and very ambitious. You get a sense of security from achieving prestige and position in the outside world, rather than creating a cozy nest or cuddling romantically by the fire. Though you are dutiful toward those you love, your heart is in your climb to the top of the business or social ladder. Concrete achievement and improving your position in life bring you great satisfaction.

MOON IN AQUARIUS. This is a gregarious moon, happiest when surrounded by people. You're everybody's buddy, as long as no one gets too close. You'd rather stay pals. You make your own rules in emotional situations; you may have a radically different life-or love-style. Intimate relationships may feel too confining, for you need plenty of space.

MOON IN PISCES. This watery moon needs an emotional anchor to help you keep grounded in reality. Otherwise, you tend to escape to a fantasy world through intoxicating substances. Creative work could give you a far more productive way to express yourself and get away from it all. Working in a healing or helping profession is also good for you because you get satisfaction from helping the underdog. But, though you naturally attract people with sob stories, try to cultivate friends with a positive upbeat point of view.

Mercury: Your Mind Power

Mercury rules how your mind operates and how you communicate. Do you have a more disciplined, focused, one-track mind, or does your mind jump from idea to idea easily, perhaps a bit scattered? Or are you a visionary, poetic type? Do you communicate easily in speech or writing, or are you the type that spends a great deal of time thinking before you speak?

Since Mercury never moves more than a sign away from

the sun, check your sun sign and the signs preceding and following it to see which Mercury position most applies to you.

MERCURY IN ARIES never shies away from a confrontation. You say what you think; you are active and assertive. Your mind is sharp, alert, and impatient, but you may not be thorough.

MERCURY IN TAURUS is deliberate and thorough, with good concentration. You'll take the slow, methodical approach and leave no stone unturned. You'll see a problem through to the end, stick with a subject till you become an expert. You may talk very slowly, but in a melodious voice.

MERCURY IN GEMINI is a quick study. You can handle many subjects at once, jumping from one to the other easily. You may, however, spread yourself too thin. You express yourself easily both verbally and in writing. You are a "people person" who enjoys having others buzzing around and you are also skilled at communicating with a large audience.

MERCURY IN CANCER has great empathy for others—you can read their feelings. Your mind works intuitively rather than logically. And your thoughts are always colored by your emotions. You have an excellent memory and imagination.

MERCURY IN LEO has a flair for dramatic expression, and can hold the attention of others (and sometimes hog the limelight). This is also a placement of mental overconfidence. You think big and prefer to skip the details. However, this might make you an excellent salesperson or public speaker.

MERCURY IN VIRGO is a strong position. You're a natural critic, with an analytic, orderly mind. You pay attention to details and have a talent for thorough analysis and good organization, though you tend to focus on the practical side of things. Teaching and editing come naturally to you.

MERCURY IN LIBRA is a smooth talker, with a graceful gift of gab. Though gifted in diplomacy and debate, you may vacillate in making decisions, forever juggling the pros and cons. You speak in elegant, well-modulated tones.

MERCURY IN SCORPIO has a sharp mind that can be sarcastic and given to making cutting remarks. You have a penetrating insight and will stop at nothing to get to the heart of matters. You are an excellent and thorough investigator, researcher, or detective. You enjoy problems that challenge your skills in digging and probing.

MERCURY IN SAGITTARIUS has a great sense of humor but a tendency toward tactlessness. You enjoy telling others what you see as the truth "for their own good." This can either make you a great teacher or visionary, like poet Robert Bly, or it can make you dogmatic. When you feel you're in the right, you may expound endlessly on your own ideas. Watch a tendency to puff up ideas unrealistically (however, this talent could make you a super salesman).

MERCURY IN CAPRICORN has excellent mental discipline. You take a serious, orderly approach and play by the rules. You have a super-organized mind that grasps structures easily, though you may lack originality. You have a dry sense of humor.

MERCURY IN AQUARIUS is "exalted" and quite at home in this analytical sign. You have a highly original point of view, combined with good mental focus. An independent thinker, you'll break the rules, if this will help make your point. You are, however, fixed mentally, and reluctant to change your mind once it is made up. Therefore, you could sometimes come across as a "know it all."

MERCURY IN PISCES has a poetic mind that is receptive to psychic, intuitive influences. You may be vague, unclear in your expression and forgetful of details and find it difficult to work within a structure, but you are strong on creative communication and thinking. You'll express yourself in a very sympathetic, caring way. You should find work that uses your imaginative talents.

What Do You React To? What Attracts You? Look for Venus

Venus will show what turns a person on. It is the planet of romantic love, pleasure, and artistry. It shows your tastes and what you'll attract to you without trying. Venus will show you how to charm others in a way that's suited to you.

You can find your Venus placement on the chart in this book. Look for the year of your birth in the lefthand column, then follow the line across the page until you read the time of your birthday. The sign heading that column will be your Venus. If you were born on a day when Venus was changing signs, check the signs preceding or following that day. Here are the roles your Venus plays—and sings.

VENUS IN ARIES. Scarlett O'Hara probably had Venus here! You love a challenge that adds spice to life; you might even pick a fight now and then to "shake 'em up." Since a good chase revs up your romantic motor, you could abandon a romance if the going becomes too smooth. You're first on the block with the newest styles, and first out the door if you're bored or ordered around.

VENUS IN TAURUS. Venus is literally at home in Taurus. It's a terrific placement for a "material girl" or boy, an interior designer or a musician. You love to surround yourself with the very finest smells, tastes, sounds, visuals, textures. You'd run from an austere lifestyle or uncomfortable surroundings. Creature comforts turn you on. And so does a beautiful, secure nest—and nest egg. Not one to rush about, you take time to enjoy your pleasures and treasures.

VENUS IN GEMINI. You're a sparkler, like singer Cher, who loves the night life, with constant variety, and a frequent change of scenes and loves. You like lots of stimulation, a varied social life; you are better at light flirtations than at serious romances. You may be attracted to younger, playful lovers who have the pep and energy to keep up with you.

VENUS IN CANCER. You can be "daddy's girl" or "mama's boy," like the late Liberace. You love to be babied, coddled, and protected in a cozy, secure home. You are attracted to those who make you feel secure, well provided for. You could also have a secret love life or clandestine arrangement with a "sugar daddy." You love to "mother" others as well.

VENUS IN LEO. You're an "uptown" girl or boy who loves "Putting on the Ritz," where you can consort with elegant people, dress extravagantly, and be the center of attention. Think of Coco Chanel, who piled on the jewelry and decorated tweed suits with gold braid. You dress and act like a star, but you might often be more attracted to hangers-on and flatterers, rather than to those who can offer you a relationship with solid value.

VENUS IN VIRGO. This Venus is attracted to perfect order, but underneath your pristine white dress is some naughty black lace! You fall for those who you can make over or improve in some way. You may also fancy those in the medical profession. Here Venus may express itself best through some kind of service, by giving loving support. You may find it difficult to show your true feelings, to really let go in intimate moments. "I Can't Get No Satisfaction" could sometimes be your theme song.

VENUS IN LIBRA. "I Feel Pretty" sings this Venus. You love a beautiful, harmonious, luxurious atmosphere. Many artists and musicians thrive with this Venus, with its natural feeling for the balance of colors and sounds. In love, you make a very compatible partner in a supportive relationship where there are few confrontations. You can't stand arguments or argumentative people. The good looks of your partner may also be a deciding factor.

VENUS IN SCORPIO. "All or Nothing at All" could be your theme song. This Venus wants "Body and Soul." You're a natural detective who's attracted to a mystery. You know how to keep a secret, and have quite a few of your own. This is a very intense placement, where you can be preoccupied with sex and power. Living dangerously adds spice to your life, but don't get burned. All that's intense appeals to you: heady perfume, deep rich colors, dark woods, spicy foods.

VENUS IN SAGITTARIUS. "On the Road Again" sums up your Venus personality. Travel, athletics, New Age philosophies, and a casual, carefree lifestyle appeal to you. You are attracted to exciting, idealistic types who give you plenty of space. Large animals, especially horses, are part of your life. You probably have a four-wheel drive vehicle or a motorized skateboard—anything to keep moving.

VENUS IN CAPRICORN. "Diamonds Are a Girl's Best Friend" could characterize this ambitious Venus. You may seem cool and calculating, but underneath you're insecure and want a substantial relationship you can count on. It wouldn't hurt if your beloved could help you up the ladder professionally, either. This Venus is often attracted to objects and people of a different generation (like Clark Gable, you could marry someone much older—or younger)—antiques; traditional clothing (sometimes worn in a very "today" way, like Diane Keaton); and dignified, conservative behavior are trademarks.

VENUS IN AQUARIUS. "Just Friends, Lovers No More" is often what happens with Venus in Aquarius. You love to be surrounded by people, but are uncomfortable with intense emotions (steer clear of Venus in Scorpio!). You like a spontaneous lifestyle, full of surprises. You make your own rules in everything you do, including love. The avant-garde, high technology, and possibly unusual sexual experiences attract you.

VENUS IN PISCES. "Why not Take All of Me?" sings this exalted Venus, who loves to give. You may have a collection of stray animals, lost souls, the underprivileged, the lonely. (Try to assess their motives in a clear light.) You're a natural for theater, film, anything involving fantasy. Psychic or spiritual life also draws you, as does selfless service for a needy cause.

Your Drive and Motivation Come From Mars

Mars shows what you'll go for. This planet is your driving force, your active sexuality, what makes you run, your kind of energy. To find your Mars, refer to the Mars chart in this book. If the following description of your Mars sign doesn't ring true, you may have been born on a day when Mars was changing signs, so check the adjacent sign descriptions.

MARS IN ARIES runs in high gear, showing the full force of its energy. You have a fiery, explosive disposition, but are also very courageous, with enormous drive. You'll tackle problems head on and mow down anything that stands in your way. Though you're supercharged and can jump-start others, you are short on follow-through, especially when a situation requires diplomacy, patience, and tolerance.

MARS IN TAURUS could claim the motto, "Persistence alone is omnipotent." You're in it for the long haul, and you win the race with a slow, steady pace. Gifted with stamina and focus, this Mars may not be first out of the gate, but you're sure to finish. You tend to wear away or outlast your foes rather than bowl them over. Like Bruce Willis, this Mars is supersensual sexually—you take your time and enjoy yourself all the way. You'll probably accumulate many collections and material possessions.

MARS IN GEMINI holds the philosophy that "two loves are better than one," which could mean trouble. Your restless nature searches out stimulation and will switch rather than fight. Your life gets complicated, but that only makes it more interesting for you. You have a way with words and can "talk" with your hands. Since you tend to go all over the lot in your interests, you may have to work to develop focus and concentration.

MARS IN CANCER is given, in its fall, to moods and can be quite crabby. This may be due to a fragile sense of security. You are quite self-protective and secretive about your life, which might make you appear untrustworthy or manipulative to others. Try not to take things so much to heart—cultivate a sense of impersonality or detachment. Sexually, you are tender and sensitive, a very protective lover.

MARS IN LEO fills you with self-confidence and charisma. You'll use your considerable drive to get attention, coming on strong with show-biz flair, like Cher, who has this placement. In fact, you'll head right for the spotlight. Sexually, you're a giver—but you do demand the royal treatment in return. You enjoy giving orders and can create quite a scene if you're disobeyed. At some point, you may have to learn some lessons in humility.

MARS IN VIRGO is a worker bee, a "Felix Unger" character who notices every detail. This is a thorough, painstaking Mars that worries a great deal about making mistakes—this "worrier" tendency may lead to very tightly strung nerves under your controlled facade. Your energy can be expressed positively in a field like teaching or editing, but your tendency to fault-find could make you a hard-to-please lover. Learning to delegate and praise, rather than do everything perfectly yourself, could make you easier to live with. You enjoy good mental companionship, with less emphasis on sex and no emotional turmoil. If you do find the perfect lover, you'll tend to take care of that person.

MARS IN LIBRA is a passive-aggressor who avoids confrontations and charms people into doing what you want. You are best off in a position where you can exercise your great diplomatic skills. Mars is in its detriment in Libra, and expends much energy deciding which course of action to take. However, setting a solid goal in life—perhaps one that expresses your passion for beauty, justice, or art—could give you the vantage point you need to achieve success. In love, like Michael Douglas, you'll go for beauty in your partner and surroundings.

MARS IN SCORPIO has a powerful drive that could become an obsession. So learn to use this energy wisely and well, for Mars in Scorpio hates to compromise, loves with all-or-nothing fever (while it lasts), and can get jealous or manipulative if you don't get your way! But your powerful concentration and nonstop stamina is an asset in challenging fields like medicine or scientific research. You're the master planner, a super-strategist who, when well directed, can achieve important goals, like actors Larry Hagman and Bill Cosby, and scientist Jonas Salk.

MARS IN SAGITTARIUS is the conquering hero set off on a crusade. You're great at getting things off the ground. Your challenge is to consider the consequences of your actions. In love with freedom, you don't always make the best marriage partner. "Love 'em and leave 'em" could be your motto. You may also gravitate toward risk and adventure, and may have great athletic skill. You're best off in a situation where you can express your love of adventure, philosophy, and travel, or where you can use artistic talents to elevate the lives of others, like Johann Sebastian Bach.

MARS IN CAPRICORN is exalted, a "chief executive" placement that gives you a drive for success and the discipline to achieve it. You deliberately aim for status and a high position in life, and you'll keep climbing, despite the odds. This Mars will work for what you get. You are well organized and persistent—a winning combination. Sexually, you have a strong, earthy drive, but you may go for someone who can be useful to you, rather than someone flashy or fascinating.

MARS IN AQUARIUS Is a visionary and often a revolutionary who stands out from the crowd. You are innovative and highly original in your methods. Sexually, you could go for unusual relationships, like Hugh Hefner or Howard Hughes. You have a rebellious streak and like to shake people up a bit. Intimacy can be a problem—you may keep lots of people around you or isolate yourself to keep others from getting too close.

MARS IN PISCES likes to play different roles. Your ability to tune in and project others' emotions makes you a natural actor. There are many film and television personalities with this placement, such as Mary Tyler Moore, Jane Seymour, Cybill Shepherd, Burt Reynolds, and Jane Fonda. You understand how to use glamour and illusion for your own benefit. You can switch emotions on and off quickly, and you're especially good at getting sympathy. You'll go for romance, though real-life relationships never quite live up to your fantasies.

Your Enthusiasm and
Sales Ability Come from Jupiter

Are you enthusiastic, optimistic, willing to take a risk? Look for Jupiter. This planet is often viewed as the "Santa Claus" of the horoscope, a jolly, happy planet that brings good luck, gifts, success, and opportunities. Jupiter also embodies the functions of the higher mind, where you do complex, expansive thinking, and deal with the big overall picture rather than with the specifics (the province of Mercury).

Be sure to look up your Jupiter "lucky spot" in the tables in this book. But bear in mind that Jupiter gives growth without discrimination or discipline. A person with a strong Jupiter may be weak in common sense. This is also the place where you could have too much of a good thing, resulting in extravagance, excess pounds, laziness, or carelessness.

JUPITER IN ARIES. You have big ambitions and won't settle for second place. You are luckiest when you are pioneering an innovative project, when you are pushing to be "first." You can break new ground with this placement, but watch a tendency to be pushy and arrogant. You'll also need to learn patience and follow through in the house where Jupiter falls in your horoscope.

JUPITER IN TAURUS. You have expensive tastes and like to surround yourself with the luxuries money can buy. You acquire beauty and comfort in all its forms. You could tend to expand physically from overindulgence in good tastes! Dieting could be a major challenge. Land and real estate are especially lucky for you.

JUPITER IN GEMINI. You love to be in the center of a whirlwind of activity, talking a blue streak, with all phone lines busy. You have great facility in expressing yourself verbally or in writing. Work that involves communicating or manual dexterity is especially lucky for you. Watch a tendency to be too restless—slow down from time to time. Try not to spread yourself too thin.

JUPITER IN CANCER. This Jupiter has a big safe-deposit box, an attic piled to overflowing with boxes of treasures. You may still have your christening dress or your beloved high school sweater. This Jupiter loves to accumulate things, to save for a rainy day, or to gather collections. Negatively, you could be a hoarder with closets full of things you'll never use. Protective, nurturing Jupiter in Cancer often has many mouths to feed, human or animal. Naturally, this placement produces great restauranteurs and hotel keepers. The shipping business is also a good bet.

JUPITER IN LEO. Naturally warm, romantic, and playful, you can't have too much attention or applause. You bask in the limelight while others are still trying to find the stage. Politics or show business—anywhere you can perform for an audience—are lucky for you. You love the good life and are happy to share your wealth with others. Negatively, you could be extravagant and tend to hog center stage. Let others take a bow from time to time. Also, be careful not to overdo or overspend.

JUPITER IN VIRGO. You like to work! In fact, work can be more interesting than play for you. You have a sharp eye for details and pick out every flaw! Be careful not to get caught up in nitpicking. You expect nothing short of perfection from others. Finding practical solutions to problems and helping others make the most of themselves are better uses for this Jupiter. Consider a health field such as nutrition, medicine, or health education.

JUPITER IN LIBRA. You function best when you have a stimulating partner. You also need harmonious, beautiful surroundings. Chances are, you have closets full of fashionable clothes. The serious side of this Jupiter has an excellent sense of fair play, and can be a good diplomat or judge. Careers in law, the arts, or fashion are favored.

JUPITER IN SCORPIO. You love the power of handling other people's money—or lives. Others see you as having nerves of steel. You have luck in detective work, sex-related ventures, psychotherapy, research, the occult, or tax work—anything that involves a mystery. You're always going to extremes, as testing the limits gives you a thrill.

Your timing is excellent—you'll wait for the perfect moment to make your moves. Negatively, this Jupiter could use power to achieve selfish ends.

JUPITER IN SAGITTARIUS. In its strongest place, Jupiter compels you to expand your mind, travel far from home, collect college degrees. This is the placement of the philosopher, the gambler, the animal trainer, the publisher. You have an excellent sense of humor and a cheerful disposition. This placement often works with animals, especially horses, in some way.

JUPITER IN CAPRICORN. You are luckiest working in an established situation, within a traditional structure. In the sign of caution and restraint, Jupiter is thrifty rather than a big spender. You accumulate duties and responsibilities, which is fine for business leadership. You'll expand in any area where you can achieve respect, prestige, or social position. People with this position are especially concerned that nothing be wasted. You might have great luck in a recycling or renovation business.

JUPITER IN AQUARIUS. You are lucky when doing good in the world. You are extremely idealistic and think in the most expansive terms about improving society at large. This is an excellent position for a politician or labor leader. You're everybody's buddy who can relate to people of diverse backgrounds. You are luckiest when you can operate away from rigid rules and conservative organizations.

JUPITER IN PISCES. You work best in a creative field or in one where you are helping the downtrodden. You exude sympathy and gravitate toward the underdog. Watch a tendency to be too self-sacrificing, overly emotional. You should also be careful not to overindulge in alcohol or drugs. Some lucky work areas: oil, perfume, dance, footwear, alcohol, pharmaceuticals, and the arts, especially film.

Can You Get the Job Done?
Saturn Will Tell

Saturn is the planet of discipline, organization, and determination. It will show your ability to follow through and structure a project. It will also reveal your fears, and what you're afraid will be taken away from you.

Saturn has suffered from a bad reputation, always cast as the heavy in the horoscope. However, the flip side of Saturn is the teacher, the one whose class is the toughest in school, but, when you graduate, you never forget the lessons well learned. (They are the ones you came here on this planet to learn.) And the tests of Saturn, which come at regular seven-year exam periods, are the ones you need to pass to survive as a conscious, independent adult. Saturn gives us the grade we've earned—so, if we have studied and prepared for our tests, we needn't be afraid of the big bad wolf.

Your Saturn position can illuminate your fears, your hangups, your important lessons in life. Remember that Saturn is concerned with your maturity, what you need to know to survive in the world. Be sure to look it up in the Saturn chart in this book.

SATURN IN ARIES. "Don't push me around!" says this Saturn, which puts the brakes on Aries natural drive and enthusiasm. You'll have to learn to cooperate, tone down self-centeredness, and respect authorities, in order to get the job done. Bill Cosby, who has this placement, may have had the same lessons to learn.

SATURN IN TAURUS. "How am I going to pay the rent?" You'll have to stick out some lean periods and get control of your material life. Learn to use your talents to their fullest potential. In the same boat, Ben Franklin had the right idea: "A penny saved is a penny earned."

SATURN IN GEMINI. You're a deep thinker, with lofty ideals—a good position for scientific studies. You may be quite shy, speak slowly, or have fears about communicating, like Eleanor Roosevelt. Yet when you master these, you'll be able to sway the masses, just like she did. You'll tend to take shelter in abstract ideas, like Sigmund Freud, when dealing with emotional issues.

SATURN IN CANCER. Some very basic fears could center on your early home environment, overcoming a negative childhood influence to establish a sense of security.

You may fear being mothered or smothered and be tested in your female relationships. You may have to learn to be objective and distance yourself emotionally when threatened or when dealing with negative feelings such as jealousy or guilt. Bette Midler and Diane Keaton have this placement.

SATURN IN LEO. This placement can bring up ego problems. If you have not received the love you crave, you could be an overly strict, dictatorial parent. You may demand respect and a position of leadership at any cost. You may have to watch a tendency toward rigidity and withholding affection. You may have to learn to relax, have fun, lighten up!

SATURN IN VIRGO. You can be very hard on yourself, making yourself sick to your stomach by worrying about every little detail. You must learn to set priorities, discriminate, and laugh!

SATURN IN LIBRA. You may have your most successful marriage (or your first) later in life, because you must learn to stand on your own first. How to relate to others is one of your major lessons. Your great sense of fairness makes you a good judge or lawyer, or a prominent diplomat, like former Secretary of State Henry Kissenger.

SATURN IN SCORPIO. Your tests come when you handle situations involving control or power over others. You could fear depending on others financially or sexually, or there could be a blurring of the lines between sex and money. Sexual tests, periods of celibacy (resulting from fear of "merging" with another), or sex for money, are some ways this could manifest.

SATURN IN SAGITTARIUS. You accept nothing at face value. You are the opposite of the happy-go-lucky Sagittarius. With Saturn here, your beliefs must be fully examined and tested. Firsthand experience, without the guidance of dogma, gurus, or teachers, is your best education. This Saturn has little tolerance for another authority. You won't follow a dream unless you understand the idea behind it.

SATURN IN CAPRICORN. Saturn, which rules Capricorn, is sensitive to public opinion and achieving a high-status image. You are not a big risk taker because you do not want to compromise your position. In its most powerful place, Saturn is the teacher par excellence, giving structure and form to your life. Your persistence will assure you a continual climb to the top.

SATURN IN AQUARIUS. This is a Greta Garbo position, where you feel like an outsider, one who doesn't fit into the group. There may be a lack of trust in others, a kind of defensiveness that could engender defensiveness in return. Not a superficial social butterfly, your commitment to groups must have depth and humanitarian meaning.

SATURN IN PISCES. This position generates a feeling of helplessness, of being a victim of circumstances. You could underestimate yourself, lack a sense of self-power. However, this can give great wisdom if you can manage, like Edgar Cayce, to look inward, with contemplation and meditation, rather than outward, for solutions.

The Outer Planets: Uranus, Neptune, and Pluto

The three outer planets—Uranus, Neptune, and Pluto—are slow moving but powerful forces in our lives. Since they stay in a sign at least seven years, you'll share the sign placement with everyone you went to school with and probably your brothers and sisters. However, the specific place (house) in the horoscope where each one operates is yours alone, and depends on your moment in time—the exact time you were born. That's why it's important to have an exact birthchart. Look at the charts on pages 94–97 to find the signs of your outer planets.

Can You Work Independently? Are You a Rebel? An Original? Look at Uranus.

Uranus can be an excellent indicator of whether you stand out in a crowd. This is a brilliant, highly original, unpredictable planet who shakes us out of a rut and propels us forward.

URANUS IN ARIES. Yours was the generation that pioneered in electronics, developing the first computers and high-tech gadgets. Your powerful mixture of fire (Aries) and electricity (Uranus) propels you into exploring the unknown. Those of you born here, like Jacqueline Onassis, Andy Warhol, and Yoko Ono, probably have had sudden, violent changes in your lives and have a very headstrong, individualistic streak.

URANUS IN TAURUS. This generation became the "hippies" who rejected the establishment. The rise of communism and socialism happened during this period. You have bright ideas about making money and are a natural entrepreneur, but can have sudden financial shakeups.

URANUS IN GEMINI. The age of information begins. This generation was the first to be brought up on television. You stock up on cordless telephones, answering machines, faxes, modems, and car phones—any new way to communicate. You have an inquiring, curious, highly original mind. You're the talk-show person.

URANUS IN CANCER. You have unorthodox ideas about parenting, shelter, food, and child rearing. You are the "New Age" people, fascinated with the subconscious, memories, dreams, and psychic research. During this time period, the home was transformed with electronic gadgets. Many of you are sure to have home computers.

URANUS IN LEO. This period coincided with the rise of rock and roll and the heyday of Hollywood. Self-expression led to the exhibitionism of the Sixties. Electronic media was used skillfully for self-promotion and self-expression. This generation, now in your thirties, will have unusual love affairs and extraordinary children. You'll show the full force of your personality in a unique way.

URANUS IN VIRGO. This generation arrived at a time of student rebellions, the civil rights movement, and general acceptance of health foods. You'll be concerned with pollution and cleaning up the environment. You may revolutionize the healing arts, making nontraditional methods acceptable. This generation also has campaigned against the use of dangerous pesticides and smoking in public spaces.

URANUS IN LIBRA. Born at a time when the divorce rate soared and the women's liberation movement gained ground, this generation will have some revolutionary ideas about marriage and partnerships. You may have an on-again, off-again relationship, prefer unusual partners, or prefer to stay uncommitted. This generation will pioneer concepts in justice and revolutionize the arts.

URANUS IN SCORPIO. Uranus here shook up our sexual ideas. And this generation, just beginning to enter adulthood, will have unorthodox sex lives. You'll delve beneath the surface of life to explore life after death past lives and mediumship. This time period signaled the public awareness of the "New Age." Body and mind control will be an issue with the generation. You may make great breakthroughs in scientific research and the medical field, especially in surgery.

URANUS IN SAGITTARIUS. This generation rebels against orthodoxy and may invent some unusual modes of religion, education, or philosophy. In Sagittarius, Uranus will make breakthroughs in long-distance travel—these children may be the first to travel in outer space. When this placement happened earlier, the Wright Brothers began to fly and the aviator Charles Lindbergh was born.

URANUS IN CAPRICORN. For the past few years, Uranus is shaking up the established structures of society in Capricorn. Stock market ups and downs, the Berlin Wall crumbling, and new practical high-tech gadgets changed our lives. Long-established financial and technological structures, like Pan Am airlines, are suddenly disappearing. Those born with this placement will take an innovative approach to their careers. Capricorn likes tradition, while Uranus likes change. Therefore, this generation's task is to reconcile the two forces.

URANUS IN AQUARIUS. Uranus shines brightest in Aquarius, the sign it rules. During its previous transit, innovators such as Orson Welles and Leonard Bernstein were born, and breakthroughs in science and technology changed the way we view the world. Uranus will enter Aquarius again starting this year and lasting until 2002, when we can look forward to this planet performing at its most revolutionary, eccentric, and brilliant peak. Though this planet promises many surprises in store, we can be sure that the generation born during this time will be very concerned with global issues that are shared by all humanity, and with experimentation and innovation on every level.

URANUS IN PISCES. Many of the first television personalities were born with this placement, because this was the first generation to exploit the electronic media. This was the time of Prohibition (Pisces rules alcohol) and the development of the film industry (also Pisces-ruled). The next go-round, in the early 2000s, could bring on the Hollywood of the twenty-first century!

Are You Imaginative?
What Are Your Dreams, Fantasies, Ideals?
Neptune Will Tell

Neptune shows how well you and those of your generation create a world of illusion (very useful in creative work). Do you have an innate glamour you can tap? With Neptune, what you see is not what you get. Neptune is the planet of dissolution (it dissolves hard reality). It is not interested in the world at face value; it dons tinted glasses or blurs the facts with the haze of an intoxicating substance. Where Neptune is, you don't see things quite clearly. This planet's function is to express our visions, and it is most at home in Pisces, which it rules.

Neptune was in the following signs in this century:

NEPTUNE IN CANCER. Family ties were glamorized and extended to the nation. Motherhood and home cooking were cast in a rosy glow (Julia Child was born with this placement). People born then waved the flag, read Dr.

Spock, and watched Walt Disney. Many gave their lives for their homeland.

NEPTUNE IN LEO. Neptune in Leo brought the lavish spending and glamour of the 1920s, which blurred the harsh realities of the age. When Neptune left Leo and moved into Virgo in 1929, the stock market fell. This Neptune, which favored the entertainment industry, brought the golden age of Broadway and the rise of the star system. Those born with this placement have a flair for drama and may idealize fame without realizing there is a price to pay.

NEPTUNE IN VIRGO. Neptune in Virgo glamorizes health and fitness (Jane Fonda). This generation invented fitness videos, marathon running, and television sports. You may include psychotherapy as part of your mental-health regime. You glamorized the workplace and many became workaholics.

NEPTUNE IN LIBRA. Born at a time when "Ozzie and Harriet" was the marital ideal, this generation went on to glamorize "relating" in ways that idealized sexual equality and is still trying to find its balance in marriage. There have been many divorces as this generation tries to adapt traditional marriage to modern times and allow both sexes free expression.

NEPTUNE IN SCORPIO. This generation was born at a time which glamorized sex and drugs, and matured when the price was paid in AIDS and drug wars. The Berlin Wall was erected when they were born, torn down when they matured. Because of your intense powers of regeneration, part of your mission will be healing and transforming the earth after damage resulting from the delusions of the past is revealed.

NEPTUNE IN SAGITTARIUS. Spiritual and philosophical values were glamorized in the "New Age" period. Neptune brought out the truth-teller who revealed Watergate and unethical conduct in business. Space travel became a reality and children born with the placement could travel mentally or physically to other worlds.

NEPTUNE IN CAPRICORN. Now in Capricorn, Neptune brings illusions of material power, which were tested as Saturn passed by and were then shaken up by Uranus. It is a time when spiritual interests are commercialized and gain respectability. The business world, however, has been rocked with scandals and broken illusions, as management distances itself from the product and becomes engrossed in power plays. Those born during this period will embody these Neptune energies in some way and express them at maturity.

How Do You Handle Power?
Find Pluto in Your Chart!

Pluto is slow-moving, covering only seven signs in the past century. It tells lots about how your generation handles power, what makes it seem "cool" to others. This planet brings deep subconscious feelings to light, digging out our secrets though painful probing, to effect a total transformation. Nothing escapes—or is sacred—with Pluto.

PLUTO IN GEMINI. Some of our most transformative writers were born with Pluto in Gemini, such as Hemingway and F. Scott Fitzgerald. Sex taboos were broken by other writers such as Henry Miller, D. H. Lawrence and James Joyce. Muckraking journalism became an agent for transformation. Psychoanalysis (talk therapy) was developed.

PLUTO IN CANCER. Motherhood, security, and the breast became fetishes for this generation; it was also the generation that saw the rise of women's rights and of dictators who swayed the masses with emotional appeals and the rise of nationalism. This generation is deeply sentimental, placing great value on emotional security. This was also the time of the depression, the deprivation of food and security. This is the sign of mother power; intense, emotional sympathy; and an understanding of where others are emotionally dependent. Power issues center around using the understanding of where others need mothering to either "feed" them psychologically or literally, or to manipulate them.

PLUTO IN LEO. Self-expression becomes a power play for this generation, which invented rock and roll. The rise of television and the development of the entertainment business emphasize Leo's transformative power. This was the generation that "did its own thing" and demanded sexual freedom. These people will go to great lengths to get attention and recognition. This desire for personal recognition can lead to self-aggrandizement and extremes of self-promotion, such as baring innermost secrets on a talk show or to a tabloid. This generation also produced some of the most flamboyant entrepreners of the 80s—the big-spending billionaires who lived in the grand style. Pluto in Leo loves to see itself in everything. As this generation ages, it will remain extremely visible and demanding of attention.

PLUTO IN VIRGO. This generation returned to traditional values and became workaholics. Fitness, health, and career interests took over mass consciousness. To increase efficiency, this generation stocked up on high-tech gadgets such as faxes, computer dictionaries, time planners, and portable telephones. This generation uses power by discrimination. These became the "yuppies" who want the best of everything. A keen, judgmental mind, good organizational skills, and an extremely dutiful attitude characterize their exercise of power.

PLUTO IN LIBRA. This generation is just beginning to come into its own. At their birthtime, there was landmark legislation on life-or-death issues such as abortion and euthanasia. The ERA and gay rights movements were coming into mass attention. Marriage is being redefined as an equal partnership and parental roles are being shared. There may be a compulsive need to be in a relationship and to link with others. This generation will exercise power in a diplomatic way, working well in partnerships rather than independently. This is more of a "we" person than an independent operator.

PLUTO IN SCORPIO. Pluto has been in its ruling sign of Scorpio for the past seven years, and during this time has come as close to earth as its irregular orbit will allow. So it is no wonder that we have experienced the full force of this tiny planet. Somewhere in each of our lives, we have felt Pluto's transforming power, especially in 1989, when Pluto was at its perhelion.

For those of you who have felt "nuked" by Pluto (Scorpios and those with Scorpio rising, especially), it may be helpful to remember one of the key symbols for Scorpio—the phoenix rising from the ashes. Pluto clears the decks in order to create anew. In the Scorpio area of your life, you will go through changes in order to be "born again" and to make way for a period of optimism and expansion. Scorpion themes such as sexuality, birth, and death—and the transcendence of death—will be reflected in the way this generation exercises power.

PLUTO IN SAGITTARIUS (January 17, 1995—2008). This should signal a time of great optimism and spiritual development, bringing the century to an exciting close. The generation born now will be expansive on a mass level. In Sagittarius, the traveler, there's a good possibility that Pluto, the planet of extremes, will make space travel a reality for many of us. Look for new dimensions in publishing, emphasis on higher education, and a concern with animal rights issues. Religion will have a new emphasis in our lives and we'll certainly be developing far-reaching philosophies designed to elevate our lives with a new sense of purpose.

CHAPTER 6

How Your Rising Sign Can Change Your Outward Image

At the moment you were born, when you assumed a physical body and became an independent person, an astrological sign—that is, a specific thirty-degree portion of the zodiac—was passing over the eastern horizon. Called your "rising sign" or ascendant, this sign is very important in your horoscope because it sets your horoscope (or "astrological life") in motion. In effect, it says, "Here I am!" as it announces your arrival in the world.

Rising signs change every two hours with the Earth's rotation. If you were born early in the morning when the sun was on the horizon (which makes your sun sign also your rising sign), then you will come across to others like the prototype of your sun sign. That is also why we call those born with their sun sign on the horizon a "double Aquarius" or a "double Virgo." You have twice as much input from that sign.

If you were born with another sign on the horizon, you will advertise yourself more like that other sign. This other sign will mask slightly—or completely disguise—your basic sun-sign character. If people have difficulty guessing your sun sign, this is probably the reason, particularly if you have a very outgoing ascendant, such a Leo ascendant, and a rather shy sun sign, like Virgo.

On the other hand, a rather conservative Capricorn ascendant can tone down the intensity of a Scorpio or make a jovial Sagittarian seem far more serious than he really is. Your rising sign is your "cover" or mask. Often a person will project just one facet of a rising sign. For instance, one person with a Sagittarius rising would be a lover of horses and a world traveler; another with the same ascendant would project the more spiritual side of this sign.

In your horoscope chart, the other signs follow the rising sign in sequence, rotating counterclockwise over the houses of your chart and coloring each one with their personality. Therefore, the rising sign sets up the tone of your chart. It rules the first house, which is the physical body (your appearance) and also influences your style, tastes, health, and physical environment (where you are most comfortable working and living).

You'll find your rising sign on the chart on pages 69-70. Since rising signs move rapidly, you should know your birthtime as close to the minute as possible. If you are unsure about the exact time, but know within a few hours, check the following descriptions to see which is most like the personality you project.

ARIES RISING. You'll be the most aggressive version of your sun sign, coming across as a go-getter—headed for the fast track, dynamic, energetic, and assertive. Billy Graham and Bette Midler show the sparkle and fire of this ascendant. But since you can also be somewhat impatient and combative, try to either consider where the other person is coming from or head for an area where your feistiness will be appreciated. With this ascendant, you may prefer the color red—or wear it a lot—instinctively grabbing for the red sweater or tie. Many of you walk with your head thrust forward like the ram. You may also have prominent eyebrows or a very wide browline. At some point in your life, you may acquire a facial scar or a head injury.

TAURUS RISING. There is nothing lightweight about the impression you give. You have a strong, steady presence; you are not easily dismissed. You are more sensual, patient, and pleasure oriented than others of your sign. You love good food and may be an excellent cook. Green thumbs are also common with this nature-loving ascendant. You may have a very unusual and memorable voice and great concentration and stamina, like TV news anchor Dan Rather. Though your frame is often stocky, with a tendency to put on weight, some curvaceous beauty queens and sex goddesses are born with this placement.

GEMINI RISING. You're a great talker, in constant motion. You're a quick thinker and fast learner, like comedienne Phyllis Diller and rock star and songwriter Bruce Springsteen. On the minus side, you could come across as nervous, scattered, a jack-of-all-trades. Play up your analytical mind and your ability to communicate and to adapt to different people and environments. This ascendant could also give you writing talent or an affinity for work that uses your hands, such as massage or piano playing. Learning a keyboard is second nature to you. You gesture often and probably have light coloring and fine features.

CANCER RISING. You may come across as sensitive and caring, one who enjoys taking care of others. You may seem a bit moodier than others of your sign and more self-protective, like actor John Travolta. You have very quick responses to emotional situations. You are also very astute businesswise, with a sharp sense of what will sell, like H. Ross Perot, a double Cancer. You may choose work dealing with hotels or shelter business, decorating or working with children. Physically, you may be a lunar type, with a large chest area, a round face, and delicate sensitive skin. Or you may be a "crab" type, with wide-set eyes and prominent bone structure.

LEO RISING. You project a regal air of authority, which instills confidence in your abilities. You come across as someone who can take charge. You are very poised in the spotlight and you know how to present yourself to play up your special star quality, like Ava Gardner, ballerina Cynthia Gregory, or Marilyn Monroe. You attract attention and you tend to take center stage graciously. In business, you can be the epitome of executive style.

VIRGO RISING. Your style may be rather conservative, restrained, and classic, but your intelligence and your analytical ability shine brightly. You seem well organized, with a no-nonsense air of knowing what you're doing. Never one to slack off, you're a hard worker who gets on with it. Your manner may be a bit aloof, and you can be critical of others who don't share your sense of mastery of your craft, of doing it to perfection. But this critical quality serves you well as an editor, writer, or teacher. You may also be drawn to the health or service fields. A high-profile example: George Bush.

LIBRA RISING. You come across as charming, attractive, well dressed, and diplomatic. Like Nancy Reagan, the first impression you give is one of social ease and harmony. You enjoy working with others and it shows. You thrive in partnerships and relationships, rather than going it alone. You may have aesthetic concerns, such as fashion or design, or you could gravitate to the diplomatic or legal fields. Physically, you'll have delicate, harmonious features; graceful gestures; and a lovely, often dimpled, smile.

SCORPIO RISING. Even if you don't say a word, your presence carries a charge of excitement and an air of mystery. Margaret Thatcher and Jacqueline Kennedy Onassis are terrific examples. Intense and charismatic, you'll make your presence felt with a penetrating gaze. Be careful not to come on too overwhelmingly strong. You might consider toning down your intensity, tempering it with a touch of humor. Less open than others of your sign, you can be very manipulative when chasing your goals. You project an air of subtle sexuality, of a secret agenda that could fascinate others. Sexual expression will be an important issue for you. You may wear a great deal of the "no-color," black.

SAGITTARIUS RISING. This ascendant can push normally home-loving signs to exotic locales. Always on the go, you have energy to burn. You're a bouncy, athletic version of your sign, like Ted Turner, with an upbeat personality that exudes cheerful optimism. You adore competitive sports that require lots of leg power. You may also be drawn to horses or horse-related activities. You are frank and direct in manner and don't hesitate to say what you think, even if it means stepping on some tender toes. Travel excites you—the more exotic the destination, the better. You may be attracted to idealistic or philosophical activities, or to teaching, publishing, or religious careers. Your sense of humor wins fans, but some of you may have to work on developing tact and diplomacy. Another famous example: Raquel Welch.

CAPRICORN RISING. You are the serious, hard-working type with a very sharp business sense. (*Cosmopolitan* editor Helen Gurley Brown, who has this ascendant, has called herself a "mouseburger"). But you could also have the traditional flair of Fred Astaire. A great organizer, you function well in a structured or corporate environment. Not a frivolous type, you aim to be taken seriously, like Paul Newman. You'll easily adapt to present the classiest impression appropriate to your business. You understand how to delegate and to use the talents of others, which could land you a leadership position. You prefer a traditional atmosphere, antiques, and possessions of "quiet quality." Take special care of your knees, teeth and bone structure, which are vulnerable areas.

AQUARIUS RISING. Like daredevil Evil Knievel, you're charismatic and individualistic—you know how to get attention, sometimes in a startling way that shakes everyone up. You'll dress to please yourself—never mind the dress code. Be sure to find a business that appreciates your eccentric side, one with a cause or principles you believe in. Your job should give you plenty of space and allow you to work independently. You'll make your own rules and probably won't take well to authority or outside discipline—you know what's best for you, anyway. You may be attracted to a high-tech career or to one that probes the depths of the mind in some way.

PISCES RISING. You'll express the most artistic, romantic, and imaginative side of your sun sign. Like Phil Donohue, you'll come across as empathetic, a good listener who is able to cue in to where others are coming from—a valuable interview asset. You may be quite dramatic, and present yourself as a "character," like baseball's Yogi Berra or author Norman Mailer. You are very happy on the water, or in a home that overlooks water. You might gravitate to the theater, dance or film worlds, or to any creative environment. Or you could take another Pisces tack and show your more spiritual side, dedicating yourself to helping others. Beautiful eyes and talented dancing feet are frequent gifts of this ascendant. One of your most vulnerable points is your supersensitivity to drugs, chemicals, or alcohol. High-profile example: Richard Pryor.

	1 AM	2 AM	3 AM	4 AM	5 AM	6 AM	7 AM	8 AM	9 AM	10 AM	11 AM	12 NOON
Jan 1	Lib	Sc	Sc	Sc	Sag	Sag	Cap	Cap	Aq	Aq	Pis	Ar
Jan 9	Lib	Sc	Sc	Sag	Sag	Sag	Cap	Cap	Aq	Pis	Ar	Tau
Jan 17	Sc	Sc	Sc	Sag	Sag	Cap	Cap	Aq	Aq	Pis	Ar	Tau
Jan 25	Sc	Sc	Sc	Sag	Sag	Sag	Cap	Cap	Aq	Pis	Ar	Tau
Feb 2	Sc	Sc	Sag	Sag	Cap	Cap	Aq	Pis	Pis	Ar	Tau	Gem
Feb 10	Sc	Sag	Sag	Sag	Cap	Cap	Aq	Pis	Ar	Tau	Tau	Gem
Feb 18	Sc	Sag	Sag	Cap	Cap	Aq	Pis	Pis	Ar	Tau	Gem	Gem
Feb 26	Sag	Sag	Sag	Cap	Aq	Aq	Pis	Ar	Tau	Tau	Gem	Gem
Mar 6	Sag	Sag	Cap	Cap	Aq	Pis	Pis	Ar	Tau	Gem	Gem	Can
Mar 14	Sag	Cap	Cap	Aq	Aq	Pis	Ar	Tau	Tau	Gem	Gem	Can
Mar 22	Sag	Cap	Cap	Aq	Pis	Ar	Ar	Tau	Gem	Gem	Can	Can
Mar 30	Cap	Cap	Aq	Pis	Pis	Ar	Tau	Tau	Gem	Can	Can	Can
Apr 7	Cap	Cap	Aq	Pis	Ar	Ar	Tau	Gem	Gem	Can	Can	Leo
Apr 14	Cap	Aq	Aq	Pis	Ar	Tau	Tau	Gem	Gem	Can	Can	Leo
Apr 22	Cap	Aq	Pis	Ar	Ar	Tau	Gem	Gem	Gem	Can	Leo	Leo
Apr 30	Aq	Aq	Pis	Ar	Tau	Tau	Gem	Can	Can	Can	Leo	Leo
May 8	Aq	Pis	Ar	Ar	Tau	Gem	Gem	Can	Can	Leo	Leo	Leo
May 16	Aq	Pis	Ar	Tau	Gem	Gem	Can	Can	Can	Leo	Leo	Vir
May 24	Pis	Ar	Ar	Tau	Gem	Gem	Can	Can	Leo	Leo	Leo	Vir
June 1	Pis	Ar	Tau	Gem	Gem	Can	Can	Can	Leo	Leo	Vir	Vir
June 9	Ar	Ar	Tau	Gem	Gem	Can	Can	Leo	Leo	Leo	Vir	Vir
June 17	Ar	Tau	Gem	Gem	Can	Can	Can	Leo	Leo	Vir	Vir	Vir
June 25	Tau	Tau	Gem	Gem	Can	Can	Leo	Leo	Leo	Vir	Vir	Lib
July 3	Tau	Gem	Gem	Can	Can	Can	Leo	Leo	Vir	Vir	Vir	Lib
July 11	Tau	Gem	Gem	Can	Can	Leo	Leo	Leo	Vir	Vir	Lib	Lib
July 18	Gem	Gem	Can	Can	Can	Leo	Leo	Vir	Vir	Vir	Lib	Lib
July 26	Gem	Gem	Can	Can	Leo	Leo	Vir	Vir	Vir	Lib	Lib	Lib
Aug 3	Gem	Can	Can	Can	Leo	Leo	Vir	Vir	Vir	Lib	Lib	Sc
Aug 11	Gem	Can	Can	Leo	Leo	Leo	Vir	Vir	Lib	Lib	Lib	Sc
Aug 18	Can	Can	Can	Leo	Leo	Vir	Vir	Vir	Lib	Lib	Sc	Sc
Aug 27	Can	Can	Leo	Leo	Leo	Vir	Vir	Vir	Lib	Lib	Sc	Sc
Sept 4	Can	Can	Leo	Leo	Leo	Vir	Vir	Vir	Lib	Lib	Sc	Sc
Sept 12	Can	Leo	Leo	Leo	Vir	Vir	Lib	Lib	Lib	Sc	Sc	Sag
Sept 20	Leo	Leo	Leo	Vir	Vir	Vir	Lib	Lib	Sc	Sc	Sc	Sag
Sept 28	Leo	Leo	Leo	Vir	Vir	Lib	Lib	Lib	Sc	Sc	Sag	Sag
Oct 6	Leo	Leo	Vir	Vir	Vir	Lib	Lib	Sc	Sc	Sc	Sag	Sag
Oct 14	Leo	Vir	Vir	Vir	Lib	Lib	Lib	Sc	Sc	Sc	Sag	Cap
Oct 22	Leo	Vir	Vir	Vir	Lib	Lib	Lib	Sc	Sc	Sc	Sag	Cap
Oct 30	Vir	Vir	Vir	Lib	Lib	Sc	Sc	Sc	Sag	Sag	Cap	Cap
Nov 7	Vir	Vir	Lib	Lib	Lib	Sc	Sc	Sc	Sag	Sag	Cap	Cap
Nov 15	Vir	Vir	Vir	Lib	Sc	Sc	Sc	Sag	Sag	Cap	Cap	Aq
Nov 23	Vir	Lib	Lib	Lib	Sc	Sc	Sag	Sag	Sag	Cap	Cap	Aq
Dec 1	Vir	Lib	Lib	Sc	Sc	Sc	Sag	Sag	Cap	Cap	Aq	Aq
Dec 9	Lib	Lib	Lib	Sc	Sc	Sag	Sag	Sag	Cap	Cap	Aq	Pis
Dec 18	Lib	Lib	Sc	Sc	Sc	Sag	Sag	Cap	Cap	Aq	Aq	Pis
Dec 28	Lib	Lib	Sc	Sc	Sag	Sag	Sag	Cap	Aq	Aq	Pis	Ar

RISING SIGNS—P.M. BIRTHS

	1 PM	2 PM	3 PM	4 PM	5 PM	6 PM	7 PM	8 PM	9 PM	10 PM	11 PM	12 MIDNIGHT
Jan 1	Tau	Gem	Gem	Can	Can	Can	Leo	Leo	Vir	Vir	Vir	Lib
Jan 9	Tau	Gem	Gem	Can	Can	Leo	Leo	Leo	Vir	Vir	Vir	Lib
Jan 17	Gem	Gem	Can	Can	Can	Leo	Leo	Vir	Vir	Vir	Lib	Lib
Jan 25	Gem	Gem	Can	Can	Leo	Leo	Leo	Vir	Vir	Lib	Lib	Lib
Feb 2	Gem	Can	Can	Can	Leo	Leo	Vir	Vir	Vir	Lib	Lib	Sc
Feb 10	Gem	Can	Can	Leo	Leo	Leo	Vir	Vir	Lib	Lib	Lib	Sc
Feb 18	Can	Can	Can	Leo	Leo	Vir	Vir	Vir	Lib	Lib	Sc	Sc
Feb 26	Can	Can	Leo	Leo	Leo	Vir	Vir	Lib	Lib	Lib	Sc	Sc
Mar 6	Can	Can	Leo	Leo	Vir	Vir	Vir	Lib	Lib	Sc	Sc	Sc
Mar 14	Can	Leo	Leo	Vir	Vir	Vir	Lib	Lib	Lib	Sc	Sc	Sag
Mar 22	Leo	Leo	Leo	Vir	Vir	Lib	Lib	Lib	Sc	Sc	Sc	Sag
Mar 30	Leo	Leo	Vir	Vir	Vir	Lib	Lib	Sc	Sc	Sc	Sag	Sag
Apr 7	Leo	Leo	Vir	Vir	Lib	Lib	Lib	Sc	Sc	Sc	Sag	Sag
Apr 14	Leo	Vir	Vir	Vir	Lib	Lib	Sc	Sc	Sc	Sag	Sag	Cap
Apr 22	Leo	Vir	Vir	Lib	Lib	Lib	Sc	Sc	Sc	Sag	Sag	Cap
Apr 30	Vir	Vir	Vir	Lib	Lib	Sc	Sc	Sc	Sag	Sag	Cap	Cap
May 8	Vir	Vir	Lib	Lib	Lib	Sc	Sc	Sag	Sag	Sag	Cap	Cap
May 16	Vir	Vir	Lib	Lib	Sc	Sc	Sc	Sag	Sag	Cap	Cap	Aq
May 24	Vir	Lib	Lib	Lib	Sc	Sc	Sag	Sag	Sag	Cap	Cap	Aq
June 1	Vir	Lib	Lib	Sc	Sc	Sc	Sag	Sag	Cap	Cap	Aq	Aq
June 9	Lib	Lib	Lib	Sc	Sc	Sag	Sag	Sag	Cap	Cap	Aq	Pis
June 17	Lib	Lib	Sc	Sc	Sc	Sag	Sag	Cap	Cap	Aq	Aq	Pis
June 25	Lib	Lib	Sc	Sc	Sag	Sag	Sag	Cap	Cap	Aq	Pis	Ar
July 3	Lib	Sc	Sc	Sc	Sag	Sag	Cap	Cap	Aq	Aq	Pis	Ar
July 11	Lib	Sc	Sc	Sag	Sag	Sag	Cap	Cap	Aq	Pis	Ar	Tau
July 18	Sc	Sc	Sc	Sag	Sag	Cap	Cap	Aq	Aq	Pis	Ar	Tau
July 26	Sc	Sc	Sag	Sag	Sag	Cap	Cap	Aq	Pis	Ar	Tau	Tau
Aug 3	Sc	Sc	Sag	Sag	Cap	Cap	Aq	Aq	Pis	Ar	Tau	Gem
Aug 11	Sc	Sag	Sag	Sag	Cap	Cap	Aq	Pis	Ar	Tau	Tau	Gem
Aug 18	Sc	Sag	Sag	Cap	Cap	Aq	Pis	Pis	Ar	Tau	Gem	Gem
Aug 27	Sag	Sag	Sag	Cap	Aq	Aq	Pis	Ar	Tau	Tau	Gem	Gem
Sept 4	Sag	Sag	Cap	Cap	Aq	Pis	Pis	Ar	Tau	Gem	Gem	Can
Sept 12	Sag	Sag	Cap	Aq	Aq	Pis	Ar	Tau	Tau	Gem	Gem	Can
Sept 20	Sag	Cap	Cap	Aq	Pis	Pis	Ar	Tau	Gem	Gem	Can	Can
Sept 28	Cap	Cap	Aq	Aq	Pis	Ar	Tau	Tau	Gem	Gem	Can	Can
Oct 6	Cap	Cap	Aq	Pis	Ar	Ar	Tau	Gem	Gem	Can	Can	Leo
Oct 14	Cap	Aq	Aq	Pis	Ar	Tau	Tau	Gem	Gem	Can	Can	Leo
Oct 22	Cap	Aq	Pis	Ar	Ar	Tau	Gem	Gem	Can	Can	Leo	Leo
Oct 30	Aq	Aq	Pis	Ar	Tau	Tau	Gem	Can	Can	Leo	Leo	Leo
Nov 7	Aq	Aq	Pis	Ar	Tau	Tau	Gem	Can	Can	Can	Leo	Leo
Nov 15	Aq	Pis	Ar	Tau	Gem	Gem	Can	Can	Can	Leo	Leo	Vir
Nov 23	Pis	Ar	Ar	Tau	Gem	Gem	Can	Can	Leo	Leo	Leo	Vir
Dec 1	Pis	Ar	Tau	Gem	Gem	Can	Can	Can	Leo	Leo	Vir	Vir
Dec 9	Ar	Tau	Tau	Gem	Gem	Can	Can	Leo	Leo	Leo	Vir	Vir
Dec 18	Ar	Tau	Gem	Gem	Can	Can	Can	Leo	Leo	Vir	Vir	Vir
Dec 28	Tau	Tau	Gem	Gem	Can	Can	Leo	Leo	Vir	Vir	Vir	Lib

CHAPTER 7

Look Up Your Planets

The following tables are provided so that you can look up the signs of seven major planets—Venus, Mars, Saturn, Jupiter, Uranus, Neptune, and Pluto. We do not have room for tables for the moon and Mercury, which change signs often.

How to Use the Venus Table

Find the year of your birth in the vertical column on the left, then follow across the page until you find the correct date. The Venus sign is at the top of that column.

How to Use the Mars, Saturn, and Jupiter Tables

Find the year of your birth date on the left side of each column. The dates the planet entered each sign are listed on the right side of each column. (Signs are abbreviated to the first three letters.) Your birthday should fall on or between each date listed, and your planetary placement should correspond to the earlier sign of that period.

VENUS SIGNS 1901–2000

	Aries	Taurus	Gemini	Cancer	Leo	Virgo
1901	3/29-4/22	4/22-5/17	5/17-6/10	6/10-7/5	7/5-7/29	7/29-8/23
1902	5/7-6/3	6/3-6/30	6/30-7/25	7/25-8/19	8/19-9/13	9/13-10/7
1903	2/28-3/24	3/24-4/18	4/18-5/13	5/13-6/9	6/9-7/7	7/7-8/17
						9/6-11/8
1904	3/13-5/7	5/7-6/1	6/1-6/25	6/25-7/19	7/19-8/13	8/13-9/6
1905	2/3-3/6	3/6-4/9	7/8-8/6	8/6-9/1	9/1-9/27	9/27-10/21
	4/9-5/28	5/28-7/8				
1906	3/1-4/7	4/7-5/2	5/2-5/26	5/26-6/20	6/20-7/16	7/16-8/11
1907	4/27-5/22	5/22-6/16	6/16-7/11	7/11-8/4	8/4-8/29	8/29-9/22
1908	2/14-3/10	3/10-4/5	4/5-5/5	5/5-9/8	9/8-10/8	10/8-11/3
1909	3/29-4/22	4/22-5/16	5/16-6/10	6/10-7/4	7/4-7/29	7/29-8/23
1910	5/7-6/3	6/4-6/29	6/30-7/24	7/25-8/18	8/19-9/12	9/13-10/6
1911	2/28-3/23	3/24-4/17	4/18-5/12	5/13-6/8	6/9-7/7	7/8-11/8
1912	4/13-5/6	5/7-5/31	6/1-6/24	6/24-7/18	7/19-8/12	8/13-9/5
1913	2/3-3/6	3/7-5/1	7/8-8/5	8/6-8/31	9/1-9/26	9/27-10/20
	5/2-5/30	5/31-7/7				
1914	3/14-4/6	4/7-5/1	5/2-5/25	5/26-6/19	6/20-7/15	7/16-8/10
1915	4/27-5/21	5/22-6/15	6/16-7/10	7/11-8/3	8/4-8/28	8/29-9/21
1916	2/14-3/9	3/10-4/5	4/6-5/5	5/6-9/8	9/9-10/7	10/8-11/2
1917	3/29-4/21	4/22-5/15	5/16-6/9	6/10-7/3	7/4-7/28	7/29-8/21
1918	5/7-6/2	6/3-6/28	6/29-7/24	7/25-8/18	8/19-9/11	9/12-10/5
1919	2/27-3/22	3/23-4/16	4/17-5/12	5/13-6/7	6/8-7/7	7/8-11/8
1920	4/12-5/6	5/7-5/30	5/31-6/23	6/24-7/18	7/19-8/11	8/12-9/4
1921	2/3-3/6	3/7-4/25	7/8-8/5	8/6-8/31	9/1-9/25	9/26-10/20
	4/26-6/1	6/2-7/7				
1922	3/13-4/6	4/7-4/30	5/1-5/25	5/26-6/19	6/20-7/14	7/15-8/9
1923	4/27-5/21	5/22-6/14	6/15-7/9	7/10-8/3	8/4-8/27	8/28-9/20
1924	2/13-3/8	3/9-4/4	4/5-5/5	5/6-9/8	9/9-10/7	10/8-11/12
1925	3/28-4/20	4/21-5/15	5/16-6/8	6/9-7/3	7/4-7/27	7/28-8/21

Libra	Scorpio	Sagittarius	Capricorn	Aquarius	Pisces
8/23-9/17	9/17-10/12	10/12-1/16	1/16-2/9 11/7-12/5	2/9 12/5-1/11	3/5-3/29
10/7-10/31	10/31-11/24	11/24-12/18	12/18-1/11	2/6-4/4	1/11-2/6 4/4-5/7
8/17-9/6 11/8-12/9	12/9-1/5			1/11-2/4	2/4-2/28
9/6-9/30	9/30-10/25	1/5-1/30 10/25-11/18	1/30-2/24 11/18-12/13	2/24-3/19 12/13-1/7	3/19-4/13
10/21-11/14	11/14-12/8	12/8-1/1/06			1/7-2/3
8/11-9/7	9/7-10/9 12/15-12/25	10/9-12/15 12/25-2/6	1/1-1/25	1/25-2/18	2/18-3/14
9/22-10/16	10/16-11/9	11/9-12/3	2/6-3/6 12/3-12/27	3/6-4/2 12/27-1/20	4/2-4/27
11/3-11/28	11/28-12/22	12/22-1/15			1/20-2/14
8/23-9/17	9/17-10/12	10/12-11/17	1/15-2/9 11/17-12/5	2/9-3/5 12/5-1/15	3/5-3/29
10/7-10/30	10/31-11/23	11/24-12/17	12/18-12/31	1/1-1/15 1/29-4/4	1/16-1/28 4/5-5/6
11/19-12/8	12/9-12/31		1/1-1/10	1/11-2/2	2/3-2/27
9/6-9/30	1/1-1/4 10/1-10/24	1/5-1/29 10/25-11/17	1/30-2/23 11/18-12/12	2/24-3/18 12/13-12/31	3/19-4/12
10/21-11/13	11/14-12/7	12/8-12/31		1/1-1/6	1/7-2/2
8/11-9/6	9/7-10/9 12-6/12-30	10/10-12/5 12/31	1/1-1/24	1/25-2/17	2/18-3/13
9/22-10/15	10/16-11/8	1/1-2/6 11/9-12/2	2/7-3/6 12/3-12/26	3/7-4/1 12/27-12/31	4/2-4/26
11/3-11/27	11/28-12/21	12/22-12/31		1/1-1/19	1/20-2/13
8/22-9/16	9/17-10/11	1/1-1/14 10/12-11/6	1/15-2/7 11/7-12/5	2/8-3/4 12/6-12/31	3/5-3/28
10/6-10/29	10/30-11/22	11/23-12/16	12/17-12/31	1/1-4/5	4/6-5/6
11/9-12/8	12/9-12/31		1/1-1/9	1/10-2/2	2/3-2/26
9/5-9/30	1/1-1/3 9/31-10/23	1/4-1/28 10/24-11/17	1/29-2/22 11/18-12/11	2/23-3/18 12/12-12/31	3/19-4/11
10/21-11/13	11/14-12/7	12/8-12/31		1/1-1/6	1/7-2/2
8/10-9/6	9/7-10/10 11/29-12/31	10/11-11/28	1/1-1/24	1/25-2/16	2/17-3/12
9/21-10/14	1/1 10/15-11/7	1/2-2/6 11/8-12/1	2/7-3/5 12/2-12/25	3/6-3/31 12/26-12/31	4/1-4/26
11/3-11/26	11/27-12/21	12/22-12/31		1/1-1/19	1/20-2/12
8/22-9/15	9/16-10/11	1/1-1/14 10-12/11-6	1/15-2/7 11/7-12/5	2/8-3/3 12/6-12/31	3/4-3/27

VENUS SIGNS 1901–2000

	Aries	Taurus	Gemini	Cancer	Leo	Virgo
1926	5/7-6/2	6/3-6/28	6/29-7/23	7/24-8/17	8/18-9/11	9/12-10/5
1927	2/27-3/22	3/23-4/16	4/17-5/11	5/12-6/7	6/8-7/7	7/8-11/9
1928	4/12-5/5	5/6-5/29	5/30-6/23	6/24-7/17	7/18-8/11	8/12-9/4
1929	2/3-3/7 4/20-6/2	3/8-4/19 6/3-7/7	7/8-8/4	8/5-8/30	8/31-9/25	9/26-10/19
1930	3/13-4/5	4/6-4/30	5/1-5/24	5/25-6/18	6/19-7/14	7/15-8/9
1931	4/26-5/20	5/21-6/13	6/14-7/8	7/9-8/2	8/3-8/26	8/27-9/19
1932	2/12-3/8	3/9-4/3	4/4-5/5 7/13-7/27	5/6-7/12 7/28-9/8	9/9-10/6	10/7-11/1
1933	3/27-4/19	4/20-5/28	5/29-6/8	6/9-7/2	7/3-7/26	7/27-8/20
1934	5/6-6/1	6/2-6/27	6/28-7/22	7/23-8/16	8/17-9/10	9/11-10/4
1935	2/26-3/21	3/22-4/15	4/16-5/10	5/11-6/6	6/7-7/6	7/7-11/8
1936	4/11-5/4	5/5-5/28	5/29-6/22	6/23-7/16	7/17-8/10	8/11-9/4
1937	2/2-3/8 4/14-6/3	3/9-4/17 6/4-7/6	7/7-8/3	8/4-8/29	8/30-9/24	9/25-10/18
1938	3/12-4/4	4/5-4/28	4/29-5/23	5/24-6/18	6/19-7/13	7/14-8/8
1939	4-25/5/19	5/20-6/13	6/14-7/8	7/9-8/1	8/2-8/25	8/26-9/19
1940	2/12-3/7	3/8-4/3	4/4-5/5 7/5-7/31	5/6-7/4 8/1-9/8	9/9-10/5	10/6-10/31
1941	3/27-4/19	4/20-5/13	5/14-6/6	6/7-7/1	7/2-7/26	7/27-8/20
1942	5/6-6/1	6/2-6/26	6/27-7/22	7/23-8/16	8/17-9/9	9/10-10/3
1943	2/25-3/20	3/21-4/14	4/15-5/10	5/11-6/6	6/7-7/6	7/7-11/8
1944	4/10-5/3	5/4-5/28	5/29-6/21	6/22-7/16	7/17-8/9	8/10-9/2
1945	2/2-3/10 4/7-6/3	3/11-4/6 6/4-7/6	7/7-8/3	8/4-8/29	8/30-9/23	9/24-10/18
1946	3/11-4/4	4/5-4/28	4/29-5/23	5/24-6/17	6/18-7/12	7/13-8/8
1947	4/25-5/19	5/20-6/12	6/13-7/7	7/8-8/1	8/2-8/25	8/26-9/18
1948	2/11-3/7	3/8-4/3	4/4-5/6 6/29-8/2	5/7-6/28 8/3-9/7	9/8-10/5	10/6-10/31
1949	3/26-4/19	4/20-5/13	5/14-6/6	6/7-6/30	7/1-7/25	7/26-8/19
1950	5/5-5/31	6/1-6/26	6/27-7/21	7/22-8/15	8/16-9/9	9/10-10/3
1951	2/25-3/21	3/22-4/15	4/16-5/10	5/11-6/6	6/7-7/7	7/8-11/9

Libra	Scorpio	Sagittarius	Capricorn	Aquarius	Pisces
10/6-10/29	10/30-11/22	11/23-12/16	12/17-12/31	1/1-4/5	4/6-5/6
11/10-12/8	12/9-12/31	1/1-1/7	1/8	1/9-2/1	2/2-2/26
9/5-9/28	1/1-1/3	1/4-1/28	1/29-2/22	2/23-3/17	3/18-4/11
	9/29-10/23	10/24-11/16	11/17-12/11	12/12-12/31	
10/20-11/12	11/13-12/6	12/7-12/30	12/31	1/1-1/5	1/6-2/2
8/10-9/6	9/7-10/11	10/12-11/21	1/1-1/23	1/24-2/16	2/17-3/12
	11/22-12/31				
9/20-10/13	1/1-1/3	1/4-2/6	2/7-3/4	3/5-3/31	4/1-4/25
	10/14-11/6	11/7-11/30	12/1-12/24	12/25-12/31	
11/2-11/25	11/26-12/20	12/21-12/31		1/1-1/18	1/19-2/11
8/21-9/14	9/15-10/10	1/1-1/13	1/14-2/6	2/7-3/2	3/3-3/26
		10/11-11/5	11/6-12/4	12/5-12/31	
10/5-10/28	10/29-11/21	11/22-12/15	12/16-12/31	1/1-4/5	4/6-5/5
11/9-12/7	12/8-12/31		1/1-1/7	1/8-1/31	2/1-2/25
9/5-9/27	1/1-1/2	1/3-1/27	1/28-2/21	2/22-3/16	3/17-4/10
	9/28-10/22	10/23-11/15	11/16-12/10	12/11-12/31	
10/19-11/11	11/12-12/5	12/6-12/29	12/30-12/31	1/1-1/5	1/6-2/1
8/9-9/6	9/7-10/13	10/14-11/14	1/1-1/22	1/23-2/15	2/16-3/11
	11/15-12/31				
9/20-10/13	1/1-1/3	1/4-2/5	2/6-3/4	3/5-3/30	3/31-4/24
	10/14-11/6	11/7-11/30	12/1-12/24	12/25-12/31	
11/1-11/25	11/26-12/19	12/20-12/31		1/1-1/18	1/19-2/11
8/21-9/14	9/15-10/9	1/1-1/12	1/13-2/5	2/6-3/1	3/2-3/26
		10/10-11/5	11/6-12/4	12/5-12/31	
10/4-10/27	10/28-11/20	11/21-12/14	12/15-12/31	1/1-4/4	4/6-5/5
11/9-12/7	12/8-12/31		1/1-1/7	1/8-1/31	2/1-2/24
9/3-9/27	1/1-1/2	1/3-1/27	1/28-2/20	2/21-3/16	3/17-4/9
	9/28-10/21	10/22-11/15	11/16-12/10	12/11-12/31	
10/19-11/11	11/12-12/5	12/6-12/29	12/30-12/31	1/1-1/4	1/5-2/1
8/9-9/6	9/7-10/15	10/16-11/7	1/1-1/21	1/22-2/14	2/15-3/10
	11/8-12/31				
9/19-10/12	1/1-1/4	1/5-2/5	2/6-3/4	3/5-3/29	3/30-4/24
	10/13-11/5	11/6-11/29	11/30-12/23	12/24-12/31	
11/1-1/25	11/26-12/19	12/20-12/31		1/1-1/17	1/18-2/10
8/20-9/14	9/15-10/9	1/1-1/12	1/13-2/5	2/6-3/1	3/2-3/25
		10/10-11/5	11/6-12/5	12/6-12/31	
10/4-10/27	10/28-11/20	11/21-12/13	12/14-12/31	1/1-4/5	4/6-5/4
11/10-12/7	12/8-12/31		1/1-1/7	1/8-1/31	2/1-2/24

VENUS SIGNS 1901–2000

	Aries	Taurus	Gemini	Cancer	Leo	Virgo
1952	4/10-5/4	5/5-5/28	5/29-6/21	6/22-7/16	7/17-8/9	8/10-9/3
1953	2/2-3/13	3/4-3/31	7/8-8/3	8/4-8/29	8/30-9/24	9/25-10/18
	4/1-6/5	6/6-7/7				
1954	3/12-4/4	4/5-4/28	4/29-5/23	5/24-6/17	6/18-7/13	7/14-8/8
1955	4/25-5/19	5/20-6/13	6/14-7/7	7/8-8/1	8/2-8/25	8/26-9/18
1956	2/12-3/7	3/8-4/4	4/5-5/7	5/8-6/23	9/9-10/5	10/6-10/31
			6:24-8/4	8/5-9/8		
1957	3/26-4/19	4/20-5/13	5/14-6/6	6/7-7/1	7/2-7/26	7/7-8/19
1958	5/6-5/31	6/1-6/26	6/27-7/22	7/23-8/15	8/16-9/9	9/10-10/3
1959	2/25-3/20	3/21-4/14	4/15-5/10	5/11-6/6	6/7-7/8	7/9-9/20
					9/21-9/24	9/25-11/9
1960	4/10-5/3	5/4-5/28	5/29-6/21	6/22-7/15	7/16-8/9	8/10-9/2
1961	2/3-6/5	6/6-7/7	7/8-8/3	8/4-8/29	8/30-9/23	9/24-10/17
1962	3/11-4/3	4/4-4/28	4/29-5/22	5/23-6/17	6/18-7/12	7/13-8/8
1963	4/24-5/18	5/19-6/12	6/13-7/7	7/8-7/31	8/1-8/25	8/26-9/18
1964	2/11-3/7	3/8-4/4	4/5-5/9	5/10-6/17	9/9-10/5	10/6-10/31
			6/18-8/5	8/6-9/8		
1965	3/26-4/18	4/19-5/12	5/13-6/6	6/7-6/30	7/1-7/25	7/26-8/19
1966	5/6-6/31	6/1-6/26	6/27-7/21	7/22-8/15	8/16-9/8	9/9-10/2
1967	2/24-3/20	3/21-4/14	4/15-5/10	5/11-6/6	6/7-7/8	7/9-9/9
					9/10-10/1	10/2-11/9
1968	4/9-5/3	5/4-5/27	5/28-6/20	6/21-7/15	7/16-8/8	8/9-9/2
1969	2/3-6/6	6/7-7/6	7/7-8/3	8/4-8/28	8/29-9/22	9/23-10/17
1970	3/11-4/3	4/4-4/27	4/28-5/22	5/23-6/16	6/17-7/12	7/13-8/8
1971	4/24-5/18	5/19-6/12	6/13-7/6	7/7-7/31	8/1-8/24	8/25-9/17
1972	2/11-3/7	3/8-4/3	4/4-5/10	5/11-6/11		
			6/12-8/6	8/7-9/8	9/9-10/5	10/6-10/30
1973	3/25-4/18	4/18-5/12	5/13-6/5	6/6-6/29	7/1-7/25	7/26-8/19
1974						
	55-5/31	6/1-6/25	6/26-7/21	7/22-8/14	8/15-9/8	9/9-10/2
1975	2/24-3/20	3/21-4/13	4/14-5/9	5/10-6/6	6/7-7/9	7/10-9/2
					9/3-10/4	10/5-11/9

Libra	Scorpio	Sagittarius	Capricorn	Aquarius	Pisces
9/4-9/27	1/1-1/2	1/3-1/27	1/28-2/20	2/21-3/16	3/17-4/9
	9/28-10/21	10/22-11/15	11/16-12/10	12/11-12/31	
10/19-11/11	11/12-12/5	12/6-12/29	12/30-12/31	1/1-1/5	1/6-2/1
8/9-9/6	9/7-10/22	10/23-10/27	1/1-1/22	1/23-2/15	2/16-3/11
	10/28-12/31				
9/19-10/13	1/1-1/6	1/7-2/5	2/6-3/4	3/5-3/30	3/31-4/24
	10/14-11/5	11/6-11/30	12/1-12/24	12/25-12/31	
11/1-11/25	11/26-12/19	12/20-12/31		1/1-1/17	1/18-2/11
8/20-9/14	9/15-10/9	1/1-1/12	1/13-2/5	2/6-3/1	3/2-3/25
		10/10-11/5	11/6-12/16	12/7-12/31	
10/4-10/27	10/28-11/20	11/21-12/14	12/15-12/31	1/1-4/6	4/7-5/5
11/10-12/7	12/8-12/31		1/1-1/7	1/8-1/31	2/1-2/24
9/3-9/26	1/1-1/2	1/3-1/27	1/28-2/20	2/21-3/15	3/16-4/9
	9/27-10/21	10/22-11/15	11/16-12/10	12/11-12/31	
10/18-11/11	11/12-12/4	12/5-12/28	12/29-12/31	1/1-1/5	1/6-2/2
8/9-9/6	9/7-12/31		1/1-1/21	1/22-2/14	2/15-3/10
9/19-10/12	1/1-1/6	1/7-2/5	2/6-3/4	3/5-3/29	3/30-4/23
	10/13-11/5	11/6-11/29	11/30-12/23	12/24-12/31	
11/1-11/24	11/25-12/19	12/20-12/31		1/1-1/16	1/17-2/10
8/20-9/13	9/14-10/9	1/1-1/12	1/13-2/5	2/6-3/1	3/2-3/25
		10/10-11/5	11/6-12/7	12/8-12/31	
10/3-10/26	10/27-11/19	11/20-12/13	2/7-2/25	1/1-2/6	4/7-5/5
			12/14-12/31	2/26-4/6	
11/10-12/7	12/8-12/23		1/1-1/6	1/7-1/30	1/31-2/23
9/3-9/26	1/1	1/2-1/26	1/27-2/20	2/21-3/15	3/16-4/8
	9/27-10/21	10/22-11/14	11/15-12/9	12/10-12/31	
10/18-11/10	11/11-12/4	12/5-12/28	12/29-12/31	1/1-1/4	1/5-2/2
8/9-9/7	9/8-12/31		1/1-1/21	1/22-2/14	2/15-3/10
9/18-10/11	1/1-1/7	1/8-2/5	2/6-3/4	3/5-3/29	3/30-4/23
	10/12-11/5	11/6-11/29	11/30-12/23	12/24-12/31	
	11/25-12/18	12/19-12/31		1/1-1/16	1/17-2/10
10/31-11/24					
8/20-9/13		1/1-1/12	1/13-2/4	2/5-2/28	3/1-3/24
		10/9-11/5	11/6-12/7	12/8-12/31	
			1/30-2/28	1/1-1/29	
10/3-10/26	10/27-11/19	11/20-12/13	12/14-12/31	3/1-4/6	4/7-5/4
			1/1-1/6	1/7-1/30	1/31-2/23
11/10-12/7	12/8-12/31				

VENUS SIGNS 1901–2000

	Aries	Taurus	Gemini	Cancer	Leo	Virgo
1976	4/8-5/2	5/2-5/27	5/27-6/20	6/20-7/14	7/14-8/8	8/8-9/1
1977	2/2-6/6	6/6-7/6	7/6-8/2	8/2-8/28	8/28-9/22	9/22-10/17
1978	3/9-4/2	4/2-4/27	4/27-5/22	5/22-6/16	6/16-7/12	7/12-8/6
1979	4/23-5/18	5/18-6/11	6/11-7/6	7/6-7/30	7/30-8/24	8/24-9/17
1980	2/9-3/6	3/6-4/3	4/3-5/12	5/12-6/5	9/7-10/4	10/4-10/30
			6/5-8/6	8/6-9/7		
1981	3/24-4/17	4/17-5/11	5/11-6/5	6/5-6/29	6/29-7/24	7/24-8/18
1982	5/4-5/30	5/30-6/25	6/25-7/20	7/20-8/14	8/14-9/7	9/7-10/2
1983	2/22-3/19	3/19-4/13	4/13-5/9	5/9-6/6	6/6-7/10	7/10-8/27
					8/27-10/5	10/5-11/9
1984	4/7-5/2	5/2-5/26	5/26-6/20	6/20-7/14	7/14-8/7	8/7-9/1
1985	2/2-6/6	6/8-7/6	7/6-8/2	8/2-8/28	8/28-9/22	9/22-10/16
1986	3/9-4/2	4/2-4/26	4/26-5/21	5/21-6/15	6/15-7/11	7/11-8/7
1987	4/22-5/17	5/17-6/11	6/11-7/5	7/5-7/30	7/30-8/23	8/23-9/16
1988	2/9-3/6	3/6-4/3	4/3-5/17	5/17-5/27	9/7-10/4	10/4-10/29
			5/27-8/6	8/6-9/7		
1989	3/23-4/16	4/16-5/11	5/11-6/4	6/4-6/29	6/29-7/24	7/24-8/18
1990	5/4-5/30	5/30-6/25	6/25-7/20	7/20-8/13	8/13-9/7	9/7-10/1
1991	2/22-3/18	3/18-4/13	4/13-5/9	5/9-6/6	6/6-7/11	7/11-8/21
					8/21-10/6	10/6-11/9
1992	4/7-5/1	5/1-5/26	5/26-6/19	6/19-7/13	7/13-8/7	8/7-8/31
1993	2/2-6/6	6/6-7/6	7/6-8/1	8/1-8/27	8/27-9/21	9/21-10/16
1994	3/8-4/1	4/1-4/26	4/26-5/21	5/21-6/15	6/15-7/11	7/11-8/7
1995	4/22-5/16	5/16-6/10	6/10-7/5	7/5-7/29	7/29-8/23	8/23-9/16
1996	2/9-3/6	3/6-4/3	4/3-8/7	8/7-9/7	9/7-10/4	10/4-10/29
1997	3/23-4/16	4/16-5/10	5/10-6/4	6/4-6/28	6/28-7/23	7/23-8/17
1998	5/3-5/29	5/29-6/24	6/24-7/19	7/19-8/13	8/13-9/6	9/6-9/30
1999	2/21-3/18	3/18-4/12	4/12-5/8	5/8-6/5	6/5-7/12	7/12-8/15
					8/15-10/7	10/7-11/9
2000	4/6-5/1	5/1-5/25	5/25-6/13	6/13-7/13	7/13-8/6	8/6-8/31

Libra	Scorpio	Sagittarius	Capricorn	Aquarius	Pisces
9/1-9/26	9/26-10/20	1/1-1/26	1/26-2/19	2/19-3/15	3/15-4/8
		10/20-11/14	11/14-12/6	12/9-1/4	
10/17-11/10	11/10-12/4	12/4-12/27	12/27-1/20		1/4-2/2
8/6-9/7	9/7-1/7			1/20-2/13	2/13-3/9
9/17-10/11	10/11-11/4	1/7-2/5	2/5-3/3	3/3-3/29	3/29-4/23
		11/4-11/28	11/28-12/22	12/22-1/16	
10/30-11/24	11/24-12/18	12/18-1/11			1/16-2/9
8/18-9/12	9/12-10/9	10/9-11/5	1/11-2/4	2/4-2/28	2/28-3/24
			11/5-12/8	12/8-1/23	
10/2-10/26	10/26-11/18	11/18-12/12	1/23-3/2	3/2-4/6	4/6-5/4
			12/12-1/5		
11/9-12/6	12/6-1/1			1/5-1/29	1/29-2/22
9/1-9/25	9/25-10/20	1/1-1/25	1/25-2/19	2/19-3/14	3/14-4/7
		10/20-11/13	11/13-12/9		
10/16-11/9	11/9-12/3	12/3-12/27			1/4-2/2
8/7-9/7	9/7-1/7			1/20-3/13	2/13-3/9
9/16-10/10	10/10-11/3	1/7-2/5	2/5-3/3	3/3-3/28	3/28-4/22
		11/3-11/28	11/28-12/22	12/22-1/15	
10/29-11/23	11/23-12/17	12/17-1/10			1/15-2/9
8/18-9/12	9/12-10/8	10/8-11/5	1/10-2/3	2/3-2/27	2/27-3/23
			11/5-12/10	12/10-1/16	
10/1-10/25	10/25-11/18	11/18-12/12	1/16-3/3	3/3-4/6	4/6-5/4
			12/12-1/5		
8/21-12/6	12/6-12/31	12/21-1/25/92		1/5-1/29	1/29-2/22
8/31-9/25	9/25-10/19	10/19-11/13	1/25-2/18	2/18-3/13	3/13-4/7
			11/13-12/8	12/8-1/3	
10/16-11/9	11/9-12/2	12/2-12/26	12/26-1/19		1/3-2/2
8/7-9/7	9/7-1/7			1/19-2/12	2/12-3/8
9/16-10/10	10/10-11/13	1/7-2/4	2/4-3/2	3/2-3/28	3/28-4/22
		11/3-11/27	11/27-12/21	12/21-1/15	
10/29-11/23	11/23-12/17	12/17-1/10/97			1/15-2/9
8/17-9/12	9/12-10/8	10/8-11/5	1/10-2/3	2/3-2/27	2/27-3/23
			11/5-12/12	12/12-1/9	
9/30-10/24	10/24-11/17	11/17-12/11	1/9-3/4	3/4-4/6	4/6-5/3
11/9-12/5	12/5-12/31	12/31-1/24		1/4-1/28	1/28-2/21
8/31-9/24	9/24-10/19	10/19-11/13	1/24-2/18	2/18-3/12	3/13-4/6
			11/13-12/8	12/8	

MARS SIGN 1901-2000

1901	MAR	1	Leo		APR	28	Gem
	May	11	Vir		JUN	11	Can
	JUL	13	Lib		JUL	27	Leo
	AUG	31	Scp		SEP	12	Vir
	OCT	14	Sag		OCT	30	Lib
	NOV	24	Cap		DEC	17	Scp
1902	JAN	1	Aqu	1907	FEB	5	Sag
	FEB	8	Pic		APR	1	Cap
	MAR	19	Ari		OCT	13	Aqu
	APR	27	Tau		NOV	29	Pic
	JUN	7	Gem	1908	JAN	11	Ari
	JUL	20	Can		FEB	23	Tau
	SEP	4	Leo		APR	7	Gem
	OCT	23	Vir		MAY	22	Can
	DEC	20	Lib		JUL	8	Leo
1903	APR	19	Vir		AUG	24	Vir
	MAY	30	Lib		OCT	10	Lib
	AUG	6	Scp		NOV	25	Scp
	SEP	22	Sag	1909	JAN	10	Sag
	NOV	3	Cap		FEB	24	Cap
	DEC	12	Aqu		APR	9	Aqu
1904	JAN	19	Pic		MAY	25	Pic
	FEB	27	Ari		JUL	21	Ari
	APR	6	Tau		SEP	26	Pic
	MAY	18	Gem		NOV	20	Ari
	JUN	30	Can	1910	JAN	23	Tau
	AUG	15	Leo		MAR	14	Gem
	OCT	1	Vir		MAY	1	Can
	NOV	20	Lib		JUN	19	Leo
1905	JAN	13	Scp		AUG	6	Vir
	AUG	21	Sag		SEP	22	Lib
	OCT	8	Cap		NOV	6	Scp
	NOV	18	Aqu		DEC	20	Sag
	DEC	27	Pic	1911	JAN	31	Cap
1906	FEB	4	Ari		MAR	14	Aqu
	MAR	17	Tau		APR	23	Pic

	JUN	2	Ari		MAY	4	Tau
	JUL	15	Tau		JUN	14	Gem
	SEP	5	Gem		JUL	28	Can
	NOV	30	Tau		SEP	12	Leo
1912	JAN	30	Gem		NOV	2	Vir
	APR	5	Can	1918	JAN	11	Lib
	MAY	28	Leo		FEB	25	Vir
	JUL	17	Vir		JUN	23	Lib
	SEP	2	Lib		AUG	17	Scp
	OCT	18	Scp		OCT	1	Sag
	NOV	30	Sag		NOV	11	Cap
1913	JAN	10	Cap		DEC	20	Aqu
	FEB	19	Aqu	1919	JAN	27	Pic
	MAR	30	Pic		MAR	6	Ari
	MAY	8	Ari		APR	15	Tau
	JUN	17	Tau		MAY	26	Gem
	JUL	29	Gem		JUL	8	Can
	SEP	15	Can		AUG	23	Leo
1914	MAY	1	Leo		OCT	10	Vir
	JUN	26	Vir		NOV	30	Lib
	AUG	14	Lib	1920	JAN	31	Scp
	SEP	29	Scp		APR	23	Lib
	NOV	11	Sag		JUL	10	Scp
	DEC	22	Cap		SEP	4	Sag
1915	JAN	30	Aqu		OCT	18	Cap
	MAR	9	Pic		NOV	27	Aqu
	APR	16	Ari	1921	JAN	5	Pic
	MAY	26	Tau		FEB	13	Ari
	JUL	6	Gem		MAR	25	Tau
	AUG	19	Can		MAY	6	Gem
	OCT	7	Leo		JUN	18	Can
1916	MAY	28	Vir		AUG	3	Leo
	JUL	23	Lib		SEP	19	Vir
	SEP	8	Scp		NOV	6	Lib
	OCT	22	Sag		DEC	26	Scp
	DEC	1	Cap	1922	FEB	18	Sag
1917	JAN	9	Aqu		SEP	13	Cap
	FEB	16	Pic		OCT	30	Aqu
	MAR	26	Ari		DEC	11	Pic

1923	JAN	21	Ari		JUN	26	Tau
	MAR	4	Tau		AUG	9	Gem
	APR	16	Gem		OCT	3	Can
	MAY	30	Can		DEC	20	Gem
	JUL	16	Leo	1929	MAR	10	Can
	SEP	1	Vir		MAY	13	Leo
	OCT	18	Lib		JUL	4	Vir
	DEC	4	Scp		AUG	21	Lib
1924	JAN	19	Sag		OCT	6	Scp
	MAR	6	Cap		NOV	18	Sag
	APR	24	Aqu		DEC	29	Cap
	JUN	24	Pic	1930	FEB	6	Aqu
	AUG	24	Aqu		MAR	17	Pic
	OCT	19	Pic		APR	24	Ari
	DEC	19	Ari		JUN	3	Tau
1925	FEB	5	Tau		JUL	14	Gem
	MAR	24	Gem		AUG	28	Can
	MAY	9	Can		OCT	20	Leo
	JUN	26	Leo	1931	FEB	16	Can
	AUG	12	Vir		MAR	30	Leo
	SEP	28	Lib		JUN	10	Vir
	NOV	13	Scp		AUG	1	Lib
	DEC	28	Sag		SEP	17	Scp
1926	FEB	9	Cap		OCT	30	Sag
	MAR	23	Aqu		DEC	10	Cap
	MAY	3	Pic	1932	JAN	18	Aqu
	JUN	15	Ari		FEB	25	Pic
	AUG	1	Tau		APR	3	Ari
1927	FEB	22	Gem		MAY	12	Tau
	APR	17	Can		JUN	22	Gem
	JUN	6	Leo		AUG	4	Can
	JUL	25	Vir		SEP	20	Leo
	SEP	10	Lib		NOV	13	Vir
	OCT	26	Scp	1933	JUL	6	Lib
	DEC	8	Sag		AUG	26	Scp
1928	JAN	19	Cap		OCT	9	Sag
	FEB	28	Aqu		NOV	19	Cap
	APR	7	Pic		DEC	28	Aqu
	MAY	16	Ari	1934	FEB	4	Pic

	MAR	14	Ari		NOV	19	Pic
	APR	22	Tau	1940	JAN	4	Ari
	JUN	2	Gem		FEB	17	Tau
	JUL	15	Can		APR	1	Gem
	AUG	30	Leo		MAY	17	Can
	OCT	18	Vir		JUL	3	Leo
	DEC	11	Lib		AUG	19	Vir
1935	JUL	29	Scp		OCT	5	Lib
	SEP	16	Sag		NOV	20	Scp
	OCT	28	Cap	1941	JAN	4	Sag
	DEC	7	Aqu		FEB	17	Cap
1936	JAN	14	Pic		APR	2	Aqu
	FEB	22	Ari		MAY	16	Pic
	APR	1	Tau		JUL	2	Ari
	MAY	13	Gem	1942	JAN	11	Tau
	JUN	25	Can		MAR	7	Gem
	AUG	10	Leo		APR	26	Can
	SEP	26	Vir		JUN	14	Leo
	NOV	14	Lib		AUG	1	Vir
1937	JAN	5	Scp		SEP	17	Lib
	MAR	13	Sag		NOV	1	Scp
	MAY	14	Scp		DEC	15	Sag
	AUG	8	Sag	1943	JAN	26	Cap
	SEP	30	Cap		MAR	8	Aqu
	NOV	11	Aqu		APR	17	Pic
	DEC	21	Pic		MAY	27	Ari
1938	JAN	30	Ari		JUL	7	Tau
	MAR	12	Tau		AUG	23	Gem
	APR	23	Gem	1944	MAR	28	Can
	JUN	7	Can		MAY	22	Leo
	JUL	22	Leo		JUL	12	Vir
	SEP	7	Vir		AUG	29	Lib
	OCT	25	Lib		OCT	13	Scp
	DEC	11	Scp		NOV	25	Sag
1939	JAN	29	Sag	1945	JAN	5	Cap
	MAR	21	Cap		FEB	14	Aqu
	MAY	25	Aqu		MAR	25	Pic
	JUL	21	Cap		MAY	2	Ari
	SEP	24	Aqu		JUN	11	Tau

	JUL	23	Gem	1951	JAN	22	Pic
	SEP	7	Can		MAR	1	Ari
	NOV	11	Leo		APR	10	Tau
	DEC	26	Can		MAY	21	Gem
1946	APR	22	Leo		JUL	3	Can
	JUN	20	Vir		AUG	18	Leo
	AUG	9	Lib		OCT	5	Vir
	SEP	24	Scp		NOV	24	Lib
	NOV	6	Sag	1952	JAN	20	Scp
	DEC	17	Cap		AUG	27	Sag
1947	JAN	25	Aqu		OCT	12	Cap
	MAR	4	Pic		NOV	21	Aqu
	APR	11	Ari		DEC	30	Pic
	MAY	21	Tau	1953	FEB	8	Ari
	JUL	1	Gem		MAR	20	Tau
	AUG	13	Can		MAY	1	Gem
	OCT	1	Leo		JUN	14	Can
	DEC	1	Vir		JUL	29	Leo
1948	FEB	12	Leo		SEP	14	Vir
	MAY	18	Vir		NOV	1	Lib
	JUL	17	Lib		DEC	20	Scp
	SEP	3	Scp	1954	FEB	9	Sag
	OCT	17	Sag		APR	12	Cap
	NOV	26	Cap		JUL	3	Sag
1949	JAN	4	Aqu		AUG	24	Cap
	FEB	11	Pic		OCT	21	Aqu
	MAR	21	Ari		DEC	4	Pic
	APR	30	Tau	1955	JAN	15	Ari
	JUN	10	Gem		FEB	26	Tau
	JUL	23	Can		APR	10	Gem
	SEP	7	Leo		MAY	26	Can
	OCT	27	Vir		JUL	11	Leo
	DEC	26	Lib		AUG	27	Vir
1950	MAR	28	Vir		OCT	13	Lib
	JUN	11	Lib		NOV	29	Scp
	AUG	10	Scp	1956	JAN	14	Sag
	SEP	25	Sag		FEB	28	Cap
	NOV	6	Cap		APR	14	Aqu
	DEC	15	Aqu		JUN	3	Pic

	DEC	6	Ari		MAR	12	Pic
1957	JAN	28	Tau		APR	19	Ari
	MAR	17	Gem		MAY	28	Tau
	MAY	4	Can		JUL	9	Gem
	JUN	21	Leo		AUG	22	Can
	AUG	8	Vir		OCT	11	Leo
	SEP	24	Lib	1963	JUN	3	Vir
	NOV	8	Scp		JUL	27	Lib
	DEC	23	Sag		SEP	12	Scp
1958	FEB	3	Cap		OCT	25	Sag
	MAR	17	Aqu		DEC	5	Cap
	APR	27	Pic	1964	JAN	13	Aqu
	JUN	7	Ari		FEB	20	Pic
	JUL	21	Tau		MAR	29	Ari
	SEP	21	Gem		MAY	7	Tau
	OCT	29	Tau		JUN	17	Gem
1959	FEB	10	Gem		JUL	30	Can
	APR	10	Can		SEP	15	Leo
	JUN	1	Leo		NOV	6	Vir
	JUL	20	Vir	1965	JUN	29	Lib
	SEP	5	Lib		AUG	20	Scp
	OCT	21	Scp		OCT	4	Sag
	DEC	3	Sag		NOV	14	Cap
1960	JAN	14	Cap		DEC	23	Aqu
	FEB	23	Aqu	1966	JAN	30	Pic
	APR	2	Pic		MAR	9	Ari
	MAY	11	Ari		APR	17	Tau
	JUN	20	Tau		MAY	28	Gem
	AUG	2	Gem		JUL	11	Can
	SEP	21	Can		AUG	25	Leo
1961	FEB	5	Gem		OCT	12	Vir
	FEB	7	Can		DEC	4	Lib
	MAY	6	Leo	1967	FEB	12	Scp
	JUN	28	Vir		MAR	31	Lib
	AUG	17	Lib		JUL	19	Scp
	OCT	1	Scp		SEP	10	Sag
	NOV	13	Sag		OCT	23	Cap
	DEC	24	Cap		DEC	1	Aqu
1962	FEB	1	Aqu	1968	JAN	9	Pic

	FEB	17	Ari		DEC	24	Tau
	MAR	27	Tau	1974	FEB	27	Gem
	MAY	8	Gem		APR	20	Can
	JUN	21	Can		JUN	9	Leo
	AUG	5	Leo		JUL	27	Vir
	SEP	21	Vir		SEP	12	Lib
	NOV	9	Lib		OCT	28	Scp
	DEC	29	Scp		DEC	10	Sag
1969	FEB	25	Sag	1975	JAN	21	Cap
	SEP	21	Cap		MAR	3	Aqu
	NOV	4	Aqu		APR	11	Pic
	DEC	15	Pic		MAY	21	Ari
1970	JAN	24	Ari		JUL	1	Tau
	MAR	7	Tau		AUG	14	Gem
	APR	18	Gem		OCT	17	Can
	JUN	2	Can		NOV	25	Gem
	JUL	18	Leo	1976	MAR	18	Can
	SEP	3	Vir		MAY	16	Leo
	OCT	20	Lib		JUL	6	Vir
	DEC	6	Scp		AUG	24	Lib
1971	JAN	23	Sag		OCT	8	Scp
	MAR	12	Cap		NOV	20	Sag
	MAY	3	Aqu	1977	JAN	1	Cap
	NOV	6	Pic		FEB	9	Aqu
	DEC	26	Ari		MAR	20	Pic
1972	FEB	10	Tau		APR	27	Ari
	MAR	27	Gem		JUN	6	Tau
	MAY	12	Can		JUL	17	Gem
	JUN	28	Leo		SEP	1	Can
	AUG	15	Vir		OCT	26	Leo
	SEP	30	Lib	1978	JAN	26	Can
	NOV	15	Scp		APR	10	Leo
	DEC	30	Sag		JUN	14	Vir
1973	FEB	12	Cap		AUG	4	Lib
	MAR	26	Aqu		SEP	19	Scp
	MAY	8	Pic		NOV	2	Sag
	JUN	20	Ari		DEC	12	Cap
	AUG	12	Tau	1979	JAN	20	Aqu
	OCT	29	Ari		FEB	27	Pic

	APR	7	Ari		MAR	15	Tau
	MAY	16	Tau		APR	26	Gem
	JUN	26	Gem		JUN	9	Can
	AUG	8	Can		JUL	25	Leo
	SEP	24	Leo		SEP	10	Vir
	NOV	19	Vir		OCT	27	Lib
1980	MAR	11	Leo		DEC	14	Scp
	MAY	4	Vir	1986	FEB	2	Sag
	JUL	10	Lib		MAR	28	Cap
	AUG	29	Scp		OCT	9	Aqu
	OCT	12	Sag		NOV	26	Pic
	NOV	22	Cap	1987	JAN	8	Ari
	DEC	30	Aqu		FEB	20	Tau
1981	FEB	6	Pic		APR	5	Gem
	MAR	17	Ari		MAY	21	Can
	APR	25	Tau		JUL	6	Leo
	JUN	5	Gem		AUG	22	Vir
	JUL	18	Can		OCT	8	Lib
	SEP	2	Leo		NOV	24	Scp
	OCT	21	Vir	1988	JAN	8	Sag
	DEC	16	Lib		FEB	22	Cap
1982	AUG	3	Scp		APR	6	Aqu
	SEP	20	Sag		MAY	22	Pic
	OCT	31	Cap		JUL	13	Ari
	DEC	10	Aqu		OCT	23	Pic
1983	JAN	17	Pic		NOV	1	Ari
	FEB	25	Ari	1989	JAN	19	Tau
	APR	5	Tau		MAR	11	Gem
	MAY	16	Gem		APR	29	Can
	JUN	29	Can		JUN	16	Leo
	AUG	13	Leo		AUG	3	Vir
	SEP	30	Vir		SEP	19	Lib
	NOV	18	Lib		NOV	4	Scp
1984	JAN	11	Scp		DEC	18	Sag
	AUG	17	Sag	1990	JAN	29	Cap
	OCT	5	Cap		MAR	11	Aqu
	NOV	15	Aqu		APR	20	Pic
	DEC	25	Pic		MAY	31	Ari
1985	FEB	2	Ari		JUL	12	Tau

	AUG	31	Gem		FEB	15	Pic
	DEC	14	Tau		MAR	24	Ari
1991	JAN	21	Gem		MAY	2	Tau
	APR	3	Can		JUN	12	Gem
	MAY	26	Leo		JUL	25	Can
	JUL	15	Vir		SEP	9	Leo
	SEP	1	Lib		OCT	30	Vir
	OCT	16	Scp	1997	JAN	3	Lib
	NOV	29	Sag		MAR	8	Vir
1992	JAN	9	Cap		JUN	19	Lib
	FEB	18	Aqu		AUG	14	Scp
	MAR	28	Pic		SEP	28	Sag
	MAY	5	Ari		NOV	9	Cap
	JUN	14	Tau		DEC	18	Aqu
	JUL	26	Gem	1998	JAN	25	Pic
	SEP	12	Can		MAR	4	Ari
1993	APR	27	Leo		APR	13	Tau
	JUN	23	Vir		MAY	24	Gem
	AUG	12	Lib		JUL	6	Can
	SEP	27	Scp		AUG	20	Leo
	NOV	9	Sag		OCT	7	Vir
	DEC	20	Cap		NOV	27	Lib
1994	JAN	28	Aqu	1999	JAN	26	Scp
	MAR	7	Pic		MAY	5	Lib
	APR	14	Ari		JUL	5	Scp
	MAY	23	Tau		SEP	2	Sag
	JUL	3	Gem		OCT	17	Cap
	AUG	16	Can		NOV	26	Aqu
	OCT	4	Leo	2000	JAN	4	Pic
	DEC	12	Vir		FEB	12	Ari
1995	JAN	22	Leo		MAR	23	Tau
	MAY	25	Vir		MAY	3	Gem
	JUL	21	Lib		JUN	16	Can
	SEP	7	Scp		AUG	1	Leo
	OCT	20	Sag		SEP	17	Vir
	NOV	30	Cap		NOV	4	Lib
1996	JAN	8	Aqu		DEC	23	Scp

1901	JAN	19	Cap	1930	JUN	26	Can
1902	FEB	6	Aqu	1931	JUL	17	Leo
1903	FEB	20	Pic	1932	AUG	11	Vir
1904	MAR	1	Ari	1933	SEP	10	Lib
	AUG	8	Tau	1934	OCT	11	Scp
	AUG	31	Ari	1935	NOV	9	Sag
1905	MAR	7	Tau	1936	DEC	2	Cap
	JUL	21	Gem	1937	DEC	20	Aqu
	DEC	4	Tau	1938	MAY	14	Pic
1906	MAR	9	Gem		JUL	30	Aqu
	JUL	30	Can		DEC	29	Pic
1907	AUG	18	Leo	1939	MAY	11	Ari
1908	SEP	12	Vir		OCT	30	Pic
1909	OCT	11	Lib		DEC	20	Ari
1910	NOV	11	Scp	1940	MAY	16	Tau
1911	DEC	10	Sag	1941	MAY	26	Gem
1913	JAN	2	Cap	1942	JUN	10	Can
1914	JAN	21	Aqu	1943	JUN	30	Leo
1915	FEB	4	Pic	1944	JUL	26	Vir
1916	FEB	12	Ari	1945	AUG	25	Lib
	JUN	26	Tau	1946	SEP	25	Scp
	OCT	26	Ari	1947	OCT	24	Sag
1917	FEB	12	Tau	1948	NOV	15	Cap
	JUN	29	Gem	1949	APR	12	Aqu
1918	JUL	13	Can		JUN	27	Cap
1919	AUG	2	Leo		NOV	30	Aqu
1920	AUG	27	Vir	1950	APR	15	Pic
1921	SEP	25	Lib		SEP	15	Aqu
1922	OCT	26	Scp		DEC	1	Pic
1923	NOV	24	Sag	1951	APR	21	Ari
1924	DEC	18	Cap	1952	APR	28	Tau
1926	JAN	6	Aqu	1953	MAY	9	Gem
1927	JAN	18	Pic	1954	MAY	24	Can
	JUN	6	Ari	1955	JUN	13	Leo
	SEP	11	Pic		NOV	17	Vir
1928	JAN	23	Ari	1956	JAN	18	Leo
	JUN	4	Tau		JUL	7	Vir
1929	JUN	12	Gem		DEC	13	Lib

1957	FEB	19	Vir	1973	FEB	23	Aqu
	AUG	7	Lib	1974	MAR	8	Pic
1958	JAN	13	Scp	1975	MAR	18	Ari
	MAR	20	Lib	1976	MAR	26	Tau
	SEP	7	Scp		AUG	23	Gem
1959	FEB	10	Sag		OCT	16	Tau
	APR	24	Scp	1977	APR	3	Gem
	OCT	5	Sag		AUG	20	Can
1960	MAR	1	Cap		DEC	30	Gem
	JUN	10	Sag	1978	APR	12	Can
	OCT	26	Cap		SEP	5	Leo
1961	MAR	15	Aqu	1979	FEB	28	Can
	AUG	12	Cap		APR	20	Leo
	NOV	4	Aqu		SEP	29	Vir
1962	MAR	25	Pic	1980	OCT	27	Lib
1963	APR	4	Ari	1981	Nov	27	Scp
1964	APR	12	Tau	1982	DEC	26	Sag
1965	APR	22	Gem	1984	JAN	19	Cap
	SEP	21	Can	1985	FEB	6	Aqu
	NOV	17	Gem	1986	FEB	20	Pic
1966	MAY	5	Can	1987	MAR	2	Ari
	SEP	27	Leo	1988	MAR	8	Tau
1967	JAN	16	Can		JUL	22	Gem
	MAY	23	Leo		NOV	30	Tau
	OCT	19	Vir	1989	MAR	11	Gem
1968	FEB	27	Leo		JUL	30	Can
	JUN	15	Vir	1990	AUG	18	Leo
	NOV	15	Lib	1991	SEP	12	Vir
1969	MAR	30	Vir	1992	OCT	10	Lib
	JUL	15	Lib	1993	NOV	10	Scp
	DEC	16	Scp	1994	DEC	9	Sag
1970	APR	30	Lib	1996	JAN	3	Cap
	AUG	15	Scp	1997	JAN	21	Aqu
1971	JAN	14	Sag	1998	FEB	4	Pic
	JUN	5	Scp	1999	FEB	13	Ari
	SEP	11	Sag		JUN	28	Tau
1972	FEB	6	Cap		OCT	23	Ari
	JUL	24	Sag	2000	FEB	14	Tau
	SEP	25	Cap		JUN	30	Gem

SATURN SIGN 1903–2000

1903	JAN	19	Aqu	1942	MAY	8	Gem
1905	APR	13	Pic	1944	JUN	20	Can
	AUG	17	Aqu	1946	AUG	2	Leo
1906	JAN	8	Pic	1948	SEP	19	Vir
1908	MAR	19	Ari	1949	APR	3	Leo
1910	MAY	17	Tau		MAY	29	Vir
	DEC	14	Ari	1950	NOV	20	Lib
1911	JAN	20	Tau	1951	MAR	7	Vir
1912	JUL	7	Gem		AUG	13	Lib
	NOV	30	Tau	1953	OCT	22	Scp
1913	MAR	26	Gem	1956	JAN	12	Sag
1914	AUG	24	Can		MAY	14	Scp
	DEC	7	Gem		OCT	10	Sag
1915	MAY	11	Can	1959	JAN	5	Cap
1916	OCT	17	Leo	1962	JAN	3	Aqu
	DEC	7	Can	1964	MAR	24	Pic
1917	JUN	24	Leo		SEP	16	Aqu
1919	AUG	12	Vir		DEC	16	Pic
1921	OCT	7	Lib	1967	MAR	3	Ari
1923	DEC	20	Scp	1969	APR	29	Tau
1924	APR	6	Lib	1971	JUN	18	Gem
	SEP	13	Scp	1972	JAN	10	Tau
1926	DEC	2	Sag		FEB	21	Gem
1929	MAR	15	Cap	1973	AUG	1	Can
	MAY	5	Sag	1974	JAN	7	Gem
	NOV	30	Cap		APR	18	Can
1932	FEB	24	Aqu	1975	SEP	17	Leo
	AUG	13	Cap	1976	JAN	14	Can
	NOV	20	Aqu		JUN	5	Leo
1935	FEB	14	Pic	1977	NOV	17	Vir
1937	APR	25	Ari	1978	JAN	5	Leo
	OCT	18	Pic		JUL	26	Vir
1938	JAN	14	Ari	1980	SEP	21	Lib
1939	JUL	6	Tau	1982	NOV	29	Scp
	SEP	22	Ari	1983	MAY	6	Lib
1940	MAR	20	Tau		AUG	24	Scp

1985	NOV	17	Sag		1994	JAN	28	Pic
1988	FEB	13	Cap		1996	APR	7	Ari
	JUN	10	Sag		1998	JUN	9	Tau
	NOV	12	Cap			OCT	25	Ari
1991	FEB	6	Aqu		1999	MAR	1	Tau
1993	MAY	21	Pic		2000	AUG	10	Gem
	JUN	30	Aqu			OCT	16	Tau

How to Use the Uranus, Neptune, and Pluto Tables

Find your birthday in the list following each sign.

Look up your Uranus placement by finding your birthday on the following lists.

URANUS IN ARIES BIRTH DATES

March 31–November 4, 1927
January 13, 1928–June 6, 1934
October 10, 1934–March 28, 1935

URANUS IN TAURUS BIRTH DATES

June 6, 1934–October 10, 1935
March 28, 1935–August 7, 1941
October 5, 1941–May 15, 1942

URANUS IN GEMINI BIRTH DATES

August 7–October 5, 1941
May 15, 1949–August 30, 1948
November 12, 1948–June 10, 1949

URANUS IN CANCER BIRTH DATES

August 30–November 12, 1948
June 10, 1942–August 24, 1955
January 28–June 10, 1956

URANUS IN LEO BIRTH DATES

August 24, 1955–January 28, 1956
June 10, 1956–November 1, 1961
January 10–August 10, 1962

URANUS IN VIRGO BIRTH DATES

November 1, 1961–January 10, 1962
August 10, 1962–September 28, 1968
May 20, 1969–June 24, 1969

URANUS IN LIBRA BIRTH DATES

September 28, 1968–May 20, 1969
June 24, 1969–November 21, 1974
May 1–September 8, 1975

URANUS IN SCORPIO BIRTH DATES

November 21, 1974–May 1, 1975
September 8, 1975–February 17, 1981
March 20–November 16, 1981

URANUS IN SAGITTARIUS BIRTH DATES

February 17–March 20, 1981
November 16, 1981–February 15, 1988
May 27, 1988–December 2, 1988

URANUS IN CAPRICORN BIRTH DATES

December 20, 1904–January 30, 1912
September 4–November 12, 1912
February 15–May 27, 1988
December 2, 1988–April 1, 1995
June 9, 1995–January 12, 1996

URANUS IN AQUARIUS BIRTH DATES

January 30–September 4, 1912
November 12, 1912–April 1, 1919
August 16, 1919–January 22, 1920

URANUS IN PISCES BIRTH DATES

April 1–August 16, 1919
January 22, 1920–March 31, 1927
November 4, 1927–January 13, 1928

Look up your Neptune placement by finding your birthday on the following lists.

NEPTUNE IN CANCER BIRTH DATES

July 19–December 25, 1901
May 21, 1902–September 23, 1914
December 14, 1914–July 19, 1915
March 19–May 2, 1916

NEPTUNE IN LEO BIRTH DATES

September 23–December 14, 1914
July 19, 1915–March 19, 1916
May 2, 1916–September 21, 1928
February 19, 1929–July 24, 1929

NEPTUNE IN VIRGO BIRTH DATES

September 21, 1928–February 19, 1929
July 24, 1929–October 3, 1942
April 17–August 2, 1943

NEPTUNE IN LIBRA BIRTH DATES

October 3, 1942–April 17, 1943
August 2, 1943–December 24, 1955
March 12–October 9, 1956
June 15–August 6, 1957

NEPTUNE IN SCORPIO BIRTH DATES

December 24, 1955–March 12, 1956
October 9, 1956–June 15, 1957
August 6, 1957–January 4, 1970
May 3–November 6, 1970

NEPTUNE IN SAGITTARIUS BIRTH DATES

January 4–May 3, 1970
November 6, 1970–January 19, 1984
June 23–November 21, 1984

NEPTUNE IN CAPRICORN BIRTH DATES

January 19, 1984–June 23, 1984
November 21, 1984–January 29, 1998

Find your Pluto placement in the following list:
Pluto in Gemini—Late 1800s until May 28, 1914
Pluto in Cancer—May 26, 1914–June 14, 1939
Pluto in Leo—June 14, 1939–August 19, 1957
Pluto in Virgo—August 19, 1957–October 5, 1971
                      April 17, 1972–July 30, 1972
Pluto in Libra—October 5, 1971–April 17, 1972
                  July 30, 1972–August 28, 1984
Pluto in Scorpio—August 28, 1984–January 17, 1995
Pluto in Sagittarius—starting January 17, 1995

CHAPTER 8

Astrology's Glyphs and the Myths Behind Them

Your horoscope chart is written in a special language known to astrologers all over the world. An astrologer in South America could read it as easily as an astrologer in Moscow could. However, if you don't know the meaning of the symbols covering your chart, the language of "astrologese" might look like a difficult code to crack.

If you have ordered one of the popular computer astrology programs, or if you have ordered your chart from one of the many computer services, you'll want to learn the meaning of the symbols. You probably know a few already, like the one for your sun sign, and the moon. It's easy to learn the meaning of the symbols, or "glyphs," for the other signs and planets.

Those little characters, twelve symbols for the astrological signs and 10 for planets, each contain information about their identity—and the hidden meaning of what they represent—within their design. Some are so obvious they give themselves away, like the symbol for the moon. Others take a bit of detective work, like a game of hide-and-seek. But the meaning is expressed right there in that combination of circles, wavy lines, and crosses. In fact, those readers who have already memorized the glyphs may not have realized how much of their meaning is revealed.

Let's start with the symbols for the planets. Look for them inside the "houses" (wedge-shaped segments) of your chart.

Glyphs for the Planets

Almost all the glyphs of the planets are derived from a combination of three basic forms—the circle, the half-circle or arc, and the cross (though this may not be immediately apparent because several symbols have become highly stylized over the years). Each element has a special meaning in relation to the others, which adds to the significance of the completed glyph.

The circle, with no beginning or end, is one of the oldest symbols of spirit or spiritual forces. All of the early diagrams of the heavens—spiritual territory—are shown in circular form. The arc or semicircle is the receptive symbol of the soul. The soul is finite, yet there is spiritual potential. The vertical line symbolizes movement from heaven to earth. The horizontal line describes temporal movement, in time and in space. Superimposed together, they become the cross, symbolizing manifestation in the material world.

THE SUN GLYPH ☉

The sun is always shown by this powerful solar symbol, a circle with a point in the center. It is you, your spiritual center, your infinite personality incarnating into the finite cycles of birth and death.

This symbol was brought into common use in the 16th century, after a German occultist and scholar, Cornelius Agrippa (1486–1535) wrote a book called *De Occulta Philosophia,* which became accepted as the standard work in its field. Agrippa collected many medieval astrological and magical symbols in this book, which were used by astrologers thereafter, copied from those found in Agrippa's book. In the light of what we have written about Pluto in Sagittarius in other chapters in this book, it's especially interesting that Agrippa's influential philosophical treatise was written during a previous time when Pluto was in Sagittarius (the sign that rules philosophy).

THE MOON GLYPH ☽

The easiest symbol to spot on a chart, the moon glyph is a left-facing arc stylized into the crescent moon, which perfectly captures the reactive, receptive, emotional nature of the moon.

As part of a circle, the arc symbolizes the potential fulfillment of the entire circle. It is the life force that is still incomplete. Unlike the circle, it is in a receptive state.

THE MERCURY GLYPH ☿

With a stretch of the imagination, can't you see the winged cap of Mercury the messenger? You might also think of the upturned crescent as little antennae that tune in and transmit messages from the sun, signifying that Mercury is the way you communicate, the way your mind works. The upturned arc is receiving energy into the spirit or solar disk, which will later be translated into action on the material plane, symbolized by the cross. All the elements are equally sized—because Mercury is neutral and doesn't play favorites—this planet symbolizes objective, detached, dispassionate thinking.

THE VENUS GLYPH ♀

Here the relationship is between two elements, the circle of spirit above the cross of matter. Spirit is elevated over matter, pulling it upward. Venus asks, "What is beautiful? What do you like best, what do you love to have done to you?" Venus determines both your ideal of beauty and what feels good sensually. It governs your own allure and power to attract, as well as what attracts and pleases you.

THE MARS GLYPH ♂

In this glyph, the cross of matter is stylized into an arrowhead pointed up and outward, propelled by the circle of spirit. You can deduce that Mars embodies your spiritual energy projected into the outer world. It's your assertiveness, your initiative, your aggressive drive, what you like to do to others, your temper. Your task is to use your outgoing Mars energy wisely and well.

THE JUPITER GLYPH ♃

Jupiter is the basic cross of matter, with a large stylized crescent perched on the left side of the horizontal, temporal plane. You might think of the crescent as an open hand—one meaning of Jupiter is "luck," what's handed to you. You don't work for what you get from Jupiter—it comes to you if you're open to it.

The Jupiter glyph might also remind you of a jumbo jet plane with a huge tail fin, about to take off. This is the planet of travel, mental and spiritual, of expanding your horizons via new ideas, new spiritual dimensions, and new places. Jupiter embodies the optimism and enthusiasm of the traveler about the embark on an exciting adventure.

THE SATURN GLYPH ♄

Flip Jupiter upside down and you've got Saturn. (This might not be immediately apparent, because Saturn is usually stylized into an "h" form like the one shown here.) But the principle it expresses is the opposite of Jupiter's expansive tendencies. Saturn pulls you back to earth—the receptive arc is pushed down underneath the cross of matter. Before there is any expansion, the duties and obligations of the material world must be considered. Saturn says, "Stop, wait, finish your chores before you take off!"

Saturn's glyph also resembles the sickle of old "Father Time." Saturn was first known as Chronos, the Greek god of time, for time brings all matter to an end. When it was the most distant planet (before the discovery of Uranus), it was thought to be the place where time stopped. After the soul, having departed from earth, journeyed back to the outer reaches of the universe, it finally stopped at Saturn, at the end of time.

THE URANUS GLYPH ♅

The glyph for Uranus is often stylized to form a capital "H" after Sir William Herschel, the name of the planet's discoverer. But the more esoteric version curves the two pillars of the H into crescent antennae, like satellite discs receiving signals from space, perched on the material plane of the cross of matter and pushed from below by the circle of the spirit (a bit like an orbiting satellite). Uranus channels the highest energy of all, the white electrical light of the universal spiritual sun. This pure electrical energy picks up impulses from the deepest reaches of the universe. Because it doesn't follow the ordinary drumbeat, it can't be controlled or predicted (which is also true of those who are strongly influenced by this eccentric planet). This light of spirit is manifested through the balance of polarities (the two arms of the glyph).

THE NEPTUNE GLYPH ♆

Neptune's glyph is usually stylized to look like a trident, the weapon of the Roman god Neptune. However, on a more esoteric level, it shows the large upturned crescent of the soul pierced through by the cross of matter. Neptune nails down, or materializes, soul energy, bringing impulses from the soul level into manifestation. That is why Neptune is associated with imagination, making an image of the soul. Neptune works through feeling, sensitivity and mystical capacity to bring the divine into the earthly realm.

THE PLUTO GLYPH ♇ or ♇

Pluto is written two ways. One is a composite of the letters PL, the first two letters of the word Pluto and coincidentally the initials of Percival Lowell, one of the planet's discoverers. The other, more esoteric symbol is a small circle above a large open crescent surmounting the cross of matter. This depicts Pluto's power to regenerate—you might imagine from this glyph a new little spirit emerging from the sheltering cup of the soul. Pluto rules the forces of life and death—after a Pluto experience, you are transformed, reborn in some way.

Sci-fi fans might visualize this glyph as a small satellite

being launched. It was shortly after Pluto's discovery that we learned how to harness the nuclear forces that made space exploration possible. Pluto rules the transformative power of atomic energy, which totally changed our lives and from which there was no turning back.

The Glyphs for the Signs

On your chart, the glyphs for the sign will appear after the planet. You'll see something like (moon) 23 (Taurus) 44. That means that the moon is located at 23 degrees of Taurus, 44 minutes. At the dividing points (or cusps) between the houses on your chart, you'll also see a symbol for the sign that rules each house.

Glyphs for the signs are much harder to define visually than those of the planets. Many have been passed down from ancient Egyptian and Chaldean civilizations with few modifications. Others have been adapted over the centuries. In deciphering many of the glyphs, you'll often find the dual nature of a sign revealed that is not always obvious from sun-sign descriptions. The Gemini glyph is much like a Roman numeral for two, and reveals the sign's longing for the twin soul. The Cancer glyph may be interpreted as either nurturing, like the breast, or self-protective, like the crab. Libra's glyph embodies the duality of the spirit balanced with material reality. The Sagittarius glyph shows that the aspirant must also carry along the earthy animal nature. The Capricorn sea goat climbs high, yet is pulled back by the deep waters of the unconscious. Aquarius embodies the double waves of detachment and friendliness. And finally the two fishes of Pisces, forever tied together, show the duality of the soul and spirit that must be reconciled.

THE ARIES GLYPH ♈

Since the symbol for Aries is the ram, this glyph's most obvious association is with a ram's horns, which characterizes one aspect of the Aries personality—an aggressive, me-first, leaping-head-first attitude. But the symbol may have other meanings for you, too. Some astrologers liken it to a fountain of energy, which Aries people also embody. The first sign of the zodiac bursts on the scene eagerly, ready to go. Another analogy is to the eyebrows and nose of the human head, which Aries rules, and the thinking power that is initiated in the brain.

One theory of the origin of this symbol links it to the Egyptian god Amun, represented by a ram. As Amon-Ra, this god was believed to embody the creator of the universe, the leader of all the other gods. This relates easily to the position of Aries as the leader (or first sign) of the zodiac, which begins at the spring equinox, a time of the year when nature is renewed.

THE TAURUS GLYPH ♉

This is another easy glyph to draw and identify. It takes little imagination to decipher the bull's head with long curving horns. Like the bull, the archetypal Taurus is slow to anger but ferocious when provoked, as well as stubborn, steady, and sensual. Another association is the larynx (and thyroid) of the throat area (ruled by Taurus) and the eustachian tubes running up to the ears, which coincides with the relationship of Taurus to the voice, song, and music. Many famous singer, musicians, and composers have prominent Taurus influences.

Many ancient religions involve a bull as a central figure in certain rites of fertility or initiation, usually symbolizing the victory of man over his animal nature. Another possible origin is in the sacred bull of Egypt, who embodied the incarnate form of Osiris, god of death and resurrection. In early Christian imagery, the Taurean bull represented St. Luke.

THE GEMINI GLYPH ♊

The standard glyph immediately calls to mind the Roman numeral for two and the symbol for Gemini, the "twins." In almost all images for this sign, the relationship between two persons is emphasized. This is the sign of communication, human contact brings with it the desire to share. Many of the figurative images for Gemini show twins with their arms around each other, emphasizing that they are sharing the same ideas and the same ground. In the glyph, the top line indicates mental communication, while the bottom line indicates shared physical space.

The most prevalent Gemini legend is that of the twin sons, Castor and Pollux, one of whom had a mortal father, while the other was the son of Zeus, king of the gods. When it came time for the mortal twin to die, his grief-stricken brother pleaded with Zeus, who agreed to let them spend half the year on earth, in mortal form, and half in immortal life with the gods on Mt. Olympus. This reflects the basic nature of humankind, which possesses an immortal soul, yet is also subject to the limits of mortality.

THE CANCER GLYPH ♋

Two convenient images relate to the Cancer glyph. The easiest to picture is the curving claws of the Cancer symbol, the crab. Like the crab, Cancer's element is water. This sensitive sign also has a hard protective shell to protect its tender interior. It is wily to escape predators, scampering sideways and hiding shyly under rocks. The crab also responds to the cycles of the moon, as do all shellfish. The other image is that of two female breasts, which Cancer rules, showing that this is a sign that nurtures and protects others as well as itself.

In ancient Egypt, Cancer was also represented by the scarab beetle, a symbol of regeneration and eternal life.

THE LEO GLYPH ♌

Lions have belonged to the sign of Leo since earliest times, and it is not difficult to imagine the king of beasts with his sweeping mane and curling tail from this glyph. The upward sweep of the glyph easily describes the positive energy of Leos; the flourishing tail, their flamboyant qualities. Another analogy, which is a stretch, is that of a heart leaping up with joy and enthusiasm—also very typical of Leo. Notice that the Leo glyph seems to be an extension of Cancer's glyph; however, in the Cancer glyph, the figures are folding inward, protectively, while the Leo glyph expresses energy outward and there is no duality in the symbol (or in Leo). In early Christian imagery, the winged Leo lion represented St. Mark.

THE VIRGO GLYPH ♍

You can read much into this mysterious glyph. The initials of "Mary Virgin," female genitalia, and a young woman holding a staff of wheat are common interpretations. The "M" shape might also remind you that Virgo is ruled by Mercury. The cross beneath the symbol could indicate the grounded, practical nature of this earth sign.

The earliest zodiacs link Virgo with the Egyptian goddess Isis, who gave birth to the god Horus after her husband Osiris had been killed, in the archetype of a miraculous conception. There are many statues of Isis nursing her baby son, which are reminiscent of medieval Virgin and Child motifs. This sign has also been associated with the image of the Holy Grail, when the Virgo symbol was substituted with a chalice.

THE LIBRA GLYPH ♎

It is not difficult to read the standard image for Libra, the scales, into this glyph. There is another meaning, however, that is equally relevant: the setting sun as it descends over the horizon. Libra's natural position on the zodiac wheel is the descendant or sunset position (as Aries' natural position is the ascendant, or rising sign). Both images relate to Libra's personality. Libra is always weighing pros and cons for a balanced decision. In the sunset image, the sun (male) hovers over the horizontal Earth (female) before setting. Libra is the space between these lines, harmonizing yin and yang, spiritual and material, ideal and real worlds. The glyph has also been linked to the kidneys, which are ruled by Libra.

THE SCORPIO GLYPH ♏

With its barbed tail, this glyph is easy to identify with the sign of the Scorpion. It also represents the male sexual parts, over which the sign rules. However, some earlier symbols for Scorpio, such as the Egyptian, represent it as an erect serpent. You can also draw the conclusion that Mars is its ruler by the arrowhead.

Another image for Scorpio, which is not identifiable in this glyph, is the eagle. Scorpios can go to extremes, soaring like the eagle or self-destructing like the Scorpion. In early Christian imagery, which often used zodiacal symbols, the Scorpio eagle was chosen to symbolize the intense apostle St. John the Evangelist.

THE SAGITTARIUS GLYPH ♐

This glyph is one of the easiest to spot and draw—an upward pointing arrow lifting up a cross. The arrow is pointing skyward, while the cross represents the four elements of the material world, which the arrow must convey. Elevating materiality into spirituality is an important Sagittarius quality, which explains why this sign is associated with higher learning, religion, philosophy, travel—the aspiring professions. Sagittarians can also send barbed arrows of frankness in their pursuit of truth. (This is also the sign of the super-salesman.)

Sagittarius is symbolically represented by the centaur, a mythological creature who is half-man, half-horse, aiming his arrow toward the skies. Though Sagittarius is motivated by spiritual aspiration, it also must balance the powerful appetites of the animal nature. The centaur Chiron, a figure in Greek mythology, became a wise teacher, after many adventures and world travels.

THE CAPRICORN GLYPH ♑

One of the most difficult symbols to draw, this glyph may take some practice. It is a representation of the seagoat: a mythical animal that is a goat with a curving fish's tail. The goat part of Capricorn wants to leave the waters of the emotions and climb to the elevated areas of life. But the fish part is the unconscious, the deep chaotic psychic level that draws the goat back. Capricorn is often trying to escape the deep, feeling part of life by submerging himself in work, steadily climbing to the top. To some people, the glyph represents a seated figure with a bent knee, since Capricorn governs the knee area of the body.

An interesting aspect of this figure is how the sharp

pointed horns of this figure, which represent the penetrating, shrewd, conscious side of Capricorn, contrast with the swishing tail, which represents its serpentine, unconscious, emotional force. One Capricorn legend dates from Roman times. The earthy fertility god, Pan, tried to save himself from uncontrollable life forces by jumping into the Nile. His upper body then turned into a goat, while the lower part became a fish. Then Jupiter gave him a save have in the skies, as a constellation.

THE AQUARIUS GLYPH ≈

This ancient water symbol can be traced back to an Egyptian hieroglyph representing streams of life force. Symbolized by the water bearer, Aquarius is distributor of the waters of life—the magic liquid of regeneration. The two waves can also be linked to the positive and negative charges of the electrical energy that Aquarius rules, a sort of universal wavelength. Aquarius is tuned in intuitively to higher forces via this electrical force. The duality of the glyph could also refer to the dual nature of Aquarius, a sign that runs hot and cold, is friendly but also detached in the mental world of air signs.

In Greek legends, Aquarius was represented by Ganymedes, who was carried to heaven by an eagle in order to become the cup bearer of Zeus, and to supervise the annual flooding of the Nile. The sign became associated with aviation and notions of flight.

THE PISCES GLYPH)(

Here is an abstraction of the familiar image of Pisces, two fishes swimming in opposite directions, bound together by a cord. The fishes represent spirit, which yearns for the freedom of heaven, while the soul remains attached to the desires of the temporal world. During life on earth, the spirit and the soul are bound together, and when they complement each other, instead of pulling in opposite directions, this facilitates the creative expression for which Pisceans are known. The ancient version of this glyph, taken from the Egyptians, had no connecting line, which was added in the fourteenth century.

Another interpretation is that the left fish indicates the

direction of involution or the beginning of a cycle; the right-hand fish, the direction of evolution, the way to completion of a cycle. It's an appropriate meaning for Pisces, the last sign of the zodiac.

CHAPTER 9

Ten Sure-fire Ways to Thrive in '95!

Wouldn't you like to use the power of the planets to help you achieve your goals? By flowing with the major planetary movements of 1995, you can master your own particular universe. Scheduling activities to coincide with the most favorable cosmic trends is a technique that rulers, presidents, and financiers have been using for centuries. Now you have the same kind of information that was once a highly guarded secret available right in this chapter.

Some very predictable movements of the planet Mercury, for instance, could cause your big plans to stall or go into reverse motion. Perhaps someone might not get an urgent message on time. Or a plane trip might be unaccountably delayed. Knowing what Mercury's up to in advance, you'll double check reservations, and give yourself plenty of options and a double dose of patience. Other planetary movements could bring a situation you've been barely tolerating to a dramatic head, causing tempers to flare. That's when your Dr. Jekyll turns into Mr. Hyde and comes out of hiding. However, these topsy-turvy times might also serve a useful purpose, by forcing you to slow down, reevaluate your life, or blast yourself out of a rut.

Several kinds of events can throw your daily life off track. One possible cause is a retrograding planet. Periodically, most planets seem to tread backward (retrograde) from our point of view on Earth. (Planets don't actually move backward; it just looks that way from here.) If you have a new project planned for those times, you'll know enough to provide for possible delays and tie-ups. On the other hand, you'll have much more success with the kinds of activities that require reaction rather than direct action. If you learn not to push against the tide, but to flow with it, you'll have a big advantage!

Here's our ten-point plan for getting the most out of '95:

1. Promote Yourself When You'll Be Most Attractive to Others

When Venus is in your sign, you can be sure that your charm will be appreciated. Since Venus spends about a month in each sign, time your big sales pitches for the month when it passes through your sun Sign. That's when to flirt up a storm with someone who hasn't been giving you the time of day. Socialize and network with potential clients and contacts. Wear the colors of your sun Sign and play up all your natural sun-sign charms. You'll be the flavor of the month! For example, from January 7 to February 4, Venus is passing through Sagittarius, so Sagittarians will be most appealing. But signs of the same fire-sign family as Sagittarius (Leo and Aries) will also benefit from Venus in Sagittarius. It's also good for air signs (Libra, Aquarius, and Gemini).

So it pays to look for the times when Venus is in your sign, putting a rosy glow on the signs most compatible with yours. For a brief review, fire and air signs generally click. Water and earth signs are generally compatible. The glow will "rub off" on you!

Your Venus Timetable for 1995

As the year begins: Venus is in Scorpio

January 7:	Venus moves to Sagittarius
February 4:	Venus to Capricorn
March 2:	Venus enters Aquarius
March 28:	Venus enters Pisces
April 22:	Venus to Aries
May 16:	Venus to Taurus
June 10:	Venus to Gemini
July 5:	Venus to Cancer
July 29:	Venus to Leo

August 23:	Venus to Virgo
September 16:	Venus to Libra
October 10:	Venus to Scorpio
November 3:	Venus to Sagittarius
November 27:	Venus to Capricorn
December 21:	Venus to Aquarius

2. Make Your Big Push When You'll Have Energy to Burn

Mars is often called the great motivator—it shows how to get where you want to go. It's your personal battery charger, so knowing where this planet is traveling at any given time can help you take the initiative and schedule your major moves for days when you can get ahead fast. At other times, you may be much better off kicking back and reacting to what's happening around you.

Your best times to forge ahead are during the weeks when Mars is traveling through your sun sign or your Mars sign (you can look your Mars Sign up in the chapter on how to find your planets). Also consider times when Mars is in a compatible sign (fire with air signs, or earth with water signs). You'll be sure to have plenty of fuel to get where you're going.

Hold your fire, however, from January 2 until March 24 this year, when Mars retrogrades back from Virgo to Leo, especially if your sun or Mars is in either of those signs. This is the time to exercise diplomacy, let someone else run with the ball, or fight city hall. You may feel that you are not accomplishing as much as you'd like. The key here for everybody when Mars retrogrades is patience. Slow down and work off any frustrations with constructive physical activity (get on that Stairmaster; start pumping iron). It's also best to postpone buying mechanical devices (Mars-ruled) and take extra care when handling sharp objects.

Your Mars Timetable for 1995

January 2:	* Mars turns retrograde in Virgo
January 22:	* Mars retrogrades back to Leo
March 24:	Mars turns direct in Leo

May 25:	Mars reenters Virgo
July 21:	Mars to Libra
September 7:	Mars to Scorpio
October 20:	Mars to Sagittarius
November 30:	Mars to Capricorn

3. Play Your Cards on Your Best Days Every Month and Your High Times Each Year

Your birthday is literally a new birth, when you begin a new solar cycle. This is truly the high time of the year, when the qualities of your sun sign predominate in the overall atmosphere. Take advantage of this time to get new projects under way, especially at the time of the new moon in your sign. This is a powerful time to try new things, to take off in a different direction.

For about two days every month, as the moon passes through your sun sign, the emotional energies are in tune with you. This is also an excellent time to make your moves. Use the moon listings, which accompany your daily forecasts in this book, to schedule key activities.

4. Take It Easy During Your Personal "Low" Times

There are two times during the year when you may feel you are out of sync with what's happening around you. One time is right before your birthday, when the sun is passing through the sign preceding yours. This is a slowdown time, before the annual rebirth on your birthday. You may be feeling a bit vulnerable and reflective, more like keeping to yourself than socializing. (That's good—it's what you're supposed to do at this time!) This is a time to toss away ideas that have outlived their usefulness and unproductive ways of using your time. If you reflect on where you're going and why, then this can be one of your most profitable times of the year. It's also the ideal time to meditate and spend time in more spiritual pursuits.

The other time of year when you may feel at odds with the world is when the sun is passing through the sign opposite yours. If you are a Pisces, for instance, you may feel a sense of unease when the sun is in down-to-earth Virgo, which favors efficient, routine work, rather than creative, imaginative activity. On the other hand, this may be the perfect time to get your life in order. When the full moon is in Pisces, which occurs during this period, you Pisceans may feel especially emotional, as if you're pulled in different directions.

During each month, when the moon passes through your opposite sign, play it cool, doing a few things you've been avoiding. Pisces could clean up clutter when the moon is in Virgo; Aries might be more diplomatic when the moon is in Libra. The idea is to look at the other side of the coin and act accordingly.

5. Gear Up for Saturn's Testing Times

You'll discover strengths you didn't know you had when Saturn comes calling! With a Saturn transit, obstacles appear and our dreams often get doused with a cold splash of reality. However, if these dreams have a chance of really happening, Saturn will provide the structure that will make them materialize. So don't knock Saturn! If you pass this planet's tests, you'll be a much stronger, more grown-up, and more capable person.

Important Saturn times are those when Saturn returns to the position it occupied when you were born, every twenty-eight years or so. At these times, if you don't think about duties and obligations, settling down, and taking on responsibilities, events may force you to do so. Other significant times are when Saturn crosses your rising sign and when it passes your natal sun.

Since Saturn will be traveling through the second half of Pisces all year long, those with Pisces placements will find that they're having some of Saturn's learning experiences. You might find that you are restricted or constrained in some area of your life. (If you're astrology aware, look up the house Saturn is passing through to discover what kind of experiences to expect.) If you ask yourself what the lessons are in these experiences, you might discover that they involve adjusting your dreams to reality and dealing with the responsibilities of being an adult. You'll grow up fast during a Saturn transit.

When Saturn retrogrades, from July 6 to November 21, all signs may feel a lack of discipline. It may be difficult to get things done when you'd rather indulge yourself. You're more likely to give in to daydreaming or overspending when Saturn's restraints are lifted. (Don't worry—you'll put your nose to the grindstone later!)

The best times of this year's Saturn transit could be when Saturn sextiles Neptune (the ruler of Pisces). This happens twice this year, on June 27 and August 17). During this favorable aspect, your dreams have a good chance of becoming realities. On the other hand, it's "chin-up" time in November, when first Jupiter (November 11) and then Mars (November 15) in Sagittarius form an unfriendly angle to Saturn. Things should get back on track after November 21, when Saturn swings into forward motion.

If Saturn is putting on the brakes in your life, remember that Father Time (Saturn) is a fair teacher. You'll get the grades you earn. This planet can be very kind to those who have progressed in maturity and learned their lessons well. It is those who need to learn discipline and responsibility (not the strong points of Sagittarius and Gemini) who will face the most difficult tests.

6. Outwit Mercury Mischief!

If there's one planet that is guaranteed to cause mischief with your scheduling, it's Mercury. This little planet, which rules communications, turns retrograde three times each year for three weeks at a time, when it wreaks havoc with computers, telephones, and traffic of all kinds. People don't get your message or they misunderstand you. Your answering machine breaks down. Computer terminals at your travel agency will somehow put you on the wrong flight. Then your baggage gets lost.

Your best ammunition against the woes of Mercury retrograde is a sense of humor. This diabolical little planet seems to be saying "Don't take it all so seriously!" If traveling, carry a good book or some work to do during delays. Put on your favorite tape when stuck in traffic. Keep your options open and double-check all reservations. Try not to sign contracts or make major purchases during this period. If you're traveling for pleasure, revisit favorite places, leaving exploring the unknown for another time.

This is also a time when people or things from the past could turn up again. You might reignite a former passion or plan a reunion with school buddies. While you're cleaning out your files, you might find an important document you'd lost. Look in the back of your closet—you could uncover a forgotten dress or jacket that could be recycled now. Revisit favorite places. Spend a weekend with your first love in a small hotel filled with memories. You might run into an old friend. At work, go for repeat business. Call up customers you haven't heard from in a while, look up old business contacts, renew subscriptions to professional journals.

This year, Mercury turns retrograde in air signs (Aquarius, Gemini, and Libra), so mark the dates on your calendar. Those born in air signs could feel especially confused or unfocused. Give yourself plenty of options; double-check all communication; and try not to make commitments, sign leases, or make contracts. Instead, use this time to reevaluate your plans and strategies. And remember, in just three weeks, it will be over!

Mercury Retrogrades for 1995

January 26:	Mercury turns retrograde in Aquarius
February 16:	Mercury direct in Aquarius
May 24:	Mercury turns retrograde in Gemini
June 17:	Mercury direct in Gemini
September 22:	Mercury turns retrograde in Libra
October 14:	Mercury direct in Libra

7. Could You Get Lucky This Year? Put Your Money on Sagittarius!

Jupiter represents the principle of expansion—think of hot-air balloons, Santa Claus, and "Luck Be a Lady Tonight." The flipside of Jupiter is that there are no limits—you can expand right off the planet, which is why Jupiter is also called the gateway to heaven. Many people pass on with a Jupiter transit or overextend themselves in some way. Jupiter promotes optimism and enthusiasm, as well as overconfidence, so you'll need a good set of brakes when this planet steps on the gas.

This year, Jupiter is especially strong as it passes through the sign it rules, Sagittarius. This makes for a blast of optimism, enthusiasm, and risk taking in Sagittarian-ruled things. Since Pluto is also powering up the beginning of Sagittarius, it's fair to bet on horses, publishing ventures, higher education, gambling, the travel business, and religious-themed products.

Doing foreign business? Consider Chile, Czechoslovakia, Saudi Arabia, Spain, Toronto, Provence (France), Singapore, Stuttgart (Germany), or Madagascar—all Sagittarius-influenced.

However, be careful of overoptimism during the April 1–August 2 period, when Jupiter will be retrograding, which can deflate enthusiasm and cause powers of persuasion to fall flat. There may be delays and foul-ups in Jupiter-ruled areas, so postpone your risk-taking adventures until after Jupiter turns direct!

Another period to note is the time around November 11, when Jupiter forms a tense aspect with Saturn, which will apply the brakes to any overinflated ventures. However, if your schemes pass Saturn's test, you can be sure they're winners!

Movements of Jupiter in 1995

April 1:	Jupiter turns retrograde in Sagittarius
August 2:	Jupiter direct in Sagittarius
November 11:	Jupiter in Sagittarius squares Saturn in Pisces

8. Oh, Those Ominous Eclipses!

Eclipses have had an ominous reputation since man first panicked at the blackout of one of the celestial lights. If you've ever witnessed a total solar eclipse, you'll agree it's an awesome spectacle. Even today, people in many parts of the world cling to their superstitions about the negative effects of eclipses. During the total solar eclipse of July 1991, villagers in Mexico painted fruit trees red and wore red ribbons and underwear to deflect "evil rays." Then everyone retreated inside to track the eclipse on TV.

Could you be eclipsed by an eclipse? Not if you know how to turn one of nature's most fascinating events to your advantage. Lunar eclipses happen at the time of a full moon, when emotions would normally come to a head and be released—this is the monthly climax of events. Then, after the full moon comes a winding-down period before the next new moon starts the cycle rolling again. At a lunar eclipse, however, the release, which is usually triggered by the tension of the sun opposing the moon, is intercepted by the Earth, which passes exactly between the two bodies and cuts off the exchange of energy, like a football player intercepting a long pass. The effect can be either confusion or clarity, as subconscious energies are let loose, bringing insights and events that can change the pattern of our lives. Whether this creates disorientation or divine insight depends on each individual's reaction. However, change is the key word.

When a solar eclipse occurs, the moon is the interfering body, blocking the sun's energy from the Earth. Since this always happens at the new moon, which begins the monthly cycle, the alignment of sun and moon energies becomes super-intense, with the moon's emotional nature taking over. It's not a time for objective clarity! Emotions can get out of hand as the ego (sun) goes into hiding. But what a time for spiritual or psychic experiences!

Because the exact alignments of eclipses create such a concentration of energy, everything from birds, animals, fish—even oysters—become disoriented. But if we look behind eclipse-related crises, we often find that there is some deep, positive force activated—a change that needed to happen.

How should you handle an eclipse? Mark your calendar the week before the eclipse, a few days after the previous quarter moon, when energies start to build up. Clearly this would not be a good time to make a serious commitment, an important decision, or a major purchase that requires measured, rational thinking. Generally, stick to low-stress activities, since your energy and immune system may be lower than usual. If at all possible, avoid surgery, risky sports, handling sharp or dangerous objects. And be especially careful with any form of drug or alcohol use.

However, if you'd like to catch someone off guard, this would be the time to do it! Let the competition make a move, while you sit patiently and wait until at least three days after the eclipse before you act.

New Moons, Full Moons, and Eclipses in 1995

January 1:	New moon in Capricorn
January 16:	Full moon in Cancer
January 30:	New moon in Aquarius
February 15:	Full moon in Leo
March 1:	New moon in Pisces
March 17:	Full moon in Virgo
March 31:	New moon in Aries
**April 15:	Full moon/lunar eclipse in Libra
**April 29:	New moon/solar eclipse in Taurus
May 14:	Full moon in Scorpio
May 29:	New moon in Gemini
June 13:	Full moon in Sagittarius
June 27:	New moon in Cancer
July 12:	Full moon in Capricorn
July 27:	New moon in Leo
August 10:	Full moon in Aquarius
August 26:	New moon in Virgo
September 9:	Full moon at Pisces
September 24:	New moon in Libra
**October 8:	Full moon/lunar eclipse in Aries
**October 24:	New moon/solar eclipse in Scorpio
November 7:	Full moon in Taurus
November 22:	New moon in Scorpio again
December 7:	Full moon in Gemini
December 21:	New moon in Sagittarius

9. Process What You Learned over the Last Two Years

The outer planets, Uranus and Neptune, have been making the news since 1993, when they lined up in Capricorn for a monumental happening that takes place only once every

171 years. Many of us experienced the fallout from natural shakeups—floods, wars, personal confusion—which served to break down traditional structures in all areas of our lives, redefine our priorities, and put us on new ground for the next century. Now, as both planets prepare to leave Capricorn, you should be making significant progress based on what you've learned over the past two years.

Pay attention when both these planets turn retrograde this year. At these times, watch for delays and setbacks in areas where there have been revolutionary changes in the last two years. This is a pause to gather energy for a great shift in the atmosphere next year. During late November and December, when Venus, Mars, and Mercury pass by Uranus and Neptune, their energies will be strongly activated once again. Expect the unexpected!

In June and August, Neptune's sextile to Saturn, which is passing through Neptune-ruled Pisces, could have a very constructive effect in our lives by providing an understanding of the lessons we learned over the past two years.

Uranus, often called the awakener, has certainly done its work over the past two years. This year, it begins to move into Aquarius, the sign it rules, where its influence is strongest. More than ever, it seems to say, "Make way for the new!" This is a transition time between the breaking up of old structures and the beginning of a more expansive and more advanced era. Uranus will confirm this as it nods to Pluto on April 10 and August 7, signaling a shift in energy that should bring hope to everyone.

Movements of Uranus in 1995

April 1:	Uranus enters Aquarius, its planetary ruler
April 10:	Uranus sextiles Pluto in Sagittarius
May 5:	Uranus turns retrograde in Aquarius
June 8:	Uranus retrogrades back to Capricorn
August 7:	Uranus in Capricorn Sextiles Pluto in Scorpio again
October 6:	Uranus turns direct in Capricorn

Movements of Neptune in 1995

April 27:	Neptune turns retrograde in Capricorn
June 27:	Saturn (Pisces) sextiles Neptune (Capricorn)

August 17: Saturn (retrograding in Pisces) sextiles Neptune (Capricorn) for the second time.

October 5: Neptune turns direct in Capricorn

10. Watch Pluto Switch on a New Kind of Power!

Pluto shows where the power is on a mass level. And if you have strong Sagittarius placements, you're sure to feel the intense transformative power of Pluto in the next few years. Everyone else could also benefit by some Pluto awareness. Though this tiny planet moves very slowly through the zodiac, it's an amazingly accurate barometer of what's really happening on a deep, subconscious level. Since we've covered the main event this year (Pluto's move into Sagittarius) in a separate chapter, this should serve as an extra reminder to tune in to Pluto and mark its movements on your calendar.

After moving into Sagittarius on January 17, giving us a taste of things to come, Pluto turns retrograde on March 3, moving back to Scorpio and, after turning direct on August 8, it finally enters Sagittarius on November 10. You may be able to feel the energy as it shifts from the intensity of Scorpio to the light, jovial optimism of Sagittarius. We'll all be transformed in our attitudes toward the very serious life-and-death issues that Scorpio rules. Now we can look forward to a spiritual shift with the potential to uplift our lives!

Movements of Pluto

**January 17:	Pluto enters Sagittarius, a major event
March 3:	Pluto turns retrograde in Sagittarius
April 10:	Uranus sextiles Pluto in Sagittarius
April 21:	Pluto retrogrades back to Scorpio
August 8:	Pluto turns direct in Scorpio
November 10:	Pluto enters Sagittarius

CHAPTER 10

Find Your Love in the Sun-Sign Personals

For some lucky people, the love of their lives is waiting in their favorite newspaper or magazine. There, in the back pages, could be a "successful entrepreneur looking for a curvaceous cutie." Further down the column is a "sensuous, brilliant blonde." Or how about the sports fan who's looking for someone who likes tennis and kayaking.

Since "personals" columns are taking up more and more classified ad space, many people must be getting together via the printed media. And some love seekers include either their own astrological sign, or the sign they'd most like to meet, in their qualifications.

Astrology-savvy sleuths might be able to detect a certain sign's style from the wording of the ad. Who but a Leo would be so confident in print? And doesn't that long list of qualifications sound like a Virgo's ad? But first, you have to know what a given sun sign's line might be. One easy way to do this is to guess which sign wrote the following ads. Then ask yourself who you'd be most likely to respond to it.

The ad writer's astrological identity will be revealed at the end of the chapter.

Women Seeking Men

1. RESCUE ME! I've been looking for love in all the wrong places. I need a special someone who is successful, sincere, and ready for a permanent commitment. I'm a magical dreamer who could invent some fantasies you'd love to fulfill. If you like affectionate, adorable, offbeat ladies, who are interested in music, art, and romantic candlelit dinners, I'll be happy to start over again with you.

2. LOOKING FOR THE REAL THING. Are you a steadfast, caring go-getter, who not only appreciates the best things in life but wants to have them! Are you the ritzy romantic who'll break down my reserve, the man of substance who can also make me laugh? I'm a hard-working, ambitious professional who'll make romance a high priority with an equally accomplished soulmate. I'll give you good value if you'll cater to my needs.

3. FIRE UP YOUR ENGINE! I'm looking for my knight riding a red Miata, Jeep or dirt bike. Let's hit the road and talk. I'm a feminine feminist, financially independent and frisky. I love the simple joy of wind in my hair, would rather have a mountaintop picnic than a posh night out. My guy is in good shape, has high energy, and is brave enough to have an equal relationship. Adventure and wild passion are ahead for us both.

4. PRESCRIPTION FOR PASSION. I'm waiting for a doting doctor with a logical mind and a poetic soul. You need tender loving care from a sweet-tempered nurse who is intelligent, informed, and a good conversationalist. I need a responsible, rational Romeo who's fit physically and financially. You should be a nonsmoker, brainy, funny, and confident, but also shy, gentle, and gallant. Since casual encounters are not my style, please be serious about having a meaningful relationship.

5. WOMAN OF DEPTH, looking for a man of substance. If you're smart, sexy, and do what you do with passion, we should meet. Why settle for less? This passionate, attractive, super-sensual seductress is looking for her match. I have some wild ideas, but old-fashioned values. I'm ready to be your one-and-only, so say good-bye to all your exes, and let's get back to basics together.

6. LET'S BE FRIENDS FIRST, LOVERS LATER. I'm a loving visionary who cares about making the world a better place. I'm looking for a Renaissance man who's unconventional, bright, and strong, who dances to his own tune, a like-minded lover who will hold me lightly. If you'd like to be the wind beneath my wings, let's get together and reach for the stars.

7. BIG SPENDER WANTS MILLIONAIRE IN TRAINING. Let's conquer the world together. I'm a warm, ultra-feminine head-turner who's as gorgeous in jeans as in a ball gown. If you deserve the best, look no further. My best man has George Hamilton's wardrobe, Bill Clinton's power, and Schwartzenegger's muscles. But if you've just got a heart of gold, you might still be The One for me.

8. I'M THRILLED BY CREATURE COMFORTS. Breakfast in bed, fresh flowers, gourmet dinners, velvet gowns. I'm looking for someone to share earthly pleasures and earthy passion. Let's indulge each other! I could make beautiful music with someone who's generous, sensual, and single. You'll be rewarded with all the cuddling and laughter you can handle!

9. ARE THERE ANY GUYS LEFT who like nice old-fashioned girls like me? I'm pretty, full figured, and want a solid relationship with a man of morals, manners, and means, who can take time to be loving and tender. Please be a family man who'll bring me home to mother, introduce me to your kids, wolf down the wonderful meals I'll cook for you, and hold hands under the full moon.

10. SPORTS FAN. Blond personal trainer, 5'10", looking for someone who likes football as much as I do. Interested in meeting upbeat, honest, athletic male for tennis or biking, as well as Monday-night TV games. If you love travel to exotic places, have a sharp mind in a fit body, I'll take a gamble on you. Let's go jogging or walk our dogs together. Who knows where we'll end up?

11. DESIGNING WOMAN SEEKS A LEADING MAN. If you appreciate the finer things in life (and can afford them), let me surround you with romance. I'm a beautiful balance of cool logic and vulnerability; I love togetherness, but also need my own well-decorated space. Please be an unencumbered potential mate with good looks, good manners, and a great lifestyle. If you believe success is better when shared, then I'm the elegant lady who can take you from here to eternity.

12. GOT A TWINKLE IN YOUR EYE? Then I'll be no trivial pursuit. If we can talk a good game, then we might be lifetime playmates. You've got a lot to say and a witty way to say it; you're a playful party-goer, a sharp dresser who can make me laugh. Would a sophisticated, brainy beauty, who'll never give you a dull moment, make you happy? Then let's talk!

Men Seeking Women

1. TRY A LITTLE TENDERNESS. I'm romantic; I love moonlight and old-fashioned girls. I'm looking for someone to share long walks by the sea, old movies, and cozy candlelit dinners we'll cook together. You should be gentle and feminine, soft spoken and affectionate, with family values. We'll go antiquing, make love in a canopy bed, share our secrets. I love children, good wine, good company. Intimacy is my specialty. Let me provide a warm, supportive nest for you.

2. YOUR BEST INVESTMENT. Established professional, very financially secure, seeks an attractive, classy, charming lady to get serious about. Am interested in raising a family. You should also be marriage minded, intelligent, and well educated. I offer you a life of art, music, and mental stimulation. Please be slim, between 25–35, and physically fit. You may be a career woman by day, but be a homebody by night.

3. READ MY LIPS. Young-looking, young-at-heart, divorced male with eclectic tastes. I'm looking for a stunning, spirited companion with a zest for life. Great sense of humor a must. I'm whimsical, unencumbered, fun-loving, and communicative. Be ready for laughter and loving combined. If you like a varied menu of activities with lots of spice and sweet words, can we talk?

4. DOES KAYAKING IN ALASKA LEAVE YOU COLD? If so, you're not the spirited, adventurous, outdoor gal I'm looking for. Be in good shape or willing to get there fast. You should also like camping, animals, and weekends away from it all. If you're an optimist who cares about making the world a better place; if you're a brainy, insightful lady with great legs, then let's try out that kayak! Keep your bags packed and your passport updated.

5. LIVE OUT YOUR FANTASIES. I'm the man you meet in your dreams, the one who knows your thoughts before you speak, who treats you like the special person you are. I'll listen to your innermost confidences, give you my shoulder to cry on. Please be sweet but strong willed. Let me be the dreamer, while you be the doer. If you've been overworking, I'll de-stress you with caresses, give you the romance you've been missing.

6. LET ME BE YOUR TEDDYBEAR. I'm looking for a curvaceous cutie to huddle and cuddle with. Be my favorite pet and we'll satisfy our appetites in the kitchen and bedroom. You won't have to diet for me! I like you full figured and fabulous, wearing silk blouses, fluffy sweaters, and French perfumes. If you're a peaceful, home-loving lady with feet on the ground, let's get together. If you're a great cook, even better.

7. BE MY PRETTY WOMAN. I'll show you how beautiful life can be. Let's be Nick and Nora, Fred and Ginger, Bill and Hillary. I'm slim and handsome, and I have a passion for the arts and fine dining. I love entertaining and am as comfortable in a tux as I am in a jogging suit. I'd like a committed relationship with my female counterpart, who's up on the latest fashions and exudes elegance. Come share my social whirl!

8. WHERE'S MY QUEEN OF HEARTS? I'm a handsome, high-powered executive looking for a princess to share my castle. I'd love to hear from a beautiful, intelligent, passionate woman who feels good about herself and would like to share life's pleasures with a very generous man. If you're a warm, sunny head-turner with a radiant smile, I'll give you the royal treatment.

9. ALL OR NOTHING AT ALL. A woman of depth and sensuality who'll be my body and soulmate. If you're a one-man woman who's ready to be cherished forever, I'd like to meet you. I could get serious about someone who is intensely feminine, proud and passionate, erotically inventive. Let's rendezvous in a haunted mansion, read each other's tarot cards and snack on caviar. Wear slinky black—or nothing at all—under your trenchcoat.

10. LOOKING FOR BEAUTY AND BRAINS. Successful M.D. seeks lady to share the best things in life. I'm looking for a foxy lady who exudes style, class, and great taste in all she does. Dazzle me with your brilliant mind and fascinate me with witty conversation. You should also be in great shape, slim, and health conscious. Be conservative in public, and an uninhibited vixen in private. For Ms. Perfect, I'll cure your insecurities and be your significant other.

11. I'M OPEN-MINDED AND WILLING TO TRY ANYTHING ONCE. Surprise me! I'm slightly eccentric—a Renaissance man with Tom Selleck's looks, Einstein's mind, and Yeltsin's guts. You're your own person, strong in spirit and body. Be adventurous, unconventional, open minded, and future oriented. Material girls need not apply. Be my best friend as well as my lover, and I'll be yours for keeps.

12. LIGHT MY FIRE! I'm a strong, confident macho man who's looking for a kindred spirit to share life's challenges. You should be athletic, energetic, and ready for lots of action. If you spark my interest, I'll give you plenty of fireworks—get ready to be swept off your feet, wooed, and pursued like you've never been before. My white charger's waiting for the right fair damsel.

Who Placed the Personal Ads?

Women Seeking Men

1. Pisces
2. Capricorn
3. Aries
4. Virgo
5. Scorpio
6. Aquarius
7. Leo
8. Taurus
9. Cancer
10. Sagittarius
11. Libra
12. Gemini

Men Seeking Women:

1. Cancer
2. Capricorn
3. Gemini
4. Sagittarius
5. Pisces
6. Taurus
7. Libra
8. Leo
9. Scorpio
10. Virgo
11. Aquarius
12. Aries

CHAPTER 11

Let the Stars Guide You to Your True-Love Type

Ladies, does the sensitivity of Tom Cruise and the smooth style of Harrison Ford appeal to you most? Or do you prefer the dash of Dennis Quaid and Alec Baldwin? Guys, do you dream of Kim Basinger? Or are Julia Roberts and Demi Moore more your type?

It's amazing how many celebrities embody the qualities of their sun sign. And it's amazing, too, what your favorite celebrity's sign can reveal about your potential soulmate. To prove (or disprove) this point, circle the celebrities that appeal to you on the following lists. Some are all-time classic film personalities; others might be the talk-show host you watch most often, or the celebrity you'd like most to have dinner with. You may be surprised to find out how many of your choices fall under one or two signs. Then look up the sun sign type at the end of the lists and learn more about who really turns you on (it could be quite a different sign than the one you expect)!

Type A: Dashing and Daring

MALES

Alec Baldwin
Al Gore
Gregory Peck
Spencer Tracy
Matthew Broderick
Timothy Dalton

FEMALES

Ellen Barkin
Diana Ross
Emma Thompson
Leeza Gibbons
Paulina Porizkova
Mariah Carey

Dennis Quaid   Reba McEntire
Warren Beatty   Shannon Doherty
David Letterman   Marilu Henner
Eddie Murphy   Ali MacGraw

Type B: Earthy Sensualists

MALES   **FEMALES**

Daniel Day Lewis   Michelle Pfeiffer
Jack Nicholson   Janet Jackson
Jay Leno   Candice Bergen
Randy Travis   Andie MacDowell
Al Pacino   Debra Winger
Pierce Brosnan   Shirley Maclaine
Tony Danza   Sheena Easton
David Byrne   Cher
Billy Joel   Bea Arthur
Emilio Estevez   Jessica Lange

Type C: Charm to Spare

MALES   **FEMALES**

Tom Berenger   Elle MacPherson
Clint Eastwood   Brooke Shields
Parker Stevenson   Isabella Rossellini
Donald Trump   Nicole Kidman
Tony Geary   Joan Rivers
Tristan Rogers   Kathleen Turner
Prince   Lisa Hartman
Johnny Depp   Phylicia Rashad
Paul McCartney   Joan Collins
John Goodman   Connie Selleca

Type D: Tender and Caring

FEMALES	MALES
Princess Diana	Tom Cruise
Linda Ronstadt	Harrison Ford
Kim Alexis	Geraldo Rivera
Meryl Streep	Bill Cosby
Diahann Carroll	Jimmy Smits
Phoebe Cates	Robin Williams
Isabelle Adjani	George Michael
Jerry Hall	John Tesh
Angelica Huston	Alex Trebek
Brigitte Neilson	Sylvester Stallone

Type E: Big-time Romantics

MALES	FEMALES
Mick Jagger	Madonna
Arnold Schwartzenegger	Jackee
President Bill Clinton	Whitney Houston
Steve Martin	Lynda Carter
Kenny Rogers	Delta Burke
Peter Jennings	Connie Chung
Magic Johnson	Kathie Lee Gifford
Robert de Niro	Deborah Norville
Robert Redford	Iman
Patrick Swayze	Loni Anderson

Type F: They Love Taking Care of You

FEMALES	MALES
Shelley Long	Richard Gere
Joan Lunden	Jeremy Irons
Raquel Welch	Harry Connick, Jr.
Sophia Loren	Billy Ray Cyrus
Jacqueline Bisset	David Soul
Faith Ford	Corbin Bernson

Rebecca DeMornay
Ann Archer
Amy Irving
Linda Gray

John Ritter
Sean Connery
Michael Keaton
Mark Harmon

Type G: The Beauty Lover

MALES

Michael Douglas
Armand Assante
Julio Iglesias
Marcello Mastroianni
Luciano Pavarotti
John Lithgow
Sting
Jesse Jackson
Bryant Gumbel
Charleton Heston

FEMALES

Susan Sarandon
Sigourney Weaver
Suzanne Somers
Cheryl Tiegs
Catherine Deneuve
Heather Locklear
Brigitte Bardot
Angela Lansbury
Julie Andrews
Deborah Kerr

Type H: Intense and Passionate

FEMALES

Jodie Foster
Goldie Hawn
Roseanne Arnold
Demi Moore
Julia Roberts
Whoopi Goldberg
Meg Ryan
Mary Elizabeth
   Mastrantonio
Mary Hart
Maria Shriver

MALES

Sam Sheppard
Dan Rather
Larry King
Kevin Kline
Harry Hamlin
Burt Lancaster
Richard Burton
Danny DeVito
Pat Sajak
Ted Turner

Type I: Call Me Lucky

MALES	FEMALES
Don Johnson	Kim Basinger
Billy Idol	Darryl Hannah
Frank Sinatra	Jane Fonda
Jeff Bridges	Sinead O'Connor
John F. Kennedy, Jr.	Bette Midler
Kirk Douglas	Robin Givens
Michael Nouri	Susan Dey
Richard Pryor	Tina Turner
Phil Donohue	Teri Garr
Woody Allen	Liv Ullman

Type J: Home Is Where the Heart Is

FEMALES	MALES
Katie Courec	David Bowie
Diane Sawyer	Elvis Presley
Diane Keaton	Rod Stewart
Kirstie Alley	Denzel Washington
Victoria Principal	Ted Danson
Faye Dunaway	Nicholas Cage
Susan Lucci	Mel Gibson
Dolly Parton	Kevin Costner
Marlene Dietrich	Cary Grant
Ava Gardner	Anthony Hopkins

Type K: Mr. or Ms. Charisma

MALES	FEMALES
Clark Gable	Geena Davis
Michael Jordan	Ann Jillian
Axl Rose	Farrah Fawcett
Burt Reynolds	Morgan Fairchild
Tom Selleck	Meg Tilly
Garth Brooks	Lana Turner

Lorenzo Lamas   Cybill Shepherd
Paul Newman   Jane Seymour
Richard Dean Anderson Vanna White
John Travolta   Oprah Winfrey

Type L: The Fantasy Lover

FEMALES   **MALES**

Cindy Crawford   Michael Bolton
Drew Barrymore   Edward James Olmos
Bernadette Peters   William Hurt
Glenn Close   Raul Julia
Rue McClanahan   Chuck Norris
Sharon Stone   Billy Crystal
Paula Zahn   Erik Estrada
Faith Daniels   James Taylor
Sally Jessy Raphael   Harry Belafonte
Elizabeth Taylor   Willard Scott

• **IF MOST OF YOUR CHOICES ARE TYPE A, YOUR FANTASY SOULMATE IS ARIES.** These are the macho men and liberated women of the zodiac. You are probably also fascinated by such classic stars as Bette Davis, Marlon Brando, and Joan Crawford. Aries men are the type who sweep you off your feet, with plenty of enthusiasm. They may, however, cool down just as fast as they heated up. This sign has produced some noted playboys, including the founder of *Playboy* magazine, Hugh Hefner, as well as Warren Beatty and Marlon Brando. The women are some of the most exciting in the zodiac. These are assertive take-charge women who usually have dynamic careers. Obstacles only make life more challenging for lady Aries, who needs someone who'll let her take the lead—or have her own turf.

• **IF MOST ARE TYPE B, YOUR FANTASY SOUL-MATE IS TAURUS.** This sign experiences the world through the five senses—whatever or whoever feels good, tastes good, smells good, sounds good, looks good, is the one they love. This is the sign that stops to smell the roses, and probably planted them in the first place. This sign likes control, and stars of this sign, like Barbra Streisand and

Shirley Maclaine, usually call their own shots. Men of this sign, like Jack Nicholson and Daniel Day Lewis, have an earthy kind of sensuality. They're the type that responds to good food, comfort, and physical beauty in a woman. The gorgeous Taurus stars like Candice Bergen, Michelle Pfeiffer, and Andie McDowell have a flowerlike femininity that is down to earth and a bit maternal—someone you'd love to come home to.

• **IF MOST ARE TYPE C, YOUR FANTASY SOUL-MATE IS GEMINI.** Gemini celebrities are known for their great lines. When we say, "Can we talk?" or "Make my day," or when we mention "the art of the deal," we conjure up images of Joan Rivers, Clint Eastwood, or Donald Trump. Joan Collins's TV character on "Dynasty" was as famous for her quick wit as her beauty. Never bored or boring, Gemini values mental stimulation more than the physical pleasures or material rewards. One example is Gemini beauty Brooke Shields, who cut her career short to finish college. Rather than be typecast, Kathleen Turner and Isabella Rossellini experiment with many kinds of roles. Rare is the Gemini who has only one career or one marriage. George Bush was the exception—but he was married to Barbara, another Gemini. Variety is the key to Gemini's appeal, and it's also the secret to their ability to communicate with so many different kinds of people.

• **IF MOST ARE TYPE D, YOUR FANTASY SOUL-MATE IS CANCER.** Women born under this sign are among the most classically feminine and nurturing in the zodiac. However, that same caring nature can make them powerful mother figures, like Princess Diana, Nancy Reagan, and Imelda Marcos. If you're attracted to this type, you love their strong femininity and depth of feelings. Actresses like Meryl Streep and Angelica Huston have an intuitive understanding of character that helps them turn in award-winning performances. The Cancer male, like Robin Williams or Tom Cruise, also accesses that uncanny intuition. Here is a man who is more comfortable with women than any other sign. This man is a born romantic, whose understanding of a woman's emotions and insecurities makes him one of the zodiac's most tender and sympathetic lovers.

• **IF MOST ARE TYPE E, YOUR FANTASY SOUL-MATE IS LEO.** This sign does everything in a big way. They crave lots of attention, and you'd better be ready to provide it if you fall in love with this sign. President Bill Clinton and Arnold Schwartzenegger are prototypes of the larger-than-life Leo male. Though not on the list, Stormin' Norman Schwartzkopf is another. Even Leos who are less than impressive physically make their presence felt—Dustin Hoffman and Mick Jagger are two examples. The women of this sign are regal romantics who need a lover who knows how to pay court. Many Leo stars were beauty queens or involved with the pageants, like Delta Burke, Lynda Carter, and Kathie Lee Gifford. Many Leo stars are powerful enough to be known by only one name, like Madonna, Iman, Jackee, or Jackie O. If she can learn to share the spotlight sometimes, this sign makes a warm, loving mate who radiates positive energy.

• **IF MOST ARE TYPE F, YOUR FANTASY SOUL-MATE IS VIRGO.** It may come as a surprise that the sign of the virgin contains some of the sexiest celebrities, like Sophia Loren, Sean Connery, Raquel Welch, and Jaqueline Bisset. Yet these are not types who bestow affection lightly. There is always an idealism, a search for the perfect lover, behind their quest. The Virgo male type, like Jeremy Irons and Corbin Bernsen, appreciates brains as well as beauty—and that's a big part of his appeal. And this is one man that can sing about an "Achey Breakey Heart" (Billy Ray Cyrus) and have women lining up to cure it. Virgo women, sensuous though they may be, always have an air of discipline and discrimination. Like Raquel, they watch what they eat and exercise every day. But it's this blend of sensuality and practicality that makes this sign so appealing. If they take such good care of themselves, imagine how well they'll take care of you!

• **IF MOST ARE TYPE G, YOUR FANTASY SOUL-MATE IS LIBRA.** Libra is an aesthetic sign that is able to project an ideal kind of beauty, like Catherine Deneuve, Deborah Kerr, or Brigitte Bardot. When this sign's scales are balanced, Libra combines charm, style, and ideals of fairness. The men of this sign are often style setters, like Bryant Gumbel, Marcello Mastroianni, or Ralph Lauren, yet they always retain an air of detachment as they examine everyone and everything from many perspectives. The women are ultra-feminine but fight fiercely for justice, as shown by the Libran celebrities' roles. Sigourney Weaver in *Aliens* and Susan Sarandon in *Thelma and Louise* are two examples. And in real life, there are forceful Libra heroines like Eleanor Roosevelt and Margaret Thatcher.

• **IF MOST ARE TYPE H, YOUR FANTASY SOUL-MATE IS SCORPIO.** This category shows an attraction to intense characters. Both male and female Scorpios love to exercise power and control over others. You'll find many female Scorpio stars firmly holding the reins, involved in all aspects of their shows. Jodie Foster, Roseanne Arnold, and Goldie Hawn are all active players in the Hollywood power scene. Hillary Rodham Clinton wields Scorpio female political power. Scorpio men, like Kevin Kline, have strong sexual magnetism, even when playing comedy roles. Often they come across as low key, like Sam Sheppard or anchorman Dan Rather—but never underestimate their underlying drive. To intrigue a Scorpio, keep your air of mystery. Don't tell all. Scorpio loves to delve into your deep secrets.

• **IF MOST ARE TYPE I, YOUR FANTASY SOUL-MATE IS SAGITTARIUS.** When Frank Sinatra sings "I Did It My Way," he's singing the Sagittarius theme song. This sign hates to take orders and needs to keep some independence in any relationship. The male Sagittarius is a romantic wanderer, but so much fun that he's easier to forgive than other zodiac Don Juans. This sign is also compelled to voice its opinions, controversial as they may be. You may be attracted by the outspoken, sometimes outrageous qualities of Sagittarius stars like Sinead O'Connor, Bette Midler, and Phil Donahue. This sign is very sports minded, whether as a participant or spectator, and adores being on the road. Sagittarius women, like Jane Fonda and Liv Ullman, usually have interests that reach beyond their profession. Sagittarians are big risk takers, whether it be a new business venture or a night at the casino. Fortunately, luck usually smiles on this sign, perhaps because these folks are among the most optimistic positive thinkers of the zodiac.

• **IF MOST ARE TYPE J, YOUR FANTASY SOUL-MATE IS CAPRICORN.** It may come as a surprise that a sign that contains David Bowie, Rod Stewart, and Elvis Presley, could be called home loving and traditional. But male Capricorns like the little woman to stay in the background, helping them rise to the top, and they usually do not tolerate a two-career marriage for long. Women of this sign also combine ambition with traditional values. Dolly Parton has lovingly restored the backwoods cabin where she grew up. Throughout her long career, Marlene Dietrich returned to her husband's chicken farm and stayed married to the same man in spite of her legendary love life. This combination of the devoted girl or boy next door with worldly success is one thing that keeps Capricorn stars like Cary Grant, Ava Gardner, and Loretta Young on our mind.

• **IF MOST ARE TYPE K, YOUR FANTASY SOUL-MATE IS AQUARIUS.** Charisma is the word for the electric appeal of Aquarius, which grows ever stronger over high-tech media like television and video. This sign understands the secret of universal appeal. They're everyone's friend and can reach out to groups of people easily, like Oprah Winfrey or Paul Newman. The men of this sign easily embody an archetypal masculinity, like Clark Gable or Burt Reynolds. However, on a personal level they tend to be remote. There's always a fascinating elusive quality that can't quite be pinned down. To have a lasting relationship with this sign, you've got to be a friend as well a lover. It also helps if you share plenty of outside activities and interests—this is not a sign who'll focus on you alone.

• **IF MOST ARE TYPE L, YOUR FANTASY SOUL-MATE IS PISCES.** Pisces celebrities wrap their talent in an air of illusion. They rarely come on strong. Instead, they have an undefinable ease and glamour that lures admirers. Like the actors Michael Caine, Glen Close, or Raul Julia, Pisces artists seem to do what they do effortlessly, as if they're hardly trying. No one can guess the hard work behind their talented facade. They love to help the needy (and often attract people with problems). Pisces, like Elizabeth Taylor, will champion the most controversial causes. The Pisces female, like Cindy Crawford, epitomizes feminine glamour, but there is always a caring, emotional quality as well. The Pisces male is home loving and sensual. He's the dreamy kind of romantic, who will make you feel as if you're the center of his universe and that he understands everything you're going through. If he's in a field where he can use his creative talents, he's sure to be a success.

CHAPTER 12

The Astrology Bulletin—How to Make Your Own Astrology Connections

If you've caught the "astrology bug," you'll want to go even further than the scope of this book. Perhaps you'll begin by having your chart done, then deepen your knowledge by taking courses or attending conferences, subscribing to astrology-oriented magazines, or trying your hand at doing charts yourself on your personal computer. If you are buying a computer with astrology use in mind, you'll want to know where to find the right program for your needs and expertise.

To help you in your quest, here is what you can expect from a typical astrological reading, some tips on the newest computer programs, plus a resource list of reputable companies and organizations at the end of the chapter.

Whether you're new to astrology or already hooked, you'll find the more you get involved, the more you'll be fascinated by its accuracy and relevance to your life. And the more there is to challenge you!

When to Have a Reading

If you've been wondering about whether an astrological reading could give you the competitive edge in business, help you break through a personal dilemma, decide on the best day for a key event in your life, or help you make a career change, this may be the time to have a personal consultation. An astrologer might give you reassurance and validation at a turning point or crisis time in your life, or simply help you get where you want to go. Though you can learn much about astrology from books such as this one, or you can choose from a varied menu of computer readings (there are some quite sophisticated readings done by world-famous astrologers), nothing compares to a personal consultation with a professional astrologer who has analyzed thousands of charts and who can pinpoint the winning potential within yours. With your astrologer, you can address specific problems in your life that may be holding you back. For instance, if you are not getting along with your mate or coworker, you could leave the reading with some new insights and some constructive ways to handle the situation. There's no question that a good astrologer can help you create a more fulfilling future by understanding your own tendencies as well as your place in the cosmic scheme.

YOU'LL NEED TO GIVE THE ASTROLOGER THIS INFORMATION BEFOREHAND. Before your reading, a reputable astrologer will ask you for the date, time (as accurately as possible), and place of birth of the subject of the reading. A horoscope can be cast about anything that has a specific time and place. Most astrologers will enter this information into a computer, which will then calculate your chart in seconds. From the resulting chart, the astrologer will do an interpretation.

WHAT TO DO IF YOU ARE NOT SURE OF YOUR EXACT BIRTH TIME. If you don't know your exact birth time, you can usually find it filed at the Bureau of Vital Statistics at the city hall or county seat of the state where you were born. If you have no success in getting your time of birth, some astrologers specialize in rectification, using past events of your life to estimate an approximate birth time.

How to Find a Good Astrologer

Your first priority should be to choose a qualified astrologer. Rather than relying on hearsay or grandiose advertising claims, do this with the same care you would choose any trusted adviser such as a doctor, lawyer, or banker.

Unfortunately, anyone can claim to be an astrologer—to date, there is no licensing of astrologers or established professional criteria. However, there are nationwide organizations of serious, committed astrologers that can help you in your search.

Good places to start your investigation are organizations such as the American Federation of Astrologers or the National Council for Geocosmic Research (NCGR), which offers a program of study and certification. If you live near a major city, there is sure to be an active NCGR chapter or astrology club in your area—many are listed in astrology magazines available at your local newsstand. In response to many requests for referrals, the NCGR has compiled a directory of professional astrologers, which includes a glossary of terms and an explanation of specialties within the astrological field. Contact the NCGR headquarters (see the resource list at the end of this chapter) to order a copy.

As a potentially lucrative freelance business, astrology has always attracted self-styled experts who may not have the technique or the counseling experience to give an accurate, helpful reading. These astrologers can range from the well-meaning amateur to the charlatan or street-corner gypsy who has for many years given astrology a bad name. Be very wary of astrologers who claim to have occult powers or who make pretentious claims of celebrated clients or miraculous achievements. You can often tell from the initial phone conversation if the astrologer is legitimate. He or she should ask for your birthday time and place and conduct the conversation in a professional way. Any astrologer who gives a reading based only on your sun sign is highly suspect.

When you arrive at the reading, the astrologer should be prepared. The consultation should be conducted in a private, quiet place. The astrologer should be interested in your problems of the moment. A good reading involves feedback on your part, so if the reading is not relating to your concerns, you should let the astrologer know. You should feel free to ask questions and get clarification of technical terms. The reading should be an interaction between two people rather than a solo performance. The more you actively participate, rather than expecting the astrologer to carry the reading or come forth with oraclar predictions, the more meaningful your experience will be.

An astrologer should help you validate your current experience and be frank about possible negative happenings, but be helpful about pointing your life in the most positive direction.

In their approach to a reading, some astrologers may be more literal, some more intuitive. Those who have had counseling training may take a more psychological approach. Though some astrologers may seem to have an almost psychic ability, extrasensory perception or any other parapsychological talent is not necessary to be a good astrologer. A very accurate picture can be drawn from factual data.

An astrologer may do several charts for each client—one for the time of birth, one for the current date, and a "progressed" chart showing the evolution from the birth time to the present. According to your individual needs, there are many other possibilities, such as a chart for a different location, if you are contemplating a change of place. Relationships between any two people, things, or events can be interpreted with a "synastry" chart, which compares the chart of one birth date with the chart of another date. Another type of relationship chart is the composite chart, which uses the midpoints between planets in two individual charts to describe the relationship.

An astrologer will be particularly interested in transits—planets passing over the planets or sensitive points in your chart during the upcoming year, which signal important times for you.

Another option is a taped reading—the astrologer will mail you a previously taped reading based on your birth chart. This type of reading if more personal than a computer printout and can give you valuable insights, but it is not equivalent to a live reading, when you have a dialogue with the astrologer and can cover your specific interests.

Astrology on Your Home Computer

Your PC is an excellent tool for learning about astrology. There are basic programs especially for students, which cost under $100, such as "Chartwheels" from Astrolabe. No longer do you have to spend hours on tedious calculations or rely on guesswork when you set up a chart. The computer does this for you in seconds and runs off a great-looking chart.

Software is now available for every computer and for all levels of astrological expertise. Some will provide pages of interpretations. Others simply run off a chart with technical information. Others give you mind-boggling menus enabling you to choose from many different zodiacs, house systems, and types of charts. If, like most of our readers, you will only be using the program occasionally for fun, then you really don't need an expensive and complicated program. If you are motivated to study astrology in depth, however, you may want to investigate the more challenging programs.

There are several companies on the resource list at the end of this chapter that produce or distribute astrological software. Most are happy to offer support and advice. If you give them the make and model of your computer and your level of astrological knowledge, they will recommend a program and even help you get started. Some offer chart services to print up charts and interpretations for those who do not have a computer or do not want to invest in a program.

BUYING A COMPUTER TO DO ASTROLOGY. There are programs available for all operating systems, although most are created for IBM compatibles. At this writing, one of the top astrology software companies, Astrolabe, is offering thirty programs for IBM PC compatibles, thirteen for Macintoshes, and one for the Commodore Amiga. It also continues to stock some older programs for Apple II, earlier Commodores, and CPM-compatible machines, so don't despair if you are still working on a "dinosaur."

If you're buying a new computer and want to run state-of-the-art programs, most software vendors recommend an 80386 to 80486 processor chip, at least 640K RAM (though most current software runs on 512 K RAM), a speed of 16 megaHertz or faster, and DOS 3.3 or higher. A hard disk with 40 or more megabytes and at least one floppy are recommended. As for monitors, color displays are not necessary; however, there are some gorgeous graphic astrology charts coming out that will require an auto VGA. Otherwise, a high-resolution one-color monitor with a Hercules monographics card is fine.

If you are buying a new printer, graphics look sharpest on a laser printer, but many astrologers are very content with a 9- or 24-pin printer. Those of you who use Windows will find that several of the companies listed at the end of the chapter are now doing programs for this environment, with pull-down menus and graphics. "Solar Fire" from Astrolabe is one such program.

Where to Connect with Other Astrologers

Check your local metaphysical bookstore for flyers or a bulletin board posting astrological events in your area. Many New Age centers offer courses with astrologers visiting your area, when you can meet kindred souls.

You can contact other astrologers or learn about astrological happenings in your area and nationwide through computer networks which have astrological SIG's (Special Interest Groups). These are often reviewed or listed in astrology magazines, so, if you have a modem, why not tune in? If you already belong to a network or to Compuserve, check to see if there are astrology fans online.

Another way of finding an astrology class is to contact one of the regional astrology groups across the country that have regular meetings. Ask at your local metaphysical or New Age bookstore or look for listings in an astrology magazine such as *American Astrology* or *Dell's Horoscope*. Astrological organizations like the National Council for Geocosmic Research may give classes in your area. Several times a year, these organizations sponsor regional astrology conferences where you can meet some of the best teachers, as well as broaden your knowledge and socialize with other astrology fans.

Several astrologers are running mating-and-dating services, using astrological savvy to bring cosmically connected couples together. It is possible that one of your local astrologers is running a comparable service. This could be a "personals" column with astrological information about the participants that you then follow up on your own, or the astrologer may do a more personalized search for you, involving individual chart comparisons, personal interviews, and video interviews.

Some Other Ways to Study Astrology

First, consider attending one of the several yearly regional conferences sponsored by the major astrological organizations. Most offer programs at several levels of expertise. You could also connect with a teacher who would help you further your studies.

If you cannot go to conferences, you can still hear many of the lectures and workshops on tape cassetes in your home or car. See the resource list to order catalogues of regional and national conferences. Taped instruction is also advertised in the more specialized astrology magazines such as *Planet Earth* or *Mountain Astrologer*.

Another option, which might interest those who live in out-of-the-way places or who are unable to fit classes into their schedule, are study-by-mail courses that are offered by several astrological computing services and astrology magazines. Some courses will send you a series of tapes; others use workbooks or computer printouts.

An Astrology Resource List

Nationwide Astrology Organizations

(Conferences, Workshops, Local Meetings, Conference Tapes, Referrals)

National Council for Geocosmic Research
(For Directory of Professional Astrologers, classes, tape catalogue, and conference schedule.)
105 Snyder Avenue
Ramsey, NJ 07446
201-818-2871

American Federation of Astrologers (A.F.A.)
P.O. Box 22040
Tempe, AZ 85382

A.F.A.N.
(Networking, Legal Issues.)
8306 Wilshire Blvd.
Berkeley Hills, CA 90211

ARC Directory
(Listing of astrologers worldwide)
2920 E. Monte Vista
Tucson, AZ 85716
602-321-1114

Computer Programs

Matrix Software
(Programs for IBM Compatibles, at the student and professional level.)
315 Marion Avenue
Big Rapids, MI 49307
(1-800-PLANETS)

Astro Communications Services
(Programs for IBM compatibles and MAC, variety of computer charts, Telephone Consultations.)
Dept. AF693, PO Box 34487
San Diego, CA 92163-4487
(1-800-888-9983)

Astrolabe
(Variety of programs for all computers, beginner to professional level, wide selection of computer readings.)
Box 1750—R
Brewster, MA 02631
1-800-843-6682

A.R.T. Software
(Programs for the Mac.)
P.O. Box 191
Cumberland Center, ME 04021

Microcycles
PO Box 78219
Los Angeles, CA 90016-0219
(1-800-CYCLES)

Air Software
115 Caya Avenue
West Hartford, CT 06110
(1-800-659-1AIR)

Time Cycles Research
(Programs for the Macintosh.)
27 Dimmock Road
Waterford, CT 06385

Astro-Cartography
(Charts for location changes.)
Astro-Numeric Service
Box 336-AD
Ashland, OR 97520
1-800-MAPPING

Conference and Workshop Tapes

Pegasus Tapes
P.O. Box 419
Santa Ysabel, CA 92070

National Council for Geocosmic Research
(Conference tapes.)
NCGR Headquarters
105 Snyder Avenue
Ramsey, NJ 07446
201-818-2871

International Society for Astrological Research (ISAR)
(Lectures, workshops, seminars.)
P.O. Box 38613
Los Angeles, CA 90038

ISIS Institute
P.O. Box 21222
El Sobrante, CA 94820-1222

Astro Analytics Productions
P.O. Box 16927
Encino, CA 914116-6927
818-997-8684

Astrology Schools

New York School of Astrology
(Intensive curriculum, seminars, bookstore, conferences, public events.)
545 Eighth Avenue-10th Floor
New York, NY 10018-4307
212-947-3609

Astrology Magazines

American Astrology
475 Park Avenue South
New York, NY 10016

Dell Horoscope
P.O. Box 53352
Boulder, CO 80321-3342

Aspects
Aquarius Workshops
P.O. Box 260556
Encino, CA 91426

Planet Earth
The Great Bear
P.O. Box 5164
Eugene, OR 97405

The Mountain Astrologer
P.O. Box 11292
Berkeley, CA 94701

CHAPTER 13

Your Year-Round Calendar for Creating a Healthier Lifestyle

Of the big changes in the past few years, those involving our health care may have the greatest effect on our future well-being. At this writing, as Pluto, the planet of transformation, is winding up its trip through Scorpio, the sign that rules insurance and life-or-death matters, we are scheduled for sweeping health-care reforms. It should be no surprise that the one who designed and launched the transformation in American health care should be an intense and dedicated Scorpio, Hillary Rodham Clinton.

At the same time, Saturn is moving through Pisces, which rules hospitals. This planet calls attention to what isn't working, and while in Pisces, it calls for devotion to helping others. Over this year, many health-care institutions are sure to be reexamined and restructured. With monumental changes shaking up our health-care system, we'll be asked to take on more responsibility for our own health, beginning with adopting a healthier lifestyle.

Astrology can help you sort out your health priorities and put your life on a healthier course by getting in step with these times of reform. Since astrology began, different parts of the body, and their potential illnesses, have been associated with specific signs of the zodiac. Today's astrologers still work with these ancient associations, using them not only to locate potential health problems, but also to help clients harmonize their activities with those favored by each sign.

Using the stars as a guide, you can create your own master plan for a healthier lifestyle by focusing on the part of your body that is ruled by each sign, during that sun-sign period. For example, during Pisces, the sign that rules the feet, you might evaluate your shoes for fit and comfort or start a walking program. You could step up to an aerobics class or regular tennis games during Mars-ruled Aries, a high-energy sign. During nature-oriented Taurus, you should switch to more outdoor exercise, like hiking. This approach varies your workout routine to harmonize with the astrological atmosphere. And you'll be more likely to sustain your fitness program if there is enough variety to keep you from getting bored. If you follow this sign by sign pathway, by the end of the year you'll have improved your health from head to toe.

The following guide should help you select activities which harmonize with each sun-sign period.

Capricorn—a great time to get started! (December 22–January 19)

You couldn't pick a better time to start off on a new health and fitness regime than discipline-oriented Capricorn. Maybe that's why this is the busiest time of the year for gyms and health spas. Why not give yourself a Christmas present of a membership in a local gym or YMCA? Under Capricorn, which favors structure and organization of all kinds, you'll be motivated to start off the new year by getting into an exercise routine. However, it's important to find a plan you can stick with, so consider first consulting with a coach or a personal trainer who'll design a routine that's best for you.

Capricorn rules the skeletal structure, which makes this a great time to look at the state of your posture, your bones and joints. It's never too early to counteract osteoporosis by adding weight-bearing exercise to your routine. If your knees or joints are showing early signs of arthritis, you may need to add calcium supplements to your diet. Check your posture, which affects your looks and your health. Remember to protect your knees when you work, perhaps adding exercises to strengthen this area.

Capricorn, the sign of Father Time, brings up the subject of aging. If sags and wrinkles are keeping you from looking as young as you feel, you may want to investigate plastic surgery. Many foods have antiaging qualities and might be worth adding to your diet. Teeth are also ruled by this sign—a reminder to have regular cleanings and dental checkups.

Capricorn is also the sign of the workaholic, so be sure not to overdo in your quest for health. Keep a steady, even pace for lasting results. Remember to include pleasurable activities in your self-care program. Grim determination can be counterproductive if you're also trying to relieve tension. Take up a sport for pure enjoyment, not necessarily to become a champion.

Your Capricorn-time stress-busters: Check your office environment for hidden health saboteurs, like air quality, lighting, and comfort. Get a back-support cushion if your chair is uncomfortable. If you work at a computer, check your keyboard and the height of the computer screen for ergonomic comfort.

Aquarius—individualize! (January 20–February 18th)

Aquarius, the sign of high-tech gadgets and new ideas, should inspire you with new ways to get fit and healthy. You don't have to follow the crowd to keep fit. There are many ways to adapt your exercise routine to your personal needs. If your schedule makes it difficult to get to the gym or take regular exercise classes, look over the vast selection of exercise videos available and take class anytime you want. Or set up a gym at home with portable home exercise equipment.

New Age health treatments are favored by Aquarius, which makes this an ideal month to consider alternative approaches to health and fitness. Since Aquarius rules the circulatory system, you might benefit from a therapeutic massage, a relaxing whirlpool, or one of the new electronic massage machines.

Calves and ankles are also Aquarius territory and should be emphasized in your exercise program. Be sure your ankles are well supported, and be careful of sprains.

This is also a good time to consider the air quality around you. Aquarians are often vulnerable to airborn allergies and are highly sensitive to air pollution. Do some air quality control on your environment with an air purifier, ionizer, or humidifier. Since this is flu season, read up on ways to strengthen your immune system.

Aquarius is a sign of reaching out to others, a cue to

make your health regime more social—doing your exercises with friends could make staying fit more fun.

Pisces—feet first! (February 19–March 20)

Perhaps it's no accident that we often do spring cleaning during Pisces. The last sign of the zodiac, which rules the lymphatic system, is super-sensitive to toxins. This is the ideal time to detox your system with a liquid diet or supervised fast. This may also help you get rid of water retention, a common Pisces problem.

Feet are Pisces territory. Consider how often you take your feet for granted and how miserable life can be when your feet hurt. Since our feet reflect and affect the health of the entire body, devote some time this month to pampering them. Check your walking shoes or buy some shoes tailored for your kind of exercise. Investigate orthotics, especially if you walk or run a lot. These custom-molded inserts could make a big difference in your comfort and performance.

The soles of our feet connect with all other parts of our body, just as the sign of Pisces embodies all the previous signs. This is the theory behind reflexology, a therapeutic foot massage which treats all areas of the body via the nerve endings on the soles of the feet. For the sake of your feet, as well as your entire body, consider treating yourself to a session with a local practitioner of this technique.

Pisces is the ideal time to start walking outdoors again, enjoying the first signs of spring. Try doing local errands on foot, as much as possible.

Aries—energize! (March 21–April 19)

This Mars-ruled sign is a high-energy time of year. It's time to step up the intensity of your workouts, so you'll be in great shape for summer. Aerobics, competitive sports, activities that burn calories are all favored. Try a new sport that has plenty of action and challenge, like soccer or bike racing. Be sure you have the proper headgear, since Aries rules the head.

Healthwise, if you've been burning the candle at both ends or repressing anger, this may show up as headaches. The way to work off steam under Aries is to schedule extra time at the gym, take up a racket sport or ping pong, anything that lets you hit an object hard! Go into spring training with your local baseball team!

Taurus—back to nature! (April 20–May 20)

Spring is in full bloom, and what better time to awaken your senses to the beauty of nature? Planting a garden can be a wonderful, relaxing antidote to a stressful job. Long walks in the woods, listening to the sounds of returning birds, and smelling the spring flowers help you slow down and enjoy the pleasures of the Earth.

This is a month to enjoy all your senses: Add more beautiful music to your library, try some new recipes, take up a musical instrument, learn the art of massage. This pleasure-loving time can be one of the most sensual in your love life, so plan a weekend getaway to somewhere special with the one you love.

This is also a time to go to local farmers' markets and to add more fresh vegetables to your diet. While we're on the subject of food, you may be tempted to overindulge during the Taurus period, so be sure there are plenty of low-calorie treats available. If you are feeling too lethargic, your thyroid might be sluggish. Taurus rules the neck and throat area, which includes the thyroid glands and vocal cords.

Since we often hold tension in our neck area, pause several times during the day for a few stretches and head rolls. If you wake up with a stiff neck, you may be using the wrong kind of pillow.

Gemini—stay in touch! (May 21–June 20)

One of the most social signs, Gemini rules the nerves, our body's lines of communication. doing things with others is therapeutic now. Include friends in your exercise routines. Join a friendly exercise class or jogging group. Gemini-type sports require good timing and manual dexterity as well as communication with others, like tennis or golf.

If your nerves are on edge, you may need more fun and laughter in your life. Getting together with friends, going to parties, doing things in groups brings more perspective into your life.

Since Gemini also rules the lungs, this is an ideal time to quit smoking. Investigate natural ways to relieve tension, such as yoga or meditation. Doing things with your hands—playing the piano, typing, doing craftwork—is also helpful.

Those of you who jog may want to try hand weights during the Gemini months, or add upper-body exercises to your daily routine.

Cancer—create a healthy home! (June 21–July 22)

Good health begins at home, and Cancer is the perfect time to do some healthy housekeeping. Evaluate your home for potential toxins in the water or building material. Could you benefit from air and water purifiers, undyed sheets and towels, biodegradable cleaners? How about safer cooking utensils of stainless steel or glass?

This is also a good month for nurturing others and yourself, airing problems and providing the emotional support that should make your home a happier, more harmonious place to live.

Cancer rules digestive difficulties, especially gastric ulcers. Emotionally caused digestive problems—those stomach-knotting insecurities—can crop up under Cancer. Baby yourself with some extra pampering if you're feeling blue.

Boating and all water sports are ideal Cancer-time activities. Sometimes, just a walk by your local pond or sitting for a few moments by a fountain can do wonders to relieve stress and tension.

If you've been feeling emotionally insecure, these feelings may be sensitized now, especially near the full moon. Being with loved ones, old friends, and family could give the support you need. Plan some special family activities that bring everyone close together.

The breast area is ruled by Cancer, a reminder to have regular checkups, according to your age and family history.

Leo—heart and spine time! (July 23–August 22)

We're now in the heart of summer, the time when you need to consider your relationship to Leo's ruler, the sun. Tans look great, but in recent years we've all been cautioned about the permanent damage the sun can do. So don't leave home without a big hat or umbrella, and some sunblock formulated for your skin type.

If you've been faithful to your exercise program, you probably look great in your swimsuit. If not, now's the time to contemplate some spot-reducing exercises to zero in on problem areas. This is prime time for outdoor activity—biking, swimming, team sports—that can supplement your routine. Leos like Arnold Schwartzenegger and Madonna have profited immensely from weight training. Since this is a time to glorify the body beautiful, why not consider what a body-building regime could do for you?

Leo rules the upper back and heart, so consider your cardiovascular fitness and make your diet healthier for your heart. Are you getting enough aerobic exercise? Also, step up exercises that strengthen the Leo-ruled upper back, like swimming.

If you have planned a vacation for this month, make it a healthy one, a complete change of pace. Spend time playing with children, expressing the child within yourself. The Leo time is great for creative activities, doing whatever you enjoy most.

Virgo—analyze! (August 23–September 22)

Virgo rules the care and maintenance of the body in general, and the abdomen, digestion, lower liver and intestines in particular. This is a troubleshooting sign, the perfect time to check your progress. Schedule medical exams and diagnostic tests, and generally evaluate your health. If you need a change of diet, supplements, or special care, consult the appropriate advisers.

It's also a good time to make your life run more efficiently. It's a great comfort to know that you've got a smooth organization backing you up. Go through your files and closets to eliminate clutter; edit your drawers and toss out whatever is no longer relevant to your life.

In this back-to-school time, many of us are taking self-improvement courses. Consider a course to improve your health—nutrition, macrobiotic cooking, or massage, for example.

Libra—balance your life! (September 23–October 22)

Are your personal scales in balance? If you're overdoing in any area of your life, Libra is an excellent time to address the problem. If you have been working too hard or taking life too seriously, what you may need is a dose of culture, art, music, or perhaps some social activity.

If your body is off balance, consider yoga, spinal adjustments, or a detoxification program. Libra rules the kidneys and lower back, which respond to relaxation and tension-relieving exercises. Make time to entertain friends. Be romantic with the one you love. Harmonize your body with chiropractic work. Cleanse your kidneys with plenty of liquids.

Since this is the sign of relationships, you may enjoy working out with a partner or with loved ones. Make morning walks and weekend hikes family affairs. Take a romantic bicycle tour and picnic in the autumn countryside. Put more beauty in all areas of your life.

Libra is also the sign of grace, and what's more graceful than the dance! If ballet is not your thing, why not swing to a Latin or African beat? Dancing combines art, music, romance, relaxation, graceful movement, social contact, and exercise—what more can you ask?

Scorpio—transformation! (October 23–November 21)

If you have been keeping up an exercise program all year, you should see a real difference now, if not a total transformation. Scorpio is the sign to transform yourself—try a new hair color, get a makeover, change your style. Eliminate what's been holding you back, including self-distructive habits—Scorpio is a sign of willpower and determination.

This sign rules the regenerative and eliminative organs, so it's a great time to turn over a new leaf. Sexual activity comes under Scorpio, so this can be a passionate time for love. It's also a good time to examine your attitudes toward sex and to put safe sexual practices into your life.

It's no accident that this passionate time is football season, which reminds us that sports are a very healthy way to diffuse emotions. If you enjoy winter sports, why not start preparing for the ski slopes or ice skating? Scorpio loves intense life-or-death competition, so be sure your muscles are warmed up before going all out.

Sagittarius—set goals! (November 22–December 21)

Sagittarius, ruled by jovial Jupiter, is holiday time, a time to kick back, socialize with friends, and enjoy a whirl of parties and get-togethers. High-calorie temptations abound, so you may want to add an extra workout or two after hitting the buffet table. Or better yet, head for the dance floor instead of the hors d'oeuvres. Most people tend to loosen up on resolve around this time of year; there's just too much fun to be had.

If you can, combine socializing with athletic activities. Local football games, bike riding, hikes, and long walks with your dog in tow are just as much fun in cooler weather. Let others know that you'd like a health-promoting gift—sports equipment, a gym membership, or an exercise video—for Christmas. Plan your holiday buffet to lessen temptation with plenty of low-calorie choices.

In your workouts, concentrate on Sagittarius-ruled areas with exercises for the hips, legs, and thighs. This is a sports-loving sign, ideal for downhill or cross-country skiing, ice skating or roller blading, and basketball.

You may find the more spiritual kinds of exercise, such as yoga or tai chi, which work on the mind as well as the body, more appealing now. Once learned, these exercises can be done anywhere. Yoga exercises are especially useful for those who travel, especially those designed to release tension in the neck and back. Isometrics-type exercises, which work one muscle group against another, can be done in a car or plane seat. If you travel often, investigate equipment that fits easily in your suitcase, such as water-filled weights, jump ropes, elastic exercise bands, and home-gym devices.

This sign of expansiveness is the ideal opportunity to set your goals for next year. Ask yourself what worked best for you this year and where you want to be at the end of 1996. Most important, in holiday-loving Sagittarius, go for the health-promoting sports and activities you truly enjoy. These are the best for you in the long run, for they're the ones you'll keep doing with pleasure.

CHAPTER 14

Your Virgo Personal Life—Including Your Decision Maker

The Virgo Man: A Cool Customer

Contradicting the virgin symbol of your sign is one of the pleasures of being a Virgo man. Sean Connery epitomizes "the sexiest man in the world" type of Virgo, who becomes even more attractive with age. Part of the Virgo man's appeal is his subtlety; you never come on strong. You are more likely to have a modest facade and to be as interested in a woman's mind as her body. In fact, Virgo usually lets the opposite sex do the chasing. Though you may be sexually skilled, you prefer to keep your feelings under wraps, leave grand passion to others, and remain tantalizingly out of reach. Perhaps that's the real secret of James Bond's appeal. Larry Hagman, who created the character of J. R. Ewing on the "Dallas" TV series is another "thinking woman's" sex symbol.

The Virgo man is not always as practical, health-conscious, and coolly aloof as you may appear. Underneath, you have a vivid fantasy life, full of adventure, like the world of James Bond, and populated by perfect love partners (although the dream may get blurry at this point). You are never quite sure what the perfect partner is, but you know what she is not.

Virgo has extremely high standards in life and love. You reach your potential by seeing that everything is well run. Virgo usually chooses the functional over the flamboyant, mistrusting anything or anyone that seems uncontrollable. Your negative side is simply your good side carried to extreme—too-high standards make you overly critical of others, concern for health can become hypochondria, extreme neatness and organization can make you difficult to live with, careful budgeting can become penny pinching. The Virgo feels impelled to right whatever is not functioning, or at least to point it out. Some Virgos, like Michael Jackson, actually create their own isolated perfect worlds, where the real world is excluded—one reason why the Virgo male is often called the bachelor of the zodiac. No one quite lives up to that fantasy image.

When you are forced to deal with the real world, Virgo either becomes the efficiency expert, the demanding perfectionist, or the teacher in some way. You are best when you are improving a situation or a person either in body or mind—being the doctor or the teacher, and sometimes both at the same time.

In A Relationship

Virgo is a devoted partner when you find a mate who meets your high standards. Like everything else, you work hard at your relationships, but you may not express your tender romantic side easily. You like to have your house in order and will expect your partner to stick to your agenda. You will tolerate her having a career, as long as she also maintains a well-ordered refuge from the outside world. However, a Virgo's woman is well advised to look beneath the surface of her man and encourage you to express your erotic sensual side, those hidden "Agent 007" fantasies. Otherwise, as Virgo ages, you may decide to take a risk and live out some of your fantasies with a younger playmate. Many Virgos leave their sensible mates for a glamorous, far more risky partner who gives them a taste of adventure. As one aging Virgo entrepreneur described his glamorous second wife, "She spends all my money, but she's worth it!"

The Virgo Woman: Sensible and Sensual

Like your male counterpart, the Virgo woman is a paradox. You're renowned for being a schoolmarm type, obsessed with neatness and tidiness. However, some of the world's most seductive women were born under the sign of the virgin—Raquel Welch and Sophia Loren, for example. Looking more deeply into the lives of these beauties, we find women who are extremely health conscious, devoted to their families, and discriminating about relationships. They have cool business heads and often run multiple business ventures. These are not party girls by any means! Virgo is oriented to work, not play (the Filofax must have been invented by a Virgo). You are the type who will turn down a glamorous spontaneous invitation, or an exciting man, if you have scheduled that time to do your laundry.

When Virgo sets a goal, you proceed in a very methodical and efficient way to attain it. Your analytical mind will take it apart, piece by piece to discover what is not functioning. You do this to people, too. (Caution: Virgo's critical nature can win you points, but lose your friends.)

Beneath the cool Virgo surface, there's a romantic in hiding, one who'll risk all for love, as did Ingrid Bergman, who scandalized the nation by leaving her family to run off with her director. Virgo Greta Garbo specialized in portraying the women who lived life romantically, like Mata Hari and Anna Karenina, the direct opposite of the Virgo image, and had a controversial ménage à trois in her personal life. Virgo Lauren Bacall blazed with Humphrey Bogart on and off screen, in spite of their considerable age difference. Many Virgos choose men who are contrary to the expectations of others—someone from an entirely different race or culture may tempt you to drop your careful plans and take a chance on love.

In A Relationship

The Virgo woman appeals to both mind and body. But though you may appear supersensual, it is the rare Virgo who is promiscuous. You are more interested in commitment, in finding the perfect mate. Sometimes you miss on the first try, and sometimes, like Garbo, you never find him.

Virgo often has a high-strung temperament that zeroes in on your partner's weak points and doesn't rest until they are corrected. This constant nagging and fault finding can make you difficult to live with. A better approach is to use talent and charm to provoke others to take action or to set a good example for others to follow.

Once committed, you're an excellent companion and one of the most helpful mates in the zodiac. Since you have been very careful about giving away your heart, you'll be an adoring wife. You are a detail-minded associate, the perfect partner for a man who needs a helping hand. You will pull your weight in the relationship, stick by him in difficult times, and even support him financially if necessary. Needless to say, his life will get organized and his diet improved. Virgo is not sparing of a man's ego, and must be careful not to let criticism degenerate into nagging. Though you rarely play around, you have a surprising romantic streak, and if you get fed up with a difficult situation, you may throw over your neat and tidy lifestyle to live out a grand passion. Virgo is one of the most loyal helpmates and, when you let go and allow laughter and fun to enter your relationship, you may indeed have found the perfect marriage.

The Virgo Family

The Virgo Parent

Virgo, who enjoys providing useful service, makes a very effective parent. Your special strength is in practical matters that prepare your child for survival on his own, such as teaching him skills and providing health care and the best education possible. You'll also train your children well in the more subtle art of common sense.

Virgo's tendency to worry and be overly critical should be soft pedaled with sensitive children, who need to develop inner confidence. You'll be more comfortable with the mental side of parenting than with the emotional demands of a needy child, and may have to compromise overly high standards to give affection and praise, as well as criticism. Though you naturally focus on perfecting details, realizing that making mistakes and taking risks are an important part of education will help you prepare your child for solo flights.

The Virgo Stepparent

You're the stepparent who keeps the home running smoothly and deals with your extended family with intelligence and objectivity. You'll allow time for the children to adjust before you make friendly moves, never forcing the relationship. But you may have to tone down your tendency to give advice for their own good. Build up their confidence first, by showing warmth, caring, and encouragement. In time, the children will respect your well-considered advice and come to you for constructive, analytical opinions.

The Virgo Grandparent

You're still as sharp mentally and still as lively as ever! You know what's going on and have a well-considered opinion to offer—and, surprise, more people are paying attention now. Maybe that's because you are more relaxed, open, and warm than ever, and your self-confidence is justified by years of experience. You're especially attractive to youngsters, who come to you for advice because you're the one who knows what works and what doesn't. They'll consult with you about all manner of problems or hash over the world situation (you're right up with the latest news). Though you're still a worrier, you realize now how many imaginary problems never came to pass, and you've become more philosophical with age. You'll happily offer advice and zero in with sharp criticism when necessary, but now it's tempered with psychological wisdom that truly reflects your deep concern for the welfare of others!

Your Virgo Decision Maker!

Astrology can help you with all kinds of decisions, from what kind of clothes to wear to what color to paint your room. Here are some of the ways you can use the stars to find the style that suits you best.

How Should I Furnish My Home?

Elegant, conservative decor, with clean lines and lots of efficient storage space, should suit you best. Many Virgos prefer modern decor, such as Bauhaus, or decor with a Japanese influence, because of the clean, uncluttered lines of these styles.

Virgos have a special genius for organization and can make even the tiniest space functional and efficient. Antique secretaries, oak file cabinets, printer's trays, and closet organizers get pressed into service. Because you're a reader, there should be plenty of bookshelves and safe storage for your prized record collection.

Virgos have an eye for the perfect detail and nothing shares your environment unless it passes muster. Like Greta Garbo, who even designed her own rugs, you may prefer to craft your own furniture or cabinets. Your kitchen should be especially well planned, equipped with blenders, juicers, sprouters, and shelves of vitamins.

What Music Puts Me In A Good Mood?

Virgo's discriminating taste in music runs to string quartets, all the classics, and Puccini operas. Dvorak, Bruchner, and John Cage appeal to the more intellectual types. You'll search out the definitive recordings of your favorites and state-of-the-art sound equipment to play them perfectly. Some Virgo musicians and composers who might add variety to your collection are Michael Jackson, Elvis Costello, Maria Muldaur, Dinah Washington, Mel Torme, Paul Winter, Itzak Perlman, Barry Gibb, Bobby Short, and Michael Feinstein.

Where Should I Go On Vacation?

Consider putting yourself in top condition at a health spa here or in a fascinating foreign country. Switzerland or northern Italy have a variety of health resorts and hot springs to choose from. With your interest in history, visits to the historical landmarks or houses of the period that interests you would make a stimulating and interesting vacation. Plan a tour of antebellum mansions or English country houses. You might take a vacation course in a subject that fascinates you—something completely divorced from your business, such as a gourmet cooking course in Paris; rock climbing in Colorado; hiking through Wordsworth country, the lake district of England. Other Virgo places are Boston, Paris, Greece, and Washington, D.C.

Your bags are probably well made and sturdy as well as good looking. Save yourself some time identifying them at the baggage claim by labeling your bags with brightly colored stickers. You probably own a sturdy wheeled cart for easy baggage transport.

Save your meticulous and detailed packing lists. When you revisit the same destination or climate, your research will have been done—you'll know just what to take. Be sure to take along a good book or some stationary to make use of times when there are inevitable delays.

What Are My Best Colors?

Light, neutral earth tones are versatile, elegant Virgo colors. You also look chic in navy and white, or in all gray. (You look especially sexy in a tailored suit!) All-white linen is another Virgo look—remember Ingrid Bergman's grand entrance in *Casablanca*? Bright colors are tricky with Virgo, because the wrong shade might make you nervous. Use them as accents.

What Kind Of Clothes Should I Wear?

Simple, elegant clothes suit Virgo best. And you'll demand comfort, too. Too many accessories or too much jewelry clutter up your style. Like Ingrid Bergman or Lauren Bacall (or Greta Garbo in private life), you'll look your best in beautifully cut, uncluttered, and classic clothes. Even the most curvaceous Virgos like Raquel Welch and Sophia Loren keep their clothing styles simple, avoiding the ruffles and flourishes. Your makeup is subtle and carefully applied; you'll use earth tones rather than lavendar eye shadow. Hair is perfectly cut and groomed. Virgo finds the ideal hairstyle and sticks to it, like Claudette Colbert, who was known for her bangs, and Garbo, known for her pageboy.

Where Should I Go For Dinner?

Finding the restaurant that pleases fussy Virgo is not easy. There should be a sound level that encourages conversation, attentive service, and food that is healthy as well as delicious. For a romantic evening, try a country inn or an elegant Japanese restaurant. Perhaps your town has a health food restaurant that's sure to be run by a Virgo. Since your sign rules wheat, a pasta restaurant would be an excellent choice. As Sophia Loren once said, "All I am, I owe to pasta!"

CHAPTER 15

Getting Together—How Virgo Pairs Up with Other Signs

Here is a lineup of your sun sign's compatibility quotient with each other sign. Remember that most successful relationships have a balance of harmonious points and challenges, which stimulate you to grow and keep you from getting bored with each other. So, if the forecast for you and your beloved (or business associate) seems like an uphill struggle, take heart! Such legendary lovers as Juan and Eva Peron, President and Mrs. Ronald Reagan, Kurt Weill and Lotte Lenya, Harry and Bess Truman, Julius Caesar and Cleopatra, the Duke and Duchess of Windsor, Ruth and Billy Graham, George and Martha Washington are among the many born under supposedly incompatible sun signs.

Virgo–Aries

SMOOTH SAILING: Uninhibited Aries loves to bring out those Virgo fantasies. You're a real challenge to the sign of the ram. You'll have fun and thrills together. You'll provide the stability and financial acumen, while Aries does the selling and go-getting. This is one of those odd earth and fire attractions that often makes wonderful chemistry.

ROUGH WATERS: Virgo likes things wholesome and conservative, while Aries is always first with the newest trend. You could have serious differences in taste and style. Virgo's desire for perfection is read by Aries as a dull and definite downer, while Aries tendency to start things and leave you to finish could drive you crazy.

Virgo–Taurus

SMOOTH SAILING: You relax under Taurus's calm, steady hand. They bring out your sensual side. If you clean up all those details they hate and make sure they are healthy and wise, they'll make sure you are wealthy.

ROUGH WATERS: Your worrying, nagging, and constant criticism jangle the placid Taurus system. Those little things that irritate you seem to roll off their backs. And when you try Taurus's patience, the bull will charge. Then, watch out!

Virgo–Gemini

SMOOTH SAILING: You two have much to talk about and enjoy each other's differing points of view. Your practical approach gives Gemini balance. While they bring humor and social sparkle into your serious life. This can be a good, stimulating companionship on all levels.

ROUGH WATERS: Your negative fault finding, worrying, and nitpicking dampens Gemini enthusiasm. While their constant flighty activity gets on your nerves. Gemini goes off in a mental realm to escape, while you get an upset stomach. To make this one work, you may need outside medicine.

Virgo–Cancer

SMOOTH SAILING: You'll have the neatest home on the block. You are two people who take care of others in different ways. Virgo gives practical support; Cancer provides for emotional needs. You are both beautifully organized and really care. You can count on each other.

ROUGH WATERS: Cancer's moods can provoke Virgo criticism, which starts a vicious circle. When both of you turn negative, it becomes a contest of complaints, incessant nagging and guilt trips. You must realize that Cancer takes everything personally and learn to give praise and emotional coddling.

Virgo–Leo

SMOOTH SAILING: You provide the backup, managing the details and organization, while Leo handles the sales and public relations. You give Leo the attention they need, never the competition. And Leo makes you shine!

ROUGH WATERS: You tend to get bogged down with details, one of which is the budget. Leo can't think small, has extravagant tendencies, and feels a divine right to go first class all the way. Your constant reminders will cause roars of displeasure.

Virgo–Virgo

SMOOTH SAILING: You are both dedicated perfectionists who understand each other's needs. You'll make every effort to live up to those high standards and cater to each other. With every detail in order, you'll keep this relationship running smoothly.

ROUGH WATERS: You may fight over trivial details, like who gets the crossword puzzle. And you may try too hard to satisfy each other, and lack inspiration or passion. This pairing could be too prim and pristine to have any fun.

Virgo–Libra

SMOOTH SAILING: Libra's refined good looks and perfect sense of style are awesome. And their sweet-talk boosts your confidence. You'll also respect the intelligent way they weigh every situation before making a balanced decision.

ROUGH WATERS: Virgo criticism can set Libran scales swaying. So can their preoccupation with reality when Libra would rather concentrate on ideas. Libra wants compliments and flattery and may turn a deaf ear when you tell them something they need to hear. And their constant spending on clothes and social life is nerve racking.

Virgo–Scorpio

SMOOTH SAILING: You are both cool on the surface but have a turbulent inner life. Scorpio will psyche out your fantasies and help you live them. You don't mind them taking control and letting you handle the details. With Scorpio stamina and Virgo discipline, you'll go far.

ROUGH WATERS: Scorpio's emotional manipulations seem just too underhanded to you. And when you nag, Scorpio will retaliate with a stinging barb that penetrates all your defenses. You'd like them to be more on the level, but Scorpio will never give up that icy control.

Virgo–Sagittarius

SMOOTH SAILING: Sag badly needs your follow-through, while you could use their sense of humor and optimistic outlook as well as their superb energy and salesmanship. This is a fire–earth combo that could go far.

ROUGH WATERS: Sag seems just too irresponsible for the conventional, conservative Virgo. And Virgo's realism and eye for detail may seem narrow minded and confining to Sag. Don't gamble on this one.

Virgo–Capricorn

SMOOTH SAILING: You are two realists, high achievers with conservative values. This is a superorganized pair who expect and deliver a great deal. You'll watch the profits mount and shore each other up in tough times.

ROUGH WATERS: This is a serious pair that may badly need to lighten up and take a vacation. What do you do together when you're not working? It's up to Virgo to supply the nurturing and Capricorn to spend a little or a lot on pure pleasure.

Virgo–Aquarius

SMOOTH SAILING: This can be an interesting odd couple. Both of you are highly intelligent and enjoy exploring your many interests together. Aquarius is happy to let you organize while they handle the public. There is no jealousy here to deflect your affections.

ROUGH WATERS: Aquarius has many interests going at once and you may have to fight for attention, never mind top priority. It's tough competing with a worthy cause. Virgo seems too practical and earthbound for Aquarius, who hates to bother with details, including a budget. Are the compromises going to be worthwhile?

Virgo–Pisces

SMOOTH SAILING: Under your cool Virgo exterior, you long for romance. Pisces senses your need for affection and their delightful fantasies add a new romantic dimension to your life. You encourage their creativity and give them solid practical support.

ROUGH WATERS: The way Pisces operates can drive orderly Virgo crazy. These people seem to live by intuition, while you know that poetry won't pay the rent. If you're prepared to provide substance, this can last. But if you resent Pisces' modus operandi, or nag them too much, or try to reform them, they'll swim away.

CHAPTER 16

Your Virgo Career Potential

Where to Find Your Best Career Opportunities

Virgo keeps operations running smoothly, no matter what field you choose. Your best job is one where you can be constructive, where your critical mind can be put to good use. You need a business that needs you! Glamour jobs that depend on a flashy presentation are not for you. You are not especially interested in public pizzazz. Your key word is service, so your career should be involved with helping others improve themselves or provide a practical, useful product. You are the efficiency expert who saves the company money and time or monitors quality control. Your meticulous neatness and concern for health makes you a natural in the fitness, health, medical or nutrition fields. This is not to say that Virgo is not glamorous or creative (who could forget Bergman, Bacall, or Garbo!). But even in the arts, you are a flawless performer who takes a craftsmanlike approach. Mercury-ruled Virgos have a talent for communicating their knowledge. You are the zodiac's most natural teacher, either in the educational system, or in some facet of your job. Virgo's eye for detail is put to good use in editorial work, accounting, science, literary criticism (or any kind of criticism), and law. Avoid jobs where too much diplomacy, handholding or flattery is required. Political power plays also irritate your delicate nerves.

Virgo in Charge

The Virgo boss in a passionate perfectionist who expects others to meet your high standards. Your mind is systematic, and you are always aware of how smoothly an organization is run. When you spot an error or something out of order, you are quick to report the misdeed or flaw. But you also can be a wonderful teacher, who is known for developing your staff and eliciting peak performance. Though some may find your attention to detail irritating, others will benefit by your caring attention. You are always thinking of your subordinates' welfare, will make sure they get the requisite benefits, sick leave, vacation time, etc. As a boss, however, you may place more emphasis on efficiency than creativity.

Virgo Teamwork

The Virgo worker is an employer's dream: punctual, efficient, detail-oriented, hardworking, and willing to put in long hours. You are modest and quiet (except when something's wrong!) and do meticulously neat and thorough work. You are the perfect "right-hand person" who troubleshoots for the boss. You are best when you can organize your job your own way, rather than cope with the inefficiency and slipups of others. On a team, your critical attitude may cause friction with less scrupulous types. You'll have to learn to phrase your criticisms diplomatically—usually you will not hesitate to deflate a fragile ego. You shine in a position where others appreciate your dedication and attention to quality.

To Get Ahead Fast

Pick a job where your services are vitally needed, then show what you can do. Play up your troubleshooting talents:

- Practicality
- Analysis
- Constructive criticism
- Teaching ability
- Craftsmanship
- Organization

Famous Virgo Millionaires

Study the careers of these Virgo millionaires for tips on how to use your Virgo talents to fulfill your "champagne wishes, caviar dreams," as Virgo Robin Leach does.

John Kluge
John Guttfreund
Alfred Knopf
Henry Ford II
Peter Ueberroth
Harry Connick, Jr.
Billy Ray Cyrus
Michael Jackson
Geoffrey Beene
Brian DePalma
William Friedkin
Jimmy Connors
Duke Snider
Werner Erhard
Stephen King
Robin Leach

CHAPTER 17

Virgo Astro-Outlook for 1995

Uranus, lord of your sixth house, breaks away from Neptune, the lord of your seventh house, as March comes to close. It will be early June before Uranus returns to Capricorn. Between those two dates (over the April–May cycle), you will be given a bird's-eye view of what you can expect in new deals in marriage and other partnerships, and in contracts and agreements over the upcoming seven-year Uranian Cycle.

Your love life is stimulated as 1995 begins. Between February 5 and March 4, single Virgos can find their heart's desire. Be confident in your romantic thinking over the early months of 1995, and put yourself in places where you are likely to meet new people.

Meet any possible problem in marriage early in March. Watch expenses and protect your earning power in mid-April when an eclipse pressures finances. The solar eclipse of April 29 can bring accident-producing potential connected with travel.

Mighty Jupiter will be moving in your fourth house this year, where there is a line of good luck touching your family, residence, real estate, property, and ownership matters.

You also gain much from maintaining stability in your committed marriage or business relationships, for Saturn will be dominating your seventh house.

On and about May 29 you can discover new ways to promote your career, profession, status, and prestige. Between June 3 and June 24, you can make especially good headway.

Family stability is also at peak strength around the middle of June, and late June becomes a time of joy and delight thanks to your friends and your sense of full participation in life.

You can force issues and hold the initiative in love, sexual relationships, and friendships during July. August can be a good money-making month. Advance on the job around August 10. Then, pursue duties, responsibilities, and obligations for all they are worth over the last nine days of the month.

Don't try to go it alone during early September; instead, work closely with partners and chalk up progress and profit around the 24th.

Push savings, investments, and perhaps consider changing your broker in early October. The total eclipse of the sun on October 24 can bring pressure to everyday matters, which you generally take for granted, while communications and travel are also uncertain. Late October is not a good period for travel at all.

You have unbeatable drive in family, residential, and community matters throughout November. Where to go and how to get there is revealed between November 5 and November 9. Your love life is strongly stimulated between November 28 and December 22.

Your career should not be neglected in early December just because you swiftly involve yourself in holiday planning. And as the month moves along, your family and their good fortune top your agenda.

CHAPTER 18

Eighteen Months of Day-by-Day Predictions— July 1994 to December 1995

JULY 1994

Friday, July 1 (Moon in Aries)   It's a martial, exciting, loud, abrasive day. Savings, investments, and progressive changes are on your agenda. Aries and Sagittarius speak up and you gain from listening. Luck is with you if you take charge of your own interests, but do not force issues with younger, uncaring types. Chartreuse is your color; your number is 6.

Saturday, July 2 (Moon in Aries to Taurus 10:23 a.m.) Check the situation out with Leo. Your Virgo assets— methodism, practicality, persistence—are going to keep you in charge. Luck is with you if you budget, serve personal and family security matters, and deal with the generation gap. Lucky lottery numbers: 8, 17, 26, 35, 44, 15.

Sunday, July 3 (Moon in Taurus)   You could meet some fiery types under today's aspects. You may be surprised at the force with which others express their inner convictions. It's a good day for making quiet decisions in the privacy of your own mind. You can choose between a potentially promising project and a no-win loser. Your lucky number is 1.

Monday, July 4 (Moon in Taurus to Gemini 11:12 p.m.)   Patriotism, possessiveness, and internal pride are all the more pronounced with the moon in Taurus on Independence Day. There's a "no retreat, no surrender" attitude in things peaceful and mundane. Travel is favored and your yen to get into a rural area can be honored. Your colors are red, white, and blue; your number is 5.

Tuesday, July 5 (Moon in Gemini)   Where your boss and coworkers have been taking it easy due to the holiday, you can breeze ahead of them under these aspects. Situations that have been sluggish can suddenly show progress. Your career can be served by what you do, say, and plan now. The advisability of remaining where you live can occur to you again and again. Hot combination numbers: 7 and 9.

Wednesday, July 6 (Moon in Gemini)   Your social life picks up steam. A Cancer and a Gemini have key roles. You're bold and determined, intending to do a lot of meaningful work and to impact the setting in which you find yourself. You actually relish your work. Earth and reddish-purple are your colors. Lucky lottery numbers: 45, 6, 9, 27, 36, 18.

Thursday, July 7 (Moon in Gemini to Cancer 10:17 a.m.)   If you get bothersome jobs done today, you will have more time tomorrow to socialize on a grand scale. No snapping of fingers for service in the wrong places, please! You could find an older person out of sorts and ready to place blame wrongfully. Sky blue is your color. Hot combination numbers: 2 and 1

Friday, July 8 (Moon in Cancer)   Today's new moon illuminates friendships, the social side of your job, professional organizations in which you hold membership, and what your relationship with these should be. There is enlightenment for you in social status and prestige matters. Today is excellent for planning a large-scale entertainment. Your lucky number is 4.

Saturday, July 9 (Moon in Cancer to Leo 6:43 p.m.)   Friendships really count. Send invitations to parties and entertainment, beach and water activities are fa-

177

vored. Your cosmic code words for the day are action, water, and shouts for joy. A Cancer and a Pisces come front and center. Letter writing gets high grades, while phone calls can be exasperating. Coral is your color. Lucky lottery numbers: 6, 15, 24, 33, 42, 22.

Sunday, July 10 (Moon in Leo)   Give Leo the benefit of every doubt. Both revelations and plagues jump out of Pandora's box. What nobody wanted to face up to may now demand a showdown, as things that have been going on behind the scenes get their day in court. Your beloved understands your feelings more than you know. Mauve is your color; your lucky number is 8.

Monday, July 11 (Moon in Leo)   Another Virgo is admiring you and the work you do. You are at your best when you complete tasks and chores, but wait a little while before beginning anything new. There is a great deal of career and professional drive at work in your life, so relaxation with quiet music and a good book is in order. Reds of various hues are lucky for you; your lucky number is 3.

Tuesday, July 12 (Moon in Leo to Virgo 12:48 a.m.) Today is fine for beginning new projects and putting new shows on the road to success. You are at your best when you engage in self-promotion and self-realization. Speak up, letting the world know that you are serious and intend to get your cut of the pie. Spruce up your personal appearance. Your lucky number is 5.

Wednesday, July 13 (Moon in Virgo)   Phone and write letters, expressing your innermost needs and ideas. A heightened romance is in store for you if you keep your wits about you. You will feel loved and appreciated under these trends. Work moves along at a rewarding pace. Purple is your color. Lucky lottery numbers: 13, 16, 7, 25, 34, 43.

Thursday, July 14 (Moon in Virgo to Libra 5:15 a.m.)   It's a promising money day, so you can increase your earning power and income. The balance between earning and spending is being improved. You can gain by delegating parts of a project to others. Shopping for wardrobe items and cosmetics will be completed to your satisfaction. Raven is your color. Hot combination numbers: 9 and 4.

Friday, July 15 (Moon in Libra)   Extra cash is in the picture. A special sale, answering a weekend advertisement, or remembering money you set aside are all good possibilities. Bargains can be found along well-traveled roads. Spend as much time outdoors as possible. Watermelon is your color. Hot combination numbers: 2 and 7.

Saturday, July 16 (Moon in Libra to Scorpio 8:35 a.m.) Libra and Aquarius are assuming important roles. You can save by keeping abreast of price differences at the various shopping markets. You can put plans for a fabulous vacation together now. Efforts to avoid arguments are wise under these aspects. Your talents and ingenuity can pay off. Cherry red is your color. Lucky lottery numbers: 4, 13, 22, 31, 40, 29.

Sunday, July 17 (Moon in Scorpio)   Scorpio takes a bow. Everyday routines, usual matters, and the expected and the easy are all getting due attention under these aspects. Get outdoors to enjoy the beauty of nature and to breathe some good clean air. You'll have the feeling that things are going your way. Pink is your color; your lucky number is 6.

Monday, July 18 (Moon in Scorpio to Sagittarius 11:09 a.m.)   Change is in the offing as this day gets off to a good start. Shop for items that change the appearance of your everyday surroundings. Your decisions will be met with loving approval. Now is a favorable time for making travel plans and for inviting a loved one to visit. Melon is your color; your number is 1.

Tuesday, July 19 (Moon in Sagittarius)   Sagittarius upholds the law and can make you feel that you have been breaking it. Avoid confrontations that can veer off from simple discussions. There is an aura of suspicion coming to the fore from time to time. You yearn for genuine relaxation and can have it after dark. Apricot is your color; your number is 3.

Wednesday, July 20 (Moon in Sagittarius to Capricorn 1:30 p.m.) Take stock of your many good qualities and resolve to exert greater influence over vacillating young people. A renewed source of energy is coming your way and you may be surprised at all the pep and stamina you exude this evening. Tackle some of your foremost aspirations. Lucky lottery numbers: 5, 14, 23, 32, 41, 20.

Thursday, July 21 (Moon in Capricorn) Matters affecting your career are to the fore. Your love life will refuse to take a backseat to anything else, however, as desire and mysterious urges remind you that nature doesn't stop the biological clock. Ecstasy can be achieved this evening. Flesh is your color. Hot combination numbers: 7 and 6.

Friday, July 22 (Moon in Capricorn to Aquarius 4:38 p.m.) Today's full moon illuminates the secret sensations of your soul. There is enlightenment in love, romance, courtship, and sexuality. A job well done finally will win the recognition you deserve. When you cooperate, you will find hearty and full approval from coworkers. Capricorn is present. Jade green is your color; your lucky numbers are 9 and 3.

Saturday, July 23 (Moon in Aquarius) This morning is good for repairs and renovation on your home and the surrounding grounds. If your garden is blossoming, take a few flowers to an elderly neighbor. Check accounts for any possible error. Communications should produce for you this evening, so be decisive when asked for an opinion. Old rose is your color. Lucky lottery numbers: 2, 11, 20, 29, 38, 47.

Sunday, July 24 (Moon in Aquarius to Pisces 9:56 p.m.) Aquarius takes the lead. You come across some good health and work pointers in your newspaper and magazines today. Make either luncheon or dinner a memorable occasion for the family—a special green salad or a sugar-free layer cake may do it. You can hear others wanting changes in their lifestyle and some of this baffles you. Your lucky number is 4.

Monday, July 25 (Moon in Pisces)   Equality is the rule of thumb. Share, working in tandem, while marriage, business partnerships, contracts, and agreements are front and center. No matter how distasteful a chore may be, stick with it until you have it out of the way. Surely you know that Virgo is considered the best worker in the zodiac. Your color is cocoa; your lucky number is 8.

Tuesday, July 26 (Moon in Pisces)   Pisces and another Virgo can make things hum beautifully. New agreements can be formulated and signed today, and contracts can be given new clauses. In-laws are very much in the picture, whether near or far away. Lead and manage in close cooperation with your mate. Beige and khaki are winning colors; your lucky number is 1.

Wednesday, July 27 (Moon in Pisces to Aries 6:31 a.m.)   Aries enters the fray. You have a strong support in security matters and you know who will defend you in any crisis. You can encounter many nervous nellies under these aspects and most of them are worried about their job and their neighborhood. Helpful preventive-medicine routines can be inaugurated. Tan and rust are your colors. Lucky lottery numbers: 3, 12, 21, 30, 39, 48.

Thursday, July 28 (Moon in Aries)   Push savings, investments, and budgeting. You are at your best today when you are correcting, improving, amending, and getting new programs and projects on their way. Discuss household and kitchen budgets with your offspring. You may not approve your bank's performance. Hot combination numbers: 5 and 6.

Friday, July 29 (Moon in Aries to Taurus 6:13 p.m.)   The plans you put together this morning may not jell. Change is in the wind and others have ideas going counter to yours, but you become adept at pleasing an aggravating critic. Leo and Sagittarius come aboard. Choose the country over the seashore. Hot combination numbers: 7 and 6.

Saturday, July 30 (Moon in Taurus)   Say hello to Taurus. You are ultra-conscious of your own possessions now. You have a yen to travel. Things perking for yourself at a distance do well and people at or from a distance can bring you good luck. What you learned a long time ago can be put to good use now. Beige is your color. Lucky lottery numbers: 9, 18, 27, 36, 45, 30.

Sunday, July 31 (Moon in Taurus)   Travel, sightseeing, and dealing in long-range and long-distance matters are all favored. You are empowered to make a difficult person very happy. You can handle the carping and hectoring better than most. Speak of and demonstrate your love; these grand days can be far between. Reddish-purple and buff are your winning colors; your lucky number is 2.

AUGUST 1994

Monday, August 1 (Moon in Taurus to Gemini 7:05 a.m.) Gemini comes calling. You can make good headway in life, in your career, and where you promote your reputation as a square shooter. You begin this week with a feeling that you are on top of things and can take on all comers. You can turn the day to good account. Indigo and off-white are your winning colors; your number is 3.

Tuesday, August 2 (Moon in Gemini)   Libra and Aquarius figure prominently. Push your career interests for all they are worth. Tackle a supervisor for answers you need. Stand up for your own rights in any discussion of the work and how it should be done. Your personality is effective and you can increase your popularity. Hot combination numbers: 5 and 4.

Wednesday, August 3 (Moon in Gemini to Cancer 6:22 p.m.)   Speak up, for you can get what you want by debate and articulation. Explanations and directions are well aspected. Luck is with you where you are earning, doing your best to increase the financial take, and where you are budgeting wisely. The day is fine for buying supplies. Lucky lottery numbers: 7, 16, 25, 34, 43, 3.

Thursday, August 4 (Moon in Cancer)   A sun-in-Cancer type is in your corner and can be counted on in any crisis. Fine trends exist in companionship, outside interests, activist matters, public relations, and advertising. In love and romance, you have the initiative, and chances are good that you look better and seem to be nicer. Hot combination numbers: 9 and 3.

Friday, August 5 (Moon in Cancer)   A Pisces, a Scorpio, and a Cancer have important parts to play in this scenario. You're sympathetic, empathetic, and ultra-considerate, as friendships become all the warmer. You can gain future kudos by volunteering for charitable or humanitarian efforts now. Kelly is your color; your lucky number is 2.

Saturday, August 6 (Moon in Cancer to Leo 2:31 p.m.)   Leo wants you to complete a certain project. Fine trends exist for dealing with difficult people and for encouraging younger people to drop shyness and useless fears and uncertainties. Rewards can be splendid when wise use is made of your leisure time. Antique white is your color. Lucky lottery numbers: 4, 13, 31, 22, 40, 20.

Sunday, August 7 (Moon in Leo)   Today's new moon illuminates the projects you should protect and those you should discard. You receive enlightenment in love matters and in ways to close the generation gap. Preparation and planning can be a big part of the day. Venetian gold is your color; your lucky number is 6.

Monday, August 8 (Moon in Leo to Virgo 7:42 a.m.) Today is fine for luxury buying and sprucing up your personal appearance. You're in the driver's seat, for this is your lunar high cycle for the month of August. Don't be quick to make fun of established situations or to see humor where it may not exist. Lemon is your color; your lucky number is 1.

Tuesday, August 9 (Moon in Virgo)　　You continue in an unbeatable power cycle and should not neglect opportunities and advantages that are crying for use. Your basic personality strengths—practicality, persistence, and nose-to-the-grindstone methods—are standing you in good stead for major achievement. The earth signs are helpful—Taurus, another Virgo, and Capricorn. Hot combination numbers: 3 and 4.

Wednesday, August 10 (Moon in Virgo to Libra 11:07 a.m.)　　Push highly personalized matters. Speak up in your own behalf, do what you can to iron out any possible disagreements with supervisors and coworkers. This afternoon can afford an opportunity to join a group with interests similar to yours. Your skills were never more required. Lucky lottery numbers: 5, 14, 23, 32, 41, 10.

Thursday, August 11 (Moon in Libra)　　Libra has some financial advice for you. Accent harmony in dealing with the opposition and the competition. Try to put aside any possible anxiety or worry because money is earmarked for you. Today is not only for the present; it also leads into your future. Amber is your color. Hot combination numbers: 7 and 2.

Friday, August 12 (Moon in Libra to Scorpio 1:56 a.m.) Push financial opportunities hard. Undertake unusual tasks around the home that will make your loved ones happier, finding ways to bring sparkle and flair into routine chores. Write that overdue letter to a dear friend who has moved away. Chartreuse is your color; your number is 9.

Saturday, August 13 (Moon in Scorpio)　　If any misunderstanding has dampened a romance, this is a good day to resolve the matter. Scorpio and Taurus have key roles. Everyday routines may have to be abandoned temporarily under these trends. Revive an old wardrobe item by buying handsome accessories for it. Lucky lottery numbers: 13, 2, 11, 20, 29, 38.

Sunday, August 14 (Moon in Scorpio to Sagittarius 4:53 p.m.)　　Your learning processes are activated and it would be wise to read, chat, and listen for information. A neighbor can be helpful to you if given half the chance. Concentrate on the work you intend to do during the week ahead, as you gather your tools and records. Your lucky number is 4.

Monday, August 15 (Moon in Sagittarius)   Spend as much time outdoors as possible. Travel, sightseeing, and visiting historic places are all favored. Be sporty and athletic, appreciating the hills and valleys in the terrain. Large animals are worth watching and a trip to the racetrack will prove enjoyable. Your lucky number is 8.

Tuesday, August 16 (Moon in Sagittarius to Capricorn 8:18 p.m.)   Sagittarius and Leo have important roles. Your winning color is lapis lazuli. The family will share your joys under these aspects. Loyalty, devotion, and sharing are major trends, as puzzling questions can be discussed with new light shed on them. Silver is your color. Hot combination numbers: 1 and 5.

Wednesday, August 17 (Moon in Capricorn)   Capricorn and another Virgo figure prominently. The loving, gentle, kind, and compassionate side of your nature is accented. Tackling a new phase of your work will propel your career forward by leaps and bounds. Issue only specific orders to young people. Orange is your color. Lucky lottery numbers: 3, 12, 21, 30, 39, 48.

Thursday, August 18 (Moon in Capricorn)   All personal interests are speeded up by Mercury. You and your beloved can enhance the power of communications, achieving a special closeness under these trends. Make your intimate wishes known to your beloved in a romantic environment. Blue is your color; your number is 5.

Friday, August 19 (Moon in Capricorn to Aquarius 12:34 a.m.)   Aquarius breezes into view. Don't get too much burning sun at the beach or elsewhere for there are places where you are slow to realize your body's reaction. Some attention to your wardrobe won't be wasted. Warn a loved one, if necessary, about the questionable results of his or her dieting. Flame is your color. Hot combination numbers: 7 and 6.

Saturday, August 20 (Moon in Aquarius)   There is work facing you now that you'd rather postpone. The social tends to combat hard work. New ways for stretching your money are evident. Your efforts to help a relative in difficulty will rebound to your benefit for a long time to come. Lavender is your color. Lucky lottery numbers: 9, 45, 27, 36, 18, 20.

Sunday, August 21 (Moon in Aquarius to Pisces 6:26 a.m.) Today's full moon enlightens you in ways to gain control over your own interests and problems. There is illumination of health, work routines, and the best way to go about keeping in a good mental and physical mood. You're at your best today where you work alone. Your lucky number is 2.

Monday, August 22 (Moon in Pisces)   It's time to put things together in your marriage and other partnerships. Review contracts and agreements and decide what they will mean in the months ahead. You may be making some important decisions about living arrangements. Is there a possible move in the offing? Gold is your color; your number is 6.

Tuesday, August 23 (Moon in Pisces to Aries 2:55 p.m.)   Your highly personalized beliefs, convictions, and needs are moved to the front burner. These should be compared to the sharing that is required in partnerships, including marriage. Yet you desire to maintain a certain amount of individuality. Strive for intelligent compromise. Pink and blush are your winning colors. Hot combination numbers: 7 and 4.

Wednesday, August 24 (Moon in Aries)   The cosmic image is of a knightly Aries on horseback, so some pioneering will become you. No matter what the doomsters are saying, keep in mind that even great fortunes can be put together during a recession. You feel sure of yourself today.

186

Lemon is your color. Lucky lottery numbers: 9, 18, 27, 36, 45, 35.

Thursday, August 25 (Moon in Aries)   Accenting savings, budgets, investments, financial changes, and the drive to greater security, this is a good day for ironing out financial problems. What is going on behind the scenes will rebound to your benefit toward the end of the work day. Don't force showdowns. Pistachio is your color. Hot combination numbers: 3 and 8.

Friday, August 26 (Moon in Aries to Taurus 2:13 a.m.) Taurus has questions for you. Travel, what you have perking for yourself at a distance, and the matters of the higher mind are on the front burners. The generosity of a loved one warms your heart. Sidestep unhappy, complaining, and crowing types. Damask is your color; your lucky number is 5.

Saturday, August 27 (Moon in Taurus)   Keep on the go by changing your scene or take a short bus or train ride. There are good opportunities now for getting another slant on life. Exchange serious views with someone wearing a uniform. Cosmic code words for today are variety, value, and sightseeing. Coffee is your color. Lucky lottery numbers: 7, 16, 25, 34, 43, 27.

Sunday, August 28 (Moon in Taurus to Gemini 3:08 p.m.)   Today is excellent for viewing a mountain, in reality or via pictures. The Earth is lord in your thinking today and you honor all the new methods of protecting the environment. You can't read too much about pollution, clean air, and the warming effect. You are at your best when in full control of situations. Your color is mocha; your lucky number is 9.

Monday, August 29 (Moon in Gemini)   Gemini may disagree; it can be a case of theory versus proved dull fact. You are empowered to get your opinions across rather effectively. Writing, speaking, and teaching are all favored. You advance in your career even though this may not be evident immediately. Olive is your color; your lucky number is 4.

Tuesday, August 30 (Moon in Gemini)   Check matters out with a Leo or Aquarius. You sort and sift the dross from the true gold of life. Lean toward fresh vegetables and fruits direct from the market. Marriage and other partnerships can be served. Seek the pure, unadulterated, and basic. Earth is your color. Hot combination numbers: 6 and 5.

Wednesday, August 31 (Moon in Gemini to Cancer 3 a.m.)   This is a friendly day and your companionable ways fascinate quiet types. The social side of your job can be served admirably. Kind words directed at coworkers will make the hours happier and provide a strong sense of accomplishment. A Cancer and a Scorpio have good advice. Sky blue is your color. Lucky lottery numbers: 8, 44, 35, 26, 17, 31.

SEPTEMBER 1994

Thursday, September 1 (Moon in Cancer)   Trust the opinions of a Piscean and a Cancer. Fine trends exist for starting a financial ball rolling in the right direction. Your sense of public relations is especially good, so friendships, the social side of your job, and participation in activist matters are all favored. Your color is amber. Hot combination numbers: 7 and 9.

Friday, September 2 (Moon in Cancer to Leo 11:37 a.m.) Scorpio and Taurus come front and center. Parties, entertainment, and spending time away from work with interesting coworkers are possible today. Today you can control situations blossoming in your favor. A television show can be instrumental to your future success and peace of mind. Your lucky number is 9.

Saturday, September 3 (Moon in Leo)   Aspects favor completions, dealings with large institutions, and helping your mate with unpleasant work. You excel as a spouse and partner under these aspects. It's a fine day for dealing with what has been transpiring behind the scenes. In-laws are in a position to be helpful. Lucky lottery numbers: 2, 11, 20, 29, 38, 47.

Sunday, September 4 (Moon in Leo to Virgo 3:33 p.m.) Leo and Sagittarius have key roles. Excellent trends exist for closing out a no-win project, for rearranging furniture in your home, and serving a hot chunky soup to the wanderers who return after a day outdoors. Your reputation for self-confidence pays off. Your winning number is 4.

Monday, September 5 (Moon in Virgo) The new moon in Virgo illuminates your worries, your plans, and your decisions. You are in a powerful cycle today; tomorrow can be even better due to your self-confidence and self-reliance. Patience and perseverence will pay handsome dividends. Your color is pinecone; your lucky number is 8.

Tuesday, September 6 (Moon in Virgo to Libra 6:57 p.m.) Sound off, airing your aspirations and let the world know that you are present and want your share of the pie. Dress to be noticed and admired. Show authority and be positive and optimistic. On your menu today: old-world sausage grilled to a "T." Hot combination numbers: 1 and 8.

Wednesday, September 7 (Moon in Libra) Libra swings into action. There is good potential in your salary—increase income by keeping your nose to the grindstone. Educational interests are perking in your favor. Reason, logic, and practicality attend you. Strawberry and almond are your winning colors. Lucky lottery numbers: 3, 12, 21, 30, 39, 48.

Thursday, September 8 (Moon in Libra to Scorpio 8:26 p.m.) Venus in Scorpio increases sexual desire and urges. The fantasy of the ultimate experience can drive you on under these aspects. You realize that despite the acceptance of greed all around, money is a poor second to love, happiness, and warranted pride. Your lucky number is 5.

Friday, September 9 (Moon in Scorpio) Taurus and Scorpio are impacting your day. You concentrate on what has to be done and on your everyday and usual routines. You can also improve your leisure activities. Make notes about the shopping you want to do this month. Be careful in any work you do where there is a possibility of accident. Your lucky number is 7.

Saturday, September 10 (Moon in Scorpio to Sagittarius 10:25 a.m.) Blackberry and yellow are your winning colors. Siblings and neighbors are in the picture, so moving about in your own locality can bring joy and gains. Use your head and avoid confronting a grouchy and revengeful type. Try to make allowances for people who worry too much. Lucky lottery numbers: 10, 9, 18, 27, 36, 45.

Sunday, September 11 (Moon in Sagittarius) Check things out with Sagittarius, a great authority on family peculiarities. Residential repairs may be in order under these trends. You are adept at winning others over to your point of view, mostly because they admire your capacity for detail work. Your color is emerald; your lucky number is 2.

Monday, September 12 (Moon in Sagittarius) The outdoors is beckoning you. Fine trends exist for an Indian summer budget vacation. Hit a resort that is just about to close, but let someone else do the climbing and the handling of sharp instruments. Sports and clubs that are regrouping after the summer are represented. Claret is your color; your lucky number is 6.

Tuesday, September 13 (Moon in Sagittarius to Capricorn 1:44 a.m.) Capricorn and a Cancer have important parts to play. Your beloved may wish you would give greater and more consistent attention to marriage; but you feel that you are already giving it your all. Avoid any possible angry encounters by refusing to argue. Your color is magenta; your lucky number is 8.

Wednesday, September 14 (Moon in Capricorn) You are romantic today and seek joint adventures with your beloved. The demands of career, the larger family, and community involvements can detract from the urgency of love. A party late this evening would produce desirable results. Your winning colors are champagne and ruby. Lucky lottery numbers: 1, 10, 19, 28, 37, 46.

Thursday, September 15 (Moon in Capricorn to Aquarius 6:42 a.m.)   Refrain from being too blunt with a supervisor, employer, or coworker. Savings and investments are supported over the late afternoon. An Aquarius is in the driver's seat. It's important that you avoid questionable food today; know something about the restaurant kitchen. Scarlet is your color. Hot combination numbers: 3 and 4.

Friday, September 16 (Moon in Aquarius)   There's a newsy communication from someone who's been thinking about you. An excursion into an unfamiliar neighborhood to look at new homes is well within your scope. Bring a valuable time-saving approach to your job. Tan is your color; your lucky number is 5.

Saturday, September 17 (Moon in Aquarius to Pisces 1:31 p.m.)   Gemini and Libra have key roles. Delegate more of the routine, repetitive tasks to someone who is eager to help. You can experience a feeling of self-confidence. Your enthusiasm is therapeutic. Be careful while driving or walking in poorly lighted neighborhoods. Taupe and beige are your colors; Lucky lottery numbers: 7, 16, 25, 34, 43, 17.

Sunday, September 18 (Moon in Pisces)   Pisces and a Cancer figure prominently. Apply that special creative ability for organizing to everything you tackle today. Marriage, other partnerships, contracts, agreements, sharing, cooperating, and working in tandem are all featured. Do what you can to lessen the impact of the gender gap. Your number is 9.

Monday, September 19 (Moon in Pisces to Aries 10:30 p.m.)   Scorpio has the answer. Take an inventory of your assets to reveal more potential than you realized. Additional sources of income are possible. Do something unusual to demonstrate your affection, as cousins, former neighbors, and old schoolmates are thinking of you. Your number is 4.

Tuesday, September 20 (Moon in Aries)   Red and white are your winning colors. Aries shows up. Big gains can come through investments, improved budgeting, and a special savings plan. Try to hold positive thoughts even when you're surrounded by negative types. You can present an especially appealing image to your beloved. Your lucky number is 6.

Wednesday, September 21 (Moon in Aries)   Push for greater accumulations of money and anything else you collect. A hobby can generate money. Be ultra-conscious in heavy traffic and watch out for the freakish fall. Take things in stride and roll with the punches to come out on top. Teal blue is your color. Lucky lottery numbers: 8, 44, 35, 26, 17, 33.

Thursday, September 22 (Moon in Aries to Taurus 9:47 a.m.)   Get mundane chores out of the way early so you will be free for spiritual and social growth later on. Magic and enchantment are registered in your chart today. Give Sagittarius a break and keep Leo well informed about your intentions. These late September evenings are full of allure. Pumpkin is your color. Hot combination numbers: 1 and 5.

Friday, September 23 (Moon in Taurus)   Taurus and Libra are talking. There's a green light for travel, for getting away from it all for a few days, and for changing your image. Questions are coming at you bang-bang. Youngsters are not able to look very far beyond the end of their noses, so don't talk long-range matters with them. Pinecone is your color. Hot combination numbers: 3 and 9.

Saturday, September 24 (Moon in Taurus to Gemini 10:41 p.m.)   Wonderful rays exist for spending time at a resort or a wooded camp area—anyplace you can chart the retreat of summer and the advance of fall. News from a distance can prove fascinating. Consider changes that are taking place all around you—move one grain of sand, they say, and you change the world. Lucky lottery numbers: 5, 14, 23, 32, 41, 39.

Sunday, September 25 (Moon in Gemini)   Gemini is adapting and adjusting in ways that can inspire you. You can take a great leap forward in your career, as the good-will you spread earlier in the month pays off. Steer clear of someone who tries to buttonhole you and give a wide berth to those who want to discuss their recent surgery. Raspberry is your color; your number is 7.

Monday, September 26 (Moon in Gemini)   Mind and hands work in unison to produce fine results. Supervisors are hoping for more creativity and originality from you. Employment and career trends are good but interviews and conferences may go off on tangents. Investigate an unusual business offer that comes your way. Bay is your color, your number is 2.

Tuesday, September 27 (Moon in Gemini to Cancer 11:21 a.m.)   There are mercurial and whimsical trends to this day. Luck awaits you when you are on the move, traveling, and entertaining unusual people from a distance. If you put yourself out for others, there will be excellent compensation. You are at your best in professional matters. Hot combination numbers: 4 and 5.

Wednesday, September 28 (Moon in Cancer)   Pisces and Cancer come front and center. You awaken full of vim, vigor, and vitality. Your progress is impressive until unfair criticism stops you in your tracks. There are annoying implications to cope with, but a smile and a kind word, will stop them. Wheat is your color. Lucky lottery numbers: 6, 15, 24, 33, 42, 40.

Thursday, September 29 (Moon in Cancer to Leo 8:55 p.m.)   Give good friends the benefit of every doubt. Parties and entertainment will go well as the month winds down. Put back together anything that fell apart at the beginning of summer. You adapt well, adjust, and show enormous flexibility—and emerge a winner. Amber and cinnamon are your colors; your lucky number is 8.

Friday, September 30 (Moon in Leo)   Excellent trends exist for finishing up chores that have been neglected this month. Today is fine also for dealing with very large organizations and institutions. Secrets and what has been transpiring behind the scenes are accented. Leo and Sagittarius make dramatic entrances and exits. Violet is your color; your lucky number is 1.

OCTOBER 1994

Saturday, October 1 (Moon in Leo)   Leo leads the way. There is power for you in all chance meetings, and in taking steps to insure greater security in your home and at your place of business. A Greek recipe would go well today. You can do much to spruce up your appearance and gain from dealings with large organizations. Your color is magenta. Lucky lottery numbers: 1, 10, 19, 28, 37, 46.

Sunday, October 2 (Moon in Leo to Virgo 2:39 a.m.)   You are in your lunar high cycle now and can pretty much get what you want. You are empowered to lead, inspire, and encourage. Another Virgo can be of great assistance. Luck is with you while you are in your own territory, doing what you do well. Your enthusiasms are catching. Your lucky number is 3.

Monday, October 3 (Moon in Virgo)   Push, coax, and take advantage of each business and social encounter to plug your own products. Under prevailing aspects, nobody can put you down or take advantage of you. Check things out with Capricorn. Your color is cerulean blue. Your winning numbers are 7 and 8.

Tuesday, October 4 (Moon in Virgo to Libra 4:56 a.m.) Money comes your way through highly personalized efforts. Practicality will pay off in inviting greater security. There are many affectionate trends as you are admired for your loyalty, dedication, devotion, and sterling character. Libra comes home. Your lucky number is 9.

Wednesday, October 5 (Moon in Libra)   Today's new moon illuminates wealth production, earning power, and income matters. There is enlightenment in budgeting, paying, and collecting. Your color is flaxen. You are empowered to knock big jobs down to handling size. Your beloved understands your feelings perfectly. Lucky lottery numbers: 2, 11, 20, 29, 38, 47.

Thursday, October 6 (Moon in Libra to Scorpio 5:22 a.m.) Scorpio and Pisces have key roles. On your menu today— crepes with delicious shrimp, cream cheese, or homemade orange marmalade filling. Domestic interests are accented. You take care of immediate and pressing duties well. As evening advances, your love life expands. Hot combination numbers: 4 and 7.

Friday, October 7 (Moon in Scorpio) Studies, your learning processes, and hobbies get the green lights. Luck attends you in everyday chores, scheduled projects, and familiar and traditional duties. Shop for wardrobe accessories that make you look a little thinner and taller. Beige and mauve are winning colors. Hot combination numbers: 6 and 9.

Saturday, October 8 (Moon in Scorpio to Sagittarius 5:47 a.m.) Sagittarius shows up. You can make magnificent progress in fall cleaning. Tackle cupboards, closets, walls of bathrooms, and children's bedrooms. There are some vexations connected with shopping, entertaining, and getting the generations to cooperate. Seaweed green is your color. Lucky lottery numbers: 8, 17, 26, 35, 44, 15.

Sunday, October 9 (Moon in Sagittarius) Everyday routines and schedules are slowing down. Studies, communications, and transportation are sluggish. A Scorpio and a Sagittarius are front and center. Your family, residence, place of business, and community matters get green lights. Try to put aside resentment over the actions of a loved one. Your number is 1.

Monday, October 10 (Moon in Sagittarius to Capricorn 7:44 a.m.) What a wonderful day you have before you! Love, romance, adventure, and ecstatic experiences are in this snapshot. If you don't prepare a magnificent meal, at least serve a simple one in an elegant way. Accent harmony, agreements, promises, and favors. Good luck is wearing a dollar sign. Flame is your color; your winning numbers are 5 and 6.

Tuesday, October 11 (Moon in Capricorn)   Capricorn, another Virgo, and Taurus make this an earthy day. There should be no pretense now, no putting on of airs. Health gets good support and there is a relationship between health and happiness. Smile rather than frown. Be positive instead of negative. Show enthusiasm and, above all, make love. Hot combination numbers: 7 and 1.

Wednesday, October 12 (Moon in Capricorn to Aquarius 12:09 p.m.)   The day, the month, and the year are involved in the joys of this day. Older and younger people can have a good time together. You gain where you check the accuracy of earlier computations. Get less pleasant chores out of the way first. Be cautious around moving vehicles. Salmon is your color. Lucky lottery numbers: 9, 45, 36, 27, 18, 16.

Thursday, October 13 (Moon in Aquarius)   Studies, hobbies, communications, and short-distance travel all become sluggish with delays, postponements, and cancellations. Aquarius and Scorpio are strongly represented in the day's activities. Don't permit others to give you hazy instructions and don't give them yourself. Umber and auburn are your colors; your lucky number is 2.

Friday, October 14 (Moon in Aquarius to Pisces 7:19 p.m.)   Work routines may run into bottlenecks. Plan, program, and schedule involvements that will give you a good feeling about yourself and people generally. Social life can be therapeutic under prevailing aspects. You can easily win the attention of a newcomer. Tawny beige is your color. Hot combination numbers: 4 and 5.

Saturday, October 15 (Moon in Pisces)   Pisces and a Scorpio are in the picture. Public relations, advertising, and publicity all get green lights. Marriage, contracts, agreements, and joint endeavors are strongly featured. Close up the generation gap. Mend business and financial fences. Your winning colors are mauve and white. Lucky lottery numbers: 6, 15, 24, 33, 42, 22.

Sunday, October 16 (Moon in Pisces) Excellent trends exist for serious discussion in marriage and business agreements. Personal grooming, new cosmetics, and hairstyle are indicated. People may appear to be moping about, contributing little to the pleasure or the pressures of the day. Cerulean blue is your color; your number is 8.

Monday, October 17 (Moon in Pisces to Aries 4:56 a.m.) Today is fine for accumulated power, and investments, savings, budgets, and the cost of living are favored as well. You have the green light for implementing changes. You can get through to difficult children and teenagers by expressing yourself clearly and concisely. Aries is watching. Never were you more methodical in your work. Your color is russet; your lucky number is 3.

Tuesday, October 18 (Moon in Aries) You aren't going to let work get in the way of your love life or your concern for those in need. You can love the homeless, the rejects, and the unwanted, and you can do something constructive in their interest. Sagittarius understands you well, and Leo can help you get started on the right road. Magenta is your color; your lucky number is 5.

Wednesday, October 19 (Moon in Aries to Taurus 4:34 p.m.) The full moon illuminates your eighth house, which rules changes, security matters, physical refurbishment, and financial awareness matters. You're alert, painstaking, anxious to please. Quiet romance and a strong feeling for your parents, older relatives, and loved ones at a distance can make this an unusual day. Your color is flaxen. Lucky lottery numbers: 7, 16, 25, 34, 43, 19.

Thursday, October 20 (Moon in Taurus) Taurus and Libra come front and center. Travel, moving about within the 300-mile radius get green lights. You see the bigger picture, the long-range problems, and the assistance you might expect from a distance. You achieve by keeping ideals and convictions intact. Hot combination numbers: 9 and 4.

Friday, October 21 (Moon in Taurus)   A change of scene will do wonders for your assets. Research will go well as information flows freely. There are answers for all the questions, no matter how evasive an executive might be. You can view some changes that have been creeping into the day's routines as sneaky, but you will love them anyway. Chartreuse is your color. Hot combination numbers: 2 and 3.

Saturday, October 22 (Moon in Taurus to Gemini 5:28 a.m.)   Gemini is hale and hardy. Recent acquisitions can bring a great deal of joy. Your career won't let you escape from it. Professional, authority, status, and prestige matters remain on the front burner. Open up new lines of communication for the best results. Spearmint green is your color. Lucky lottery numbers: 4, 13, 22, 31, 40, 29.

Sunday, October 23 (Moon in Gemini)   Libra and Aquarius demonstrate togetherness as siblings and neighbors are helpful. Fine trends exist for starting the work you have to do during the week ahead. The more you warm up to what you have to do, the higher level of efficiency attends you. Put your best foot forward in new friendships. Your lucky number is 6.

Monday, October 24 (Moon in Gemini to Cancer 6:15 p.m.)   Everyday matters pick up steam. Local conditions are ideal for participation in special community projects. Courtesy must be part of your relationship with your beloved. Gather all the facts needed to make a decision before you actually make it. Turquoise is your color; your number is 1.

Tuesday, October 25 (Moon in Cancer)   A Cancer and a Scorpio figure prominently. There is strong emphasis on group activities, on membership and participation, and on the friends of your friends. Time can be at a premium now and then and that is where parents come to your assistance.

Cerulean blue is your color. Hot combination numbers: 3 and 6.

Wednesday, October 26 (Moon in Cancer)   Push your social potential for all it is worth. Accept all invitations. In your company an inquisitive and talkative type can say too much and cause general concern. You can cash in on your good reputation and on your earned status and prestige. Peach is your color. Lucky lottery numbers: 5, 14, 23, 32, 41, 30.

Thursday, October 27 (Moon in Cancer to Leo 5:05 a.m.)   Leo bounces into view and starts things perking favorably. You enjoy good relationships with large organizations and institutions today and with the friends of your friends. Many people want to get to know you better and luck is with you where you spend time with them. Banana is your color. Hot combination numbers: 7 and 8.

Friday, October 28 (Moon in Leo)   Fine rays exist for completing what should be gotten out of the way before the end of October. Secrets require a high level of discretion today. There are gossips and, even worse, drainers of your energy who tire you out by their very presence. Former neighbors can be instrumental to your good fortune. Your color is chestnut; your lucky number is 9.

Saturday, October 29 (Moon in Leo to Virgo 12:21 p.m.)   A member of the opposite sex is giving you hard-to-read signals. The fairness of your attitudes can stand out and win admiration. You can gain from what has been transpiring behind the scenes. Luck is with you where you stand up for your own rights, and where you honor responsibility and obligations. Lucky lottery numbers: 2, 11, 20, 29, 38, 47.

Sunday, October 30 (Moon in Virgo)   Now in your lunar-cycle high, you can win others over to your point of view. Another Virgo and a Capricorn can help you accomplish miracles. Push your own unique ideas and ambitions and stick to your guns, come what may, in the wake of opposition and criticism. Nutmeg is your color; your winning number is 4.

Monday, October 31 (Daylight Savings Time Ends) (Moon in Virgo to Libra 2:47 p.m.)   You are empowered to advance yourself, your career, and your social life. Where you ponder, mulling things over in your own mind and speaking out in your own behalf, you can accomplish much under the prevailing aspects. But do take the trouble to explain clearly and to air your own aspirations. Amber is your color; your lucky number is 8.

NOVEMBER 1994

Tuesday, November 1 (Moon in Libra)   There's money around that is earmarked for you. Libra and Aquarius have key roles. As total eclipse patterns form, however, it would be wise to not count on local matters being the same this time around. This is not a good cycle for forcing changes upon yourself or others. What's natural gets the green light. Your color is beige. Hot combination numbers: 7 and 6.

Wednesday, November 2 (Moon in Libra to Scorpio 4:19 p.m.)   Short-distance travel carries an increasing accident-producing potential, which can last until the fifth or sixth. Studies are pressured and it is possible to be misquoted and misinterpreted. Gossip is rife, so rumors should be questioned. People are talking a lot of nonsense. Lucky lottery numbers: 9, 18, 27, 36, 45, 2.

Thursday, November 3 (Moon in Scorpio)   The total solar eclipse pressures sexual efforts, your ability to receive and digest information, and transportation. Everyday routines and schedules are pressured. The physical can get in the way of the spiritual. Driving, walking, climbing, and descending carry accident potential. Your lucky number is 2.

Friday, November 4 (Moon in Scorpio to Sagittarius 2:46 p.m.)   In the wake of this eclipse, there can be foolish risk taking and bizarre accidents, and it is vital that you watch your driving in parking lots, school areas, and places where children loiter. On the profit side of the ledger, communications are improving and it will be less difficult to get to the heart of matters. Scorpio and Capricorn have key roles. Your lucky number is 4.

Saturday, November 5 (Moon in Sagittarius)   Freakish accidents continue to follow in the wake of the recent eclipse. It would be easy to forget filling out a form, putting something in the mail, or getting a child to wherever he should be. Domestic routines can bog you down. A Sagittarius and a Gemini can be in opposition. Lucky lottery numbers: 6, 15, 24, 33, 42, 13.

Sunday, November 6 (Moon in Sagittarius to Capricorn 3:02 p.m.)   What you do in and outside your home today is aimed at family welfare. The accent is on your home, neighborhood, and the airing of your complaints and worries. Don't permit another person to distract you from your normal performance. An Aries may want to get his or her way too much. Your lucky number is 8.

Monday, November 7 (Moon in Capricorn)   Older people tend to be wiser people, so experiences pay off well today. The past can light the future. Capricorn and another Virgo are making things earthier, including your love life. You and your beloved are one with Mother Nature. Cherry is your color; your lucky number is 3.

Tuesday, November 8 (Moon in Capricorn to Aquarius 5:48 p.m.)   Make love, be romantic, and enjoy courtship, no matter what your age. This is a good day for spontaneous social pastimes, parties, entertainments, or sports observation or participation. Your beloved can cheer you up this evening and you won't regret turning off the lights and going to bed. Hot combination numbers: 5 and 1.

Wednesday, November 9 (Moon in Aquarius)   Take the initiative in whatever you attempt today and don't let others get in on your act. Allow time for some outdoor ventures and for visiting any aging shut-in who expects to hear from you. You're loving, approving, and appreciating, and you can do well when you socialize and entertain. Silver is your color. Lucky lottery numbers: 7, 16, 25, 34, 43, 14.

Thursday, November 10 (Moon in Aquarius)   Aquarius and Libra will impact your day. Start new and up-to-date preventive-medicine routines in your life, home, and place of employment. You may have to do some extra work or pinch-hitting for others who will be out with grim colds and other viral infections. Celery is your color. Pick 5: 9, 36, 27, 18, 45.

Friday, November 11 (Moon in Aquarius to Pisces 12:04 a.m.)   Pisces lifts veils that reveal the truth. Observe health rules and urge your mate to do the same. Family chit-chat can encourage youngsters to understand the ways of the family and the real meaning of shared security. Avoid wool-gathering. Marriage is respected. Hot combination numbers: 2 and 3.

Saturday, November 12 (Moon in Pisces)   Public relations, business partnerships, and the art of sharing are all represented. Your mate has the answers you need. Don't wait for directions from higher-ups or others—just begin the task on your own. There's an enchanting aura about you today and others are tossing approving looks your way. Orange is your color. Lucky lottery numbers: 4, 13, 40, 22, 31, 20.

Sunday, November 13 (Moon in Pisces to Aries 9:44 a.m.)   Aquamarine is your color. You may have more sympathy for a complainer than he or she deserves. It's a fine cycle for sharing, assisting, and presenting work for approval. Fine trends exist for bringing parents and offspring together. Avoid talkative types who attempt to buttonhole you. Fern green is your color; your lucky number is 6.

Monday, November 14 (Moon in Aries)   Things are happening so fast that minor matters may be overlooked. Aries is way out in front. You can get along famously with relatives, including in-laws and the friends of your beloved. You are enjoying a strong sense of personal freedom; in imagination you can romp through autumnal splendor. Your lucky number is 1.

Tuesday, November 15 (Moon in Aries to Taurus 9:44 p.m.)   Good trends exist in the way you are handling your money—talks with your banker and broker will go well. Day-to-day matters are favored over the afternoon, as well as anything of a local, immediate, or pressing nature. You have unbeatable drive where you are acting upon past information and experience. Apricot is your color. Hot combination numbers: 3 and 2.

Wednesday, November 16 (Moon in Taurus)   Trust the opinions of a Taurus. Tyrian, the richest of purples, is a winning color for you. There are green lights for doing the unusual and the unfamiliar today, and travel gets good grades as well as you extend your horizons. You don't want to stand in one spot too long. Lucky lottery numbers: 5, 14, 23, 32, 41, 16.

Thursday, November 17 (Moon in Taurus)   You could encounter arrogance, envy, and jealousy over the daylight hours, and there are pretensions in the picture as well. People tend to be ultra-possessive of their friends and angry at any third-person interference. This evening can be pleasant if you reminisce and bring old memories forward. Mocha is your color. Hot combination numbers: 7 and 8.

Friday, November 18 (Moon in Taurus to Gemini 10:42 a.m.)   The full moon illuminates long-range and long-distance matters. Fine trends exist for planning some late-November gadding about. You gain from quiet approaches and attitudes. Self-confidence and enthusiasm will open new doors for you. Get into a woodsy area if possible and observe the advance of autumn. Cherry red is your color. Hot combination numbers: 9 and 3.

Saturday, November 19 (Moon in Gemini)   Gemini has all the answers. Information flows freely and some of it can be useful in your career decisions. You have the power to begin a project all over again and to succeed where you may have failed before. Luck is with you if you stick to what you have begun. Claret is your color. Lucky lottery numbers: 2, 11, 20, 29, 38, 47.

Sunday, November 20 (Moon in Gemini to Cancer 11:21 p.m.)   Be professional in everything today. Tell gossips as little as possible. Don't move from one task to another too quickly; give yourself a breather for the best results. A neighbor can seem less friendly than before. For pointers, you may call a former supervisor or employer. Cherry and green are your colors; your number is 4.

Monday, November 21 (Moon in Cancer)   The friendlier you are today, the more popular you will be. Membership and group participation get strong emphasis and give you a chance to shine. A very creative and imaginative person can spur you on to greater ambition. Luck attends you if you let the world see you in fashionable dress. Nutmeg is your color; your lucky number is 8.

Tuesday, November 22 (Moon in Cancer)   A Cancer and a Pisces bring the information and the messages. Popularity is more than a bubble today, as you find others wishing you well and anxious to please you. There is a great deal of variety and versatility connected with your afternoon and evening. Orange is your color. Hot combination numbers: 1 and 5.

Wednesday, November 23 (Moon in Cancer to Leo 10:33 a.m.)   It's vital that you live up to a contract and agreement without thought of procrastination. An old friend may contact you for a bit of reminiscing. Your winning colors are dark red and ultramarine. Lucky lottery numbers: 3, 12, 21, 30, 39, 48.

Thursday, November 24 (Moon in Leo)   Local, everyday, immediate, and pressing matters pick up steam. Your learning processes are turned on full force. Leo can help you extract additional gains from matters you ordinarily would consider finished and closed. There are excellent trends where you are shopping for intimate garments. Reddish-brown is your color; your number is 5.

Friday, November 25 (Moon in Leo) Complete, finish, present for review, and extract additional gains from projects you ordinarily would consider finished and closed. The more conscious you are of what is transpiring behind the scenes and beneath the surface, the better you are armed for the day's demands and problems. Reddish-purple is your color; your number is 7.

Saturday, November 26 (Moon in Leo to Virgo 7:09 p.m.) Now in your lunar-cycle high, you are adept at protecting all flanks. You can take up the cudgels in your own defense as you air grievances and ambitions. Luck attends you in all your personal endeavors. You're at your best when feathering your own nest. Lucky lottery numbers: 9, 18, 27, 36, 45, 34.

Sunday, November 27 (Moon in Virgo) Push for acceptance of your ideas, speaking up in your own interest. Don't permit others to say things that have nothing to do with the topic under discussion. There is a lot of miserable quibbling pointed your way, but under these aspects you are able to put things right. Pinecone is your color; your number is 2.

Monday, November 28 (Moon in Virgo to Libra 12:22 a.m.) As the month wanes, you are given new power for dealing with the cost and the standard of living, as well as with earning power, income, budgeting, and overall wealth production. Curtail affections if you feel that others are questioning your motivations. A Libra is understanding. Your color is old rose; your number is 6.

Tuesday, November 29 (Moon in Libra) Push earning power and money matters while you have plenty of financial motivation. Do not surrender any authority. There are fine trends in special sales, advertising, and publicity, allowing you to promote yourself and your product. A Libra and an Aquarius come front and center. Hot combination numbers: 8 and 9.

Wednesday, November 30 (Moon in Libra to Scorpio 2:22 a.m.) Scorpio wants to know. Pounce on sudden opportunities and create your own advantages. It's a day when you can make progress because of unusual skills, conditions, and changes. You have power in hard work, and when you strive to make others comfortable about your decisions. Blue is your color. Lucky combination numbers: 1 and 4.

DECEMBER 1994

Thursday, December 1 (Moon in Scorpio)　　Scorpio and Taurus have key roles. Narrow your sights and zero in on new opportunities. Communications, your learning processes, studies, transportation, and hobbies are featured. Don't depend on others for the answers when there are books, brochures, and other materials to be read. Your color is turquoise; your number is 1.

Friday, December 2 (Moon in Scorpio to Sagittarius 2:13 a.m.)　　Sagittarius and Gemini figure prominently. Family, residence, and community needs are high on your agenda. It can bother you that a coworker is aiming too high and often falls back upon envy and jealousy. Your winning colors are mauve and beige. Your adored one can be off on cloud nine. Hot combination numbers: 3 and 2.

Saturday, December 3 (Moon in Sagittarius)　　Assist a relative. Don't shy away from controversy and difficulty. When you do your best today, the world is going to applaud. There's nothing wrong with entertaining illusions in which you achieve a high level of importance. Carmen is your color. Lucky lottery numbers: 5, 14, 23, 32, 41, 3.

Sunday, December 4 (Moon in Sagittarius to Capricorn 1:42 a.m.)　　Work up your Christmas list of greeting cards, beginning with those that have to travel a long way. Be alert today to the admiration you read in the eyes of others, particularly those members of the opposite sex. Capricorn rides high and wide. Gold is your color; your number is 7.

Monday, December 5 (Moon in Capricorn)　　Write annual letters to those you want to stay in touch with, for luck attends you in spreading good cheer and sending love and kisses across the wide miles. Capricorn and Pisces impact your day favorably. Contact those with whom you will be performing charitable chores later on in the month. Your lucky number is 2.

Tuesday, December 6 (Moon in Capricorn to Aquarius 2:51 a.m.) Aquarius is showing new ways of doing old jobs. Resolve to do your holiday lights very differently this year. What you do to excite and thrill those who will be seeing your outdoor holiday decorations won't be wasted. Some vexations are linked to shopping. Primrose is your color; your lucky number is 4.

Wednesday, December 7 (Moon in Aquarius) Gemini has wonderful creative ideas for you. You can claim greater happiness, more thrilling love, and more lasting security under the existing aspects. Get greeting cards and letters into the mail. Buy some of the newer type decorations that can make your living quarters sparkle. There are still bargains in the larger stores. Lucky lottery numbers: 6, 15, 24, 33, 42, 13.

Thursday, December 8 (Moon in Aquarius to Pisces 7:24 a.m.) You're alert, wide awake, and anxious to get on with all the chores of this happy season. Today is fine for gift finding and buying, excellent for meeting an interesting type at the mall and having a salad or dessert. Volunteer for humanitarian jobs that are going begging. Mocha is your color; your number is 8.

Friday, December 9 (Moon in Pisces) The moon in Pisces reveals, unveils, and shows the way through any uncertainties. Information that was held back is now out in the open, for this is a "detective's moon." It's fine for running down gifts for your mate and in-laws, and for a business partner and others at work you want to please. Your color is cinnamon. Hot combination numbers: 1 and 5.

Saturday, December 10 (Moon in Pisces to Aries 4:03 p.m.) Cooperate with your mate in getting holiday decorations, tree, and outdoor lights up. If your mate has a special place to visit and wants your company, this is one of those days when marriage is definitely for two. Charitable and humanitarian arrangements can be put together. Angry reds are your colors. Lucky lottery numbers: 3, 12, 21, 30, 39, 48.

Sunday, December 11 (Moon in Aries) Aries is present. You may have intended to do it all differently but the old traditions are going to win out today and over the rest of the holiday season. Promises made today will be honored. Luck is with you where you think things through to their natural conclusions. Maroon is your color; your number is 5.

Monday, December 12 (Moon in Aries) There are wonderful bargains waiting for you in out-of-the-way places. A big-ticket item can be just what you want. Inner resources item can be better than any outside information or suggestions. Be careful nothing is misplaced. Lilac and kelly will win, but not together. Your lucky number is 9.

Tuesday, December 13 (Moon in Aries to Taurus 3:56 a.m.) If you want to get away for a few days to visit older relatives, the period from today through the sixteenth would be an ideal one. Travel, phoning, and writing long-distance letters, as well as getting gifts on their way are all part of this picture. Excellent trends exist for shopping for wardrobe accessories to improve your image. Ecru is your color; your lucky number is 2.

Wednesday, December 14 (Moon in Taurus) The day is unusual, with a break in usual routines and schedules. It's fine for taking off from work and taking care of some urgent holiday and family business. Your positive and optimistic thinking will pay handsome dividends this evening. This evening comes early and you'll enhance lovemaking if you are enthusiastic about your mate's whims. Lucky lottery numbers: 4, 13, 22, 31, 40, 20.

Thursday, December 15 (Moon in Taurus to Gemini 5 p.m.) A glorious day for moving about, seeing lots of happy faces, and shopping for items you can't buy close to home. Cultural interests and intellectual pursuits are favored, as are matters of the higher mind. But there are times when it is wise to restrain criticism of another's faults. Sand is your color; your number is 6.

Friday, December 16 (Moon in Gemini)   Gemini rushes forward. Career matters can be given a push, and there are good aspects for entertaining coworkers and others in your own home. There are humanitarian and charitable tasks going begging in your neighborhood. Can you fit some of these into your schedule? Strawberry is your color. Hot combination numbers: 8 and 9.

Saturday, December 17 (Moon in Gemini)   Check your plans out with a Libra or an Aquarius. There are some unusual pointers available if you bother to ask questions. Seek favors and preferred treatment while you are making such a good impression on others. An executive may be a little lonely and really wish you would show more warmth. Bronze and maroon are your lucky colors. Lucky lottery numbers: 1, 10, 19, 28, 37, 46.

Sunday, December 18 (Moon in Gemini to Cancer 5:25 a.m.)   The full moon at the zenith of your chart illuminates all new directions in your life, your authority, status, and prestige. You can cash in on your earning reputation and on the goodwill you have been showing. Career considerations occupy much of your thinking. Church and club holiday tasks give you a sense of renewal. Beige is your color; your lucky number is 3.

Monday, December 19 (Moon in Cancer)   Friendly Pisces and Cancer people are represented in today's blueprint. Membership and participation matters are high on your agenda. The day is fine for office, factory, and hobbygroup parties. Help members of your family to achieve some of their long-range dreams. Saffron is your color; your lucky number is 7.

Tuesday, December 20 (Moon in Cancer to Leo 4:13 p.m.)   Parties, entertainments, and good causes are represented in your day. Silver and snow are lucky colors. The social side of your job and the goodwill you and coworkers have built up all year are on the front burner now. Reds and greens are also good for you. Youngsters may be jealous of your outings. Hot combination numbers: 9 and 4.

Wednesday, December 21 (Moon in Leo)   You're fortunate to have a Leo on deck. Coral and cherry are winning colors. Today is fine for completing social and family arrangements for the rest of the month. Secrets are well protected now. The past can be reviewed and perhaps seen in more gentle lights. You boldly accept the challenges come your way. Lucky lottery numbers: 2, 11, 20, 29, 38, 47.

Thursday, December 22 (Moon in Leo)   It's a day for loving, for being happy, and for enjoying the romance you witness all about you. You feel at one with the season now and thrill to the old holiday traditions and especially to the brilliant lights you see wherever you glance. Many joys from out of long-ago Christmases are being recycled in your mind. Hot combination numbers: 4 and 3.

Friday, December 23 (Moon in Leo to Virgo 1:01 a.m.)   How fortunate that you are moving into your lunar high cycle today and it will last until the twenty-sixth! So you can have the kind of holiday you want and others will be looking to you for the right words at the right time. Go to great lengths to look rich and royal. Another Virgo should be invited. Hot combination numbers: 6 and 5.

Saturday, December 24 (Moon in Virgo)   Be yourself—dependable, constant, the best worker in the zodiac. There are many who could use a bit of help because they are not as up-to-date as you. Volunteer where you see the need is great. Supplies, distribution, and circulation are represented. Forest green is your color. Lucky lottery numbers: 8, 17, 26, 35, 44, 24.

Sunday, December 25 (Moon in Virgo to Libra 7:27 a.m.)
Keep out in front of the competition and the opposition on a day when others know better than to get in your way. You can make marvelous progress while in your lunar-cycle high and you favorably impress others. You can solve pesky

personal and household problems. Your color is maroon; your lucky number is 1.

Monday, December 26 (Moon in Libra)   Excellent financial trends exist. Good bargains can be found in the larger stores, so consider buying end-of-season wardrobe items. Individual enterprise marks these hours and prepares the way for some glorious socializing as the month wanes. Your skills and talents can be sharpened. Tawny beige and ruby are your winning colors. Pick 5: 5, 9, 12, 20, 35.

Tuesday, December 27 (Moon in Libra to Scorpio 11:17 a.m.)   Money can be made in odd and unusual ways. You can sell what you no longer need or barter successfully. Accumulated family and personal resources are there to assist you over this high-potential afternoon. Your neighborhood is spotlighted. Grayish-blue is your color. Hot combination numbers: 7 and 2.

Wednesday, December 28 (Moon in Scorpio)   Scorpio and another Virgo have key roles. You will enjoy standing out in your own neighborhood and among your own siblings. Desires of yesterday rush to the forefront. Luck attends you in all the work you are doing. Still, close friends think you keep too busy. Your color is forest. Lucky lottery numbers: 9, 27, 36, 18, 45, 34.

Thursday, December 29 (Moon in Scorpio to Sagittarius 12:46 p.m.)   You could feel ill at ease in the presence of salesmen, cranky older persons, and drop-in visitors. Things seem to "just happen" today, which can intrude on your plans. This is not the time for making loans or giving commitments that are binding. Luck may seem elusive but it is present in local, immediate, and pressing matters. Hot combination numbers: 2 and 5.

Friday, December 30 (Moon in Sagittarius)   Sagittarius can take over. Today's accent is on your family, residence, and community. You may feel that it is time to curtail the social side and pay more attention to problem children and youth in general. It can bother you if a dear one is too

211

envious or jealous. Tangerine is your color; your lucky number is 4.

Saturday, December 31 (Moon in Sagittarius to Capricorn 12:58 p.m.) Those breaths of fresh air are to be honored and appreciated. You could find that people who are important to you may seem reticient, silent, and off on cloud nine. Rather than depend on others for the answers, you're better off going to the source and reading up on what is at stake. Auburn is your color. Don't travel too far, too long, or too fast. Lucky lottery numbers: 6, 15, 24, 42, 33, 31.

JANUARY 1995

Sunday, January 1 (Moon in Capricorn) The new moon illuminates your love life and also your creativity, imagination, originality, and romantic view of things. Fine aspects exist for partying and entertaining, especially in a spontaneous way. Bring generations together and, where possible, assume the role of peacemaker. Your lucky number is 3.

Monday, January 2 (Moon in Capricorn to Aquarius 1:39 p.m.) Capricorn and Taurus give you a sense of worthiness. You reach out for love, respect, admiration, and approval and your efforts will be rewarded. Parents and offspring are with you. You have a strong desire to improve the lives of those you love. Your winning color is olive; your lucky number is 7.

Tuesday, January 3 (Moon in Aquarius) Aquarius and Libra are on your side. You face up to your overall physical well-being and the work for which you are responsible. It's a fine day to start new preventive-medicine routines at home and also away from home. For now, there is a feeling of being overwhelmed by a pileup of work. Your color is magenta. Hot combination numbers: 9 and 27.

Wednesday, January 4 (Moon in Aquarius to Pisces 4:49 p.m.) Check up on the health of an older relative and make certain that youngsters are not pushing themselves too much in sports and seasonal activities. Dietary matters are in focus under these trends. A Gemini has many interesting facts to share. Beige is your color. Lucky lottery numbers: 2, 11, 20, 29, 38, 47.

Thursday, January 5 (Moon in Pisces) Marriage, legal, public relations, and business partnership matters are in focus. It's a day for reaching out, promoting your own image, and figuring out what is transpiring behind the scenes. A Pisces and another Virgo are impacting your day. Claret red and maroon are your colors; your lucky number is 4.

Friday, January 6 (Moon in Pisces to Aries 11:56 p.m.) Share, cooperate, and deal in joint projects and entertainment. Marvelous old traditions are connected with this day in the annals of royal courts. Jesters, fools, knaves, and forfeits can make for a gala party. Be spontaneous with your invitations. However, the shadow side of people will also be revealed. Hot combination numbers: 6 and 15.

Saturday, January 7 (Moon in Aries) You warm up to outdoor sports while keeping a weather eye on the cost of living, new expenses, and the costs of seasonal activities. Changes are taking place and you can suddenly realize how varied and numerous are your options. Cherry is your color. Lucky lottery numbers: 8, 17, 26, 35, 44 and 7.

Sunday, January 8 (Moon in Aries) Aries has a dominant role. Read the financial pages of your newspaper and find an economic forecast at your newsstand. You could have a peculiar awareness that big changes are looming ahead, and this is a good day for facing up to them. You might also learn about an upcoming divorce. Your lucky number is 1.

Monday, January 9 (Moon in Aries to Taurus 10:58 a.m.) This is an apt time for working out new budgets for the year, or at least the month ahead. It is easier to get a grasp of the economic trends now than it will be later in January. Ask questions of those who tend to have financial answers. The idea is to save a little now and during the months immediately ahead. Cherry is your color; your lucky number is 5.

Tuesday, January 10 (Moon in Taurus)   Taurus and another Virgo take command. Your mind flies from subject to subject. You apply all the lessons and experiences of your past to your future. Matters of the higher mind was what the ancients called these ninth-house interests and they all can be served today. Coral is your color; your lucky number is 7.

Wednesday, January 11 (Moon in Taurus to Gemini 11:57 p.m.)   Deep thinking is going on in your mind. You are encompassing what is taking place far away, when you are certain that it can affect your profits and gains. A Capricorn will have something to say and you better listen carefully. Cerulean blue is your color. Lucky lottery numbers: 9, 18, 27, 36, 45 and 54.

Thursday, January 12 (Moon in Gemini)   Gemini has good career and professional pointers for you. You can make good headway toward your next promotion and rise in salary. Lavender and Ecru are winning colors. Talks with your boss can clear the air of misgivings and recriminations. Use your authority wisely for best results. Hot combination numbers: 2 and 11.

Friday, January 13 (Moon in Gemini)   Where weather and other seasonal problems interfered with your career and professional relationships and organizations, and tended to temper authority, you can now make corrections and improvements. Advance with self-confidence and self-reliance. Libra is aboard. Your lucky number is 4.

Saturday, January 14 (Moon in Gemini to Cancer 12:20 p.m.)   You can cash in on the good reputation you have chalked up over the past year. Be cautious when disciplining children under these aspects, no matter how angry you are about their neglect of work. Career opportunities are in focus and you may want to discuss them with a coworker. Lucky lottery numbers: 6, 15, 24, 33, 42 and 50.

Sunday, January 15 (Moon in Cancer) A Scorpio and a Cancer figure prominently. See friends. Join groups. Open your home to those who share your hobby interests. Membership and participation matters get strong support. Encourage neighbors to drop by. Your winning colors are salmon and silver; your lucky number is 8.

Monday, January 16 (Moon in Cancer to Leo 10:36 p.m.) The full moon illuminates friendships, group trends, the social side of your job, and what you can do to promote yourself via this path. Contact friends you haven't been in touch with so far this year. You can improve your public image under these aspects. Raspberry is your color; your lucky number is 3.

Tuesday, January 17 (Moon in Leo) Fine aspects exist for completing work that has been hanging fire since the beginning of the year. You want to clear the deck for future actions by presenting work for approval today, and by closing out no-win projects. Large organizations will be in agreement with you. The invisible counts more than the visible. Brown and white is right. Hot combination numbers: 5 and 41.

Wednesday, January 18 (Moon in Leo) Leo is a great assistant as you prepare for a busy lunar-cycle high period. Ask questions so that you can have a good grasp of what has been transpiring outside your view. Secrets and confidences are accented. Beige and mauve are your winning colors. Lucky lottery numbers: 7, 16, 25, 34, 43 and 50.

Thursday, January 19 (Moon in Leo to Virgo 6:39 a.m.) Now you are in your momentous lunar-cycle high and can turn things around to suit own ideas and desires. You can gain much from being yourself and accenting your personality and character. Another Virgo and a Capricorn come front and center. Your self-confidence pays well. Your lucky number is 9.

Friday, January 20 (Moon in Virgo) Hold the initiative, speak out, issue advice and even orders. There is great command in your glance and in your tone of voice under these aspects. A Taurus will help you resolve important issues. Take on City Hall, if that is what you have in mind. Ecru and bay green are winning colors; your lucky number is 2.

Saturday, January 21 (Moon in Virgo to Libra 12:54 p.m.) Take care of your health by avoiding drafts, unexpected changes in the temperature, and eating any questionable seafood. Be assertive when you are sure you are right. A little criticism may be justified if you are dealing with a constant offender. You can persuade others. Lucky lottery numbers: 4, 13, 22, 31, 40, 49.

Sunday, January 22 (Moon in Libra) Get on top of your job by putting facts and figures together this afternoon. A trend of rising wealth is just what you and your doctor ordered. New sources of capital can be announcing themselves. Go to the source when you want a real explanation. Carmen and maroon are your colors; your lucky number is 6.

Monday, January 23 (Moon in Libra to Scorpio 5:32 p.m.) Libra has the financial answers. Push earning power and income to a higher level. Gains can come from the rising value of what you own, from recently acquired possessions, and from something that has been owed to you for a long time. Your lucky colors are magenta and azure blue; your lucky number is 1.

Tuesday, January 24 (Moon in Scorpio) Narrow your sights and zero in on immediate and pressing matters. Consult siblings and neighbors before making up your mind. Talk things over with local merchants. Studies, hobbies, and your learning processes are in strong focus and become the sources of your achievement. Purple is your color; your lucky number is 3.

Wednesday, January 25 (Moon in Scorpio to Sagittarius 8:37 p.m.) The local scene is more interesting than usual. Everyday matters are reflecting more originality and imagination. A Pisces and a Cancer figure prominently. Your learning processes are strongly stimulated. Siblings and neighbors are cooperative. Claret red and yellow are your colors. Lucky lottery numbers: 5, 14, 23, 32, 41 and 50.

Thursday, January 26 (Moon in Sagittarius) Work routines and systems are sluggish. Sagittarius and Aquarius have vital roles to play. Family and residential matters have top billing. You are strongly conscious of what you own and what you love, and you support family and community values loudly. Sorrel green is your color. Hot combination numbers: 7 and 25.

Friday, January 27 (Moon in Sagittarius to Capricorn 10:26 p.m.) Aries and Leo have front seats. Take your family to a sports event. The circus, arena, racetrack, and larger animals are all in the picture. Property matters can't be overlooked. Ancestors are lurking in the shadows, pleased with what you are thinking. Your lucky color is red-brown; your lucky number is 9.

Saturday, January 28 (Moon in Capricorn) Capricorn enters the picture on a day when your love life is strongly stimulated. A trip to ecstasy should be high on your agenda. You see the romantic side of the bigger pictures. A sense of adventure underlies all partying and entertaining. Love is creative, flexible, and versatile. Lucky lottery numbers: 2, 11, 20, 29, 38, 47.

Sunday, January 29 (Moon in Capricorn) As the month opened by strengthening your love life, so it will also make this waning day of January excellent for love and pleasurable experiences. A Capricorn and a Taurus are in your corner. You see the romance of time, place, and personnel as others may not realize. Your winning color is snow and black; your winning number is 4.

Monday, January 30 (Moon in Capricorn to Aquarius 12:03 a.m.) The new moon in your sixth house, accents the work that must be done and recommends attention to health maintenance. There are opportunities for pleasing supervisors as well as for giving special service to those you love. An Aquarius and a Gemini have key roles. Your lucky color is beige; your lucky number is 8.

Tuesday, January 31 (Moon in Aquarius)   Dress appropriately and be careful of food offered in unusual and questionable places. Hygiene and sanitation are in many ways going by the board, along with courtesy, self-respect, and privacy. Your winning colors are mauve and violet; your hot combination numbers: 1 and 10.

FEBRUARY 1995

Wednesday, February 1 (Moon in Aquarius to Pisces 3:05 a.m.)   Your marital state, talks with business partners, and new revelations about what has been going on behind the scenes are all indicated. Pisces and a Cancer have key roles. You can improve your public image today and loosen up a little where children and new workers are concerned. Maroon is your color. Lucky lottery numbers: 9, 18, 27, 36, 45 and 1.

Thursday, February 2 (Moon in Pisces)   Work is sluggish and the approval you seek may be slow in coming. Your mate and others may require a little diplomacy if things are to go right. You could find considerable secretiveness and this could mean underlying fear of some variety. Lucky colors are mauve and old rose; your lucky number is 2.

Friday, February 3 (Moon in Pisces to Aries 9:12 a.m.) Sharing, cooperating, and harmonizing your efforts with those of a partner are favored. It would be difficult to go it alone under these aspects and could result in time wasted and feelings hurt. People around you may be wishing they could be elsewhere. Minds meander. Ivory is your color; your lucky number is 4.

Saturday, February 4 (Moon in Aries)   Aries and Sagittarius figure prominently. There could be savings from the way you shop and where you shop. Discussions about household budgets, investments, money due, and other money you should be collecting will produce plenty. It's time to do something about a loved one with champagne tastes and empty pockets. Lucky lottery numbers: 6, 15, 24, 33, 42 and 4.

Sunday, February 5 (Moon in Aries to Taurus 7:09 p.m.) Aries and Sagittarius figure prominently. Work on a new kitchen and automobile budget. Are energy costs so prohibitive that you should be sharing a ride to and from work? Cost of dues and license fees can be rising. Many complaints about the cost of living are in the air. Your lucky number is 8.

Monday, February 6 (Moon in Taurus) Taurus and Scorpio have key roles. Travel by car or bus is favored. Long-range interests get top billing. You may enjoy settling down before a good fire and recycling travel you did last summer. Information is flowing more freely. Research and in-depth reading are ideal activities. Your lucky number is 3.

Tuesday, February 7 (Moon in Taurus) Another Virgo has good advice for you. Matters of the higher mind, advanced educational studies, special correspondence courses are accented. You want to do your job better and have just about decided that additional study may be the right path. Taupe is your color; your hot combination numbers: 5 and 32.

Wednesday, February 8 (Moon in Taurus to Gemini 7:44 a.m.) Capricorn is on your side in any showdown. Visitors, guests, newcomers, and immigrants are all represented. Remember that a straight line remains the shortest distance between two points. You can learn by moving about today and by listening to people with foreign accents. Lucky lottery numbers: 7, 16, 25, 34, 43 and 8.

Thursday, February 9 (Moon in Gemini) Excellent trends exist in career, reputation, professionalism, wise use of authority, and in all status and prestige matters. Look well, stand tall, speak quietly and impressively. A Gemini and a Libra have key roles. Your powers of persuasion on the job are related to a rise in earning power. Your lucky number is 9.

Friday, February 10 (Moon in Gemini to Cancer 8:17 p.m.) Present work for review. Evaluate changes carefully at a time when the status quo demands special consideration. You can advance toward certain career goals, but these advances may at this time be invisible. What you feel in your bones contains the answers. Hot combination numbers: 2 and 20.

Saturday, February 11 (Moon in Cancer) A Pisces and a Cancer have front seats. It's who more than what you know, and long-term friendships are paying off handsomely. Stick with tried and true friends now. Spend quality time with kindred spirits who really know you and your dreams and aspirations. White and black are your colors. Lucky lottery numbers: 4, 13, 22, 31, 40, 45.

Sunday, February 12 (Moon in Cancer) Group activities, church and club membership and participation matters, the social side of your hobby, and political interests are all favored. You want to be one with many others under prevailing aspects. Be sure to phone a friend you haven't heard from in some time. Your lucky number is 6.

Monday, February 13 (Moon in Cancer to Leo 6:31 a.m.) Welcome a Leo and a Sagittarius. If you pounce upon some unfinished tasks, you can really make progress over the morning. Excellent trends exist for dealing with large organizations and institutions and for using your awareness in running down lies. Wear angry reds. Your lucky number is 1.

Tuesday, February 14 (Moon in Leo) Accent past experiences and old traditions that can be honored today. Much about love, romance, and a strong sense of participation can be taught to young people on St. Valentine's Day. There are some secrets and hidden facts coming to light as the day rushes along. White and scarlet are your colors; your lucky number is 3.

Wednesday, February 15 (Moon in Leo to Virgo 1:52 p.m.) The full moon illuminates the past and what you might extract from it. There is enlightenment based on past experiences. That old chestnut about what goes around comes around is a banner. Today is fine for finishing up chores that might stand in the way of all you want to achieve tomorrow. Lucky lottery numbers: 5, 14, 23, 32, 41, 47.

Thursday, February 16 (Moon in Virgo)   Work picks up steam as you enter your lunar-cycle high. It's up to you to lead, to start, to persuade, encourage, and guide others. The more you push personally, the more others will be willing to give their all. There are victories and achievements in this picture. Cerulean blue is your color; your lucky number is 7.

Friday, February 17 (Moon in Virgo to Libra 7 p.m.)   Don't let the initiative or the reins of leadership slip from your hands. Be persuasive, self-confident, and self-reliant. The more jovial and enthusiastic you are, the quicker and better others will follow and perform well. Phone often, write letters, let the world know you mean business. Your lucky number is 9.

Saturday, February 18 (Moon in Libra)   This is a big money day. You can increase your wealth production, save through wise shopping, and offer your talents and skills part-time to the man with the money bags. If you know the value of your hours, others will be quick to catch on. It's never too far to the big sales. Violet is your color. Lucky lottery numbers: 2, 11, 20, 29, 38, 47.

Sunday, February 19 (Moon in Libra to Scorpio 10:55 p.m.)   You can pick up some valuable ideas, facts, and helpful hints. Never be too proud to ask a neighbor how to do some chore that he or she seems to have mastered well. Financial discussions can lead to some interesting lessons and successes. Blueberry is your color; your lucky number is 4.

Monday, February 20 (Moon in Scorpio)   Scorpio knows how to possess each day. What you do now can have an enduring effect. Studies, hobbies, the usual, the expected, the simple, the basic are all in the picture. You can get siblings and neighbors to do their part in a project. Chestnut is your color; your lucky number is 8.

Tuesday, February 21 (Moon in Scorpio) You don't have to travel to be in your proper element and place today. The accent is on neighbors and local matters, on your siblings and the good conversations you can enjoy with them. All communications and matters pertaining to your car are favored. A Pisces and a Cancer impact your day. Your lucky number is 1.

Wednesday, February 22 (Moon in Scorpio to Sagittarius 2:13 a.m.) Sagittarius stands tall in family and community situations. Pleasing your family is high on agenda. Keeping track of any possible deterioration in the physical plant of your home would be a good idea under prevailing aspects. Pride of ownership stands you in good stead while paying the high costs of maintenance. Your color is russet. Lucky lottery numbers: 3, 12, 21, 30, 39, 48.

Thursday, February 23 (Moon in Sagittarius) Check questions out with an Aries or a Leo. You want to be given your due in family matters. Your practicality can be criticized by both older and younger loved ones. There are some attractive real estate offers at this time. Community unity is a must to keep property values up. Hot combination numbers: 5 and 23.

Friday, February 24 (Moon in Sagittarius to Capricorn 5:11 a.m.) Capricorn will take care of everything. Enjoy the romance and courtship that are stimulated by the moon. Be more creative in your lovemaking. Make your beloved and kindred spirits happy with a spontaneous party. Be close to your children and your parents. Snow and ivory are your colors; your lucky number is 7.

Saturday, February 25 (Moon in Capricorn) If possible, get away from it all with your beloved on a day that is made for joy, delight, and ecstasy. Teach youngsters to see the potential for adventure in a late winter afternoon. There's a feeling of having time on your hands. Red is your color. Lucky lottery numbers: 9, 18, 27, 36, 45 and 12.

Sunday, February 26 (Moon in Capricorn to Aquarius 8:14 a.m.) You feel right with the world and in your own earthy element. Taurus and another Virgo can increase your happiness. Parties, entertainments, sports viewing, and talks with people who feel much as you do on politics are all in order. You feel justified and entitled. Lucky colors are ecru and magenta; your lucky number is 2.

Monday, February 27 (Moon in Aquarius) Aquarius and Libra have key roles. Excellent trends exist where you are starting new and up-to-date preventive-medicine routines, and where you have the latest data on the right kinds of vegetables and fruits for you. Most forms of work tend to be therapeutic. Tangerine and black are your colors; your lucky number is 6.

Tuesday, February 28 (Moon in Aquarius to Pisces 12:16 p.m.) Gemini has the answers you need. Don't rush the season or drop winter attire. You may have to cope with some tardiness and absenteeism on the job. There are many complaints about matters over which mankind has little control. Accept changes with good humor. Claret red is your color; your lucky number is 8.

MARCH 1995

Wednesday, March 1 (Moon in Pisces) The new moon illuminates marriage, business partnerships, contracts, and agreements, and there is enlightenment in these matters, as well as in all close emotional relationships. Pisces and Scorpio have key roles. What is invisible and silent can affect your thinking. Lucky lottery numbers: 1, 10, 19, 28, 37, 46.

Thursday, March 2 (Moon in Pisces to Aries 6:30 p.m.) Talk things over with your mate. With business partners, discuss matters pertaining to supply sources and improved lighting. This is a good day for getting the approval you need to proceed with improvements and changes, and to create better working conditions. Earth brown is your color; your lucky number is 3.

Friday, March 3 (Moon in Aries)   Aries breezes onto the scene with objections, criticism, and the desire to change things. There is a good sense of adventure dominating the picture as the day advances. Fine trends exist in budgeting, saving, and investing. The changes you have been considering can be started now. Hot combination numbers: 5 and 41.

Saturday, March 4 (Moon in Aries)   Corrections and improvements are possible under these aspects. You can speed up where things have been slow. Young men seem to have a great desire to take over and exercise power. You prefer a slower, more deliberate, and just about guaranteed accurate pace. Lucky lottery numbers: 7, 16, 25, 34, 43 and 4.

Sunday, March 5 (Moon in Aries to Taurus 3:50 a.m.) Taurus stands tall during today's discussions. Travel, long-range, and long-distance matters can top your agenda. You are anxious to know what is happening at a distance that can impact your life. So, phone, write letters, ask questions. Distant relatives want to hear from you. Your lucky number is 9.

Monday, March 6 (Moon in Taurus)   Your mind can suddenly be filled with memories of the long-ago, and also of the not-so-long-ago. People at a distance have you in their mind and heart. What is happening quietly far away can suddenly impact your thinking. Fine trends exist for asking questions about your future. Olive green and earth brown are your colors; your lucky number is 4.

Tuesday, March 7 (Moon in Taurus to Gemini 3:55 p.m.)   Capricorn and a Cancer have key roles. Information can arrive unexpectedly. Researching the past and the far away will make for special contentment. Burgundy is your color. The respect you give elders is the respect you will receive from youngsters. Buy maps and luggage. Pick five: 6, 15, 24, 33, and 42.

Wednesday, March 8 (Moon in Gemini)   Gemini and Libra brighten the atmosphere. You can make amazing headway in your career under existing aspects. Talks with supervisors, the help you offer coworkers, and the impact of economic improvements are going to make this a red-letter day. Be professional and quietly authoritative. Lucky lottery numbers: 8, 17, 26, 35, 44, 51.

Thursday, March 9 (Moon in Gemini)   Push for a promotion or a raise. Discuss the possibility of being given more responsibility on the job. There are odd jobs languishing in your work area, and you can profit by picking them up and doing them. What you do to increase the quality of your product will tell the story in the long run. Your lucky number is 1.

Friday, March 10 (Moon in Gemini to Cancer 4:40 a.m.)   Parties, entertainments, and group social and political activities are accented and you tend to enjoy them and please others by your presence. Make spontaneous plans with a dear friend for a coffee or luncheon date. You want to be part of the great parade now. Your lucky number is 3.

Saturday, March 11 (Moon in Cancer)   A Cancer and a Scorpio have vital roles in the outcome. Friendships can make your day not only happier but also more profitable. You may require membership in a support group if you are to distinguish yourself artistically or in writing and any offbeat hobby. Lucky lottery numbers: 5, 14, 23, 32, 41, 50.

Sunday, March 12 (Moon in Cancer to Leo 3:28 p.m.)   Socializing on the grand public scale gets the go-ahead. The social side of your job can appeal to you and bring much pleasure. You can improve your public image; here a Pisces or another Virgo might be helpful. Reach out to find acceptance, appreciation, and approval. Your lucky number is 7.

Monday, March 13 (Moon in Leo)   Leo may try to change your mind and would keep you from completing projects, phasing out other projects, and making vital decisions about the future. It's past, past, past with Leo under these aspects. Prepare to make the changes you have in mind. Old rose and ivory will do it; your lucky number is 2.

Tuesday, March 14 (Moon in Leo to Virgo 10:54 p.m.) Today is excellent for finishing up, dealing with large organizations and institutions, and figuring out what is going on behind the scenes and beneath the surface. Present work for approval. File things away. Clear the deck for a vital lunar-cycle high period. Your colors are magenta and indigo; your lucky number is 4.

Wednesday, March 15 (Moon in Virgo) Press forward and work to win big today and tomorrow, when you are at your best in groups, on the job, and in all social situations. You are at an advantage because your rugged Virgo personality assets are really needed by the world. Show them the illogic, the unreasonableness of their actions. Lucky lottery numbers: 6, 15, 24, 33, 42 and 40.

Thursday, March 16 (Moon in Virgo) Hold the initiative and take the lead. Air your aspirations. Spruce up your personal appearance, for you are the center of attention. Make your demands, letting others know how you really feel about their questionable behavior. Your lucky colors are olive green and earth brown. Hot combination numbers: 8 and 35.

Friday, March 17 (Moon in Virgo to Libra 3:18 a.m.) The full moon illuminates your stake in the winnings, and there is grand insight as to ways in which you can increase your take in joint projects and investments. Libra enters the picture with wonderful ideas about money making and saving. Ask plenty of questions so that you get it right. Emerald and orange are your colors; your lucky number is 1.

Saturday, March 18 (Moon in Libra) Money is flowing. Some of it is earmarked for you. What you learn about your job, your career, and a more professional way of behavior will stand you in good stead for increasing wealth production and financial reward. You review well, you study, and you learn. Lucky lottery numbers: 3, 12, 21, 30, 39, 48.

Sunday, March 19 (Moon in Libra to Scorpio 5:52 a.m.) Scorpio makes awareness and transformation part of the system. Everyday matters profit from this, along with studies, learning processes, hobbies, and your input into neighborhood trends. Talk things over with a neighbor, who is also a kindred spirit. Peach is your color; your lucky number is 5.

Monday, March 20 (Moon in Scorpio) Ask Taurus about it. Narrow your sights and concentrate on what is before you and also on what has to be done today. Ward off distractions no matter how pleasant and, like your ancestors, keep your nose to the grindstone of your project. Winning colors are magenta and rainbow; your lucky number is 9.

Tuesday, March 21 (Moon in Scorpio to Sagittarius 7:57 a.m.) Aries and a Cancer have key roles. You witness many impulsive actions as spring begins, including the desire and intention of pushing the season forward and getting in a swim. It isn't wise to go against the rules of nature, time, and circumstance. Silvery white is your color. Pick five: 2, 11, 20, 29, 47.

Wednesday, March 22 (Moon in Sagittarius) Sagittarius, like the Greeks, has a word for it—and sometimes an entire philosophy. In family and community situations, you can take it all in, but withhold agreements and support. How about the roof and gutters of your home, the removal of storm windows? You enjoy what you own. Lucky lottery numbers: 4, 13, 22, 31, 40 and 10.

Thursday, March 23 (Moon in Sagittarius to Capricorn 10:31 a.m.) Welcome Capricorn, who generally appreciates your earthy qualities. You enjoy acceptance, approval, appreciation, and demonstrative affection now. There is a romantic glow about your proposals and reactions. Today is fine for parties, entertainment, and spontaneous socializing. Violet is your color; your lucky number is 6.

Friday, March 24 (Moon in Capricorn)   Make love under these trends of passion and desire. You are inclined to remember only the joys and none of the quarrels. It's a day for forgiveness and for opening up new doors in love and in the way you view your parents and your offspring. In love, there is a reason for everything. Your lucky number is 8.

Saturday, March 25 (Moon in Capricorn to Aquarius 2:10 p.m.)   Do what you can to please and support your beloved. Accept as possibly right and lovely the things that mean so much to your spouse. The sacrifices and the self-improvement and spontaneous self-corrections you engage in will prove worthwhile later on in the boudoir. Lucky lottery numbers; 1, 10, 19, 28, 37, 46.

Sunday, March 26 (Moon in Aquarius)   Aquarius and Gemini arrive on the scene. Do what you can to improve your diet. Realize that it is what we eat that determines so much of our progressive well-being. Busy-busy work can be a big bore. Marigold is your winning color; your lucky number is 3.

Monday, March 27 (Moon in Aquarius to Pisces 7:18 p.m.)   Arise early and pounce on the projects that have to be completed before the close of the month. Encourage and guide your not very enthusiastic assistants and coworkers. You could find a lot of malingering, possibly from youngsters. Fuchsia is your color; your lucky number is 7.

Tuesday, March 28 (Moon in Pisces)   Pisces is empathetic. Your marriage and your business partnerships, your contracts and agreements, can be improved under today's aspects. Synchronization of efforts and endeavors, and faith in the work you are sharing, will tell an important tale today. Your winning colors are turquoise and white; your lucky number is 9.

Wednesday, March 29 (Moon in Pisces)   Pisces and Cancer are front and center. Aquamarine and emerald are your colors. There is workable knowledge available to you that can improve sharing in marriage and cooperation in business partnerships. The favors you do your spouse now won't be wasted in the days ahead. Lucky lottery numbers: 2, 11, 20, 29, 38, 47.

Thursday, March 30 (Moon in Pisces to Aries 2:26 a.m.) Push savings and investments, pay what you owe and collect what is due you. Prepare for the big changes you want to initiate in the near future. Is your kitchen budget working out all right or do you need a new one? Are there ways in which you can save some of the rising energy costs? Pick five: 4, 13, 22, 31, 40.

Friday, March 31 (Moon in Aries)   March's second new moon brings illumination in the way you save part of what you earn. Make changes now that can result in more money in the bank. Talks with your banker and broker well may be in order under prevailing aspects. Aries and Leo have key roles. Wear a little gold. Hot combination numbers: 6 and 15.

APRIL 1995

Saturday, April 1 (Moon in Aries to Taurus 11:59 a.m.)   The person you're dealing with could have a massive ego under these trends. You could feel that you are being pushed from a favorite perch. A lot of talk about fame and fortune could be just hot air signifying very little. Don't let the pranks children are playing get you down. Cherry is your color. Lucky lottery numbers: 5, 14, 23, 32, 41, 50.

Sunday, April 2 (Moon in Taurus; Daylight Saving Time Begins)   It's a grand day, with strong stimulation from events at a distance. Today is excellent for planning a late-spring or early-summer vacation. Your mind will wander today and you may find yourself recycling travel done earlier in life. Matters of the higher mind demand concentration. Taurus is in the picture. Your lucky number is 7.

Monday, April 3 (Moon in Taurus)   News that has been slow in coming can suddenly arrive. Write, phone, keep in touch with what is taking place at a distance. Plan ahead, program the work that has to be done before midmonth. Another Virgo and a Capricorn have important roles. Scarlet is your color; your lucky number is 2.

Tuesday, April 4 (Moon in Taurus to Gemini 12:49 a.m. EDT)   Gemini enters declaiming. What you hear today can hold you in good stead later on in the month. Your career makes vital demands upon your time, but the effort will be more than worthwhile. Talks with supervisors and coworkers can produce the information you need. Carmen is your color; your lucky number is 4.

Wednesday, April 5 (Moon in Gemini)   Push career involvements with self-confidence and self-reliance. You could be given more authority under these trends. The more professional you are, the more help you will receive. Build upon your good reputation and spread cheer and goodwill. Orchid is your color. Lucky lottery numbers: 6, 15, 24, 33, 42 and 9.

Thursday, April 6 (Moon in Gemini to Cancer 1:40 p.m.)   Seminars, conferences, and interviews connected with your career will help you achieve. You are making a real contribution to the quality of your product under these aspects. Your status and prestige are represented as you tackle major projects that others shy away from. Hot combination numbers: 8 and 35.

Friday, April 7 (Moon in Cancer)   Friendships can make your day. A Cancer and a Scorpio are in the picture. Church and club membership and participation interests will hold your attention. Group activities and the social side of your job and hobbies can produce. Your winning colors are turquoise and ecru. Hot combination numbers: 1 and 10.

Saturday, April 8 (Moon in Cancer)   Relax with kindred spirits. Spend quality time with someone who really listens and who is interested in your achievements. This is a good day for celebrating some April event and for visiting people you don't see enough of. You do well in getting around restrictions. Lucky lottery numbers: 3, 12, 21, 30, 39, 48.

Sunday, April 9 (Moon in Cancer to Leo 1:16 a.m.) Here comes Leo! What you call arrogance may be fear and uncertainty at the bottom. You could be embarrassed by the way someone wears his or her heart on a sleeve. Excellent trends exist for thinking big and dramatically, closing out no-win projects, and gaining from a bit of secretiveness. Your lucky number is 5.

Monday, April 10 (Moon in Leo)   Complete work that has been hanging fire too long. Evaluate, estimate, deal in epilogues. You do well when you are dealing with large organizations and institutions, and also with self-effacing types. You may have trouble gathering opinions and preferences from others. Cherry is your color; your lucky number is 9.

Tuesday, April 11 (Moon in Leo to Virgo 9:29 a.m.) Look back over the way the month has been going and do some correcting and improving. Clear the deck for important actions over the next several days. An Aries and a Sagittarius will have good ideas. Retire early this evening, so that you can bounce and pounce tomorrow. Pick five: 2, 11, 20, 29, 38.

Wednesday, April 12 (Moon in Virgo)   You are in your lunar high cycle and can take your life in the direction you know to be the right one. The initiative is in your hands and you can air your aspirations successfully under these trends. Another Virgo and a Capricorn are helpful. Lucky lottery numbers: 4, 13, 22, 31, 40 and 10.

Thursday, April 13 (Moon in Virgo to Libra 2:20 p.m.)   Show enthusiasm for the job and the challenge, and display your own conviction that you can take on the world. You can breeze ahead of the competition and manuever around the opposition in your lunar-cycle high. Stand up to any possible criticism and speak sharply when necessary. Amber is your color; your lucky number is 6.

Friday, April 14 (Moon in Libra)   While not taking any unreasonable chances, you can gain today by believing in your own good luck. Spend in order to earn more, but pull in at the economic seams where luxuries are concerned. Do your best and then begin hugging the sidelines in all financial decisions. Pinks and marigolds are your colors; your lucky number is 8.

Saturday, April 15 (Moon in Libra to Scorpio 4:13 p.m.)   Eclipse patterns can pressure your earning power and income. What is called a sale may not really be one. Be prepared for some crooked communications. Be wary of those who have a big bite in too-ready laughter. There's injustice and unfairness in business dealings. Auburn is right for you. Lucky lottery numbers: 1, 10, 19, 28, 37, 46.

Sunday, April 16 (Moon in Scorpio)   Don't force changes upon yourself or others in the wake of yesterday's eclipse. There can be slowdowns at airports and you may not arrive on time. Court and all legal decisions will be more unpopular than popular. But there are some good efforts to avoid that final showdown in divorce cases. Your lucky number is 3.

Monday, April 17 (Moon in Scorpio to Sagittarius 4:51 p.m.)   Information and research are speeded up. Scorpio and a Taurus have key roles. You zero in on local changes and special situations, and pounce on opportunities that are just emerging. Siblings are with you in your experimentation. Immediate and pressing events can be controlled. Peach is your color; your lucky number is 7.

Tuesday, April 18 (Moon in Sagittarius)   Domestic, property, ownership, real estate, residential, and community interests are all featured in this wonderful potpourri of a day. Spring housecleaning can get under way, or at least be organized. Spruce up lawn, shrubbery, and trees, and tend your flowers well. Hot combination numbers: 9 and 36.

Wednesday, April 19 (Moon in Sagittarius to Capricorn 5:54 p.m.)   Today is perfect for family celebrations, scheduling your offspring's wedding, having heart to heart talks with troubled teenagers. What you own is increasing in value. Have a wonderful dinner at a happy table for members of your family. Strawberry pink is your color. Lucky lottery numbers: 2, 11, 20, 29, 38, 47.

Thursday, April 20 (Moon in Capricorn) Capricorn and another Virgo figure prominently. This is your day for loving and being loved. You are romantic, deeply pleased with your beloved, quite capable of overlooking glaring faults and expressing concern and consideration. Love is bonded in an unbreakable way. Amber is your color; your lucky number is 4.

Friday, April 21 (Moon in Capricorn to Aquarius 8:38 p.m.) Wonderful rays exist for a brief respite for you and your beloved away from the grind, the usual, and the familiar. Taurus and Capricorn will combine to make this an unusual day. Dining out will make for a memorable occasion and will be recycled in your memory many times. Hot combination numbers: 6 and 33.

Saturday, April 22 (Moon in Aquarius) Aquarius and Leo will add spice, light, and color to your day. It's fine for shopping for special foods in an unusual store. Get herbs, spices, imported sauces, and wines. Don't forget the ginger, and nutmeg, the Marsala and Dutch cheeses. Buy books on special cooking in line with up-to-date dietary information. Silver and pink are a good combination for you. Lucky lottery numbers: 8, 17, 26, 35, 44, 49.

Sunday, April 23 (Moon in Aquarius) Read health books and work to know what your doctor and dentist are talking about. There are jobs around the house that should not be neglected any longer. A little work while alone will bring an unusual peace of mind. Phone a dear friend who has been under the weather. Apricot is your color; your lucky number is 1.

Monday, April 24 (Moon in Aquarius to Pisces 1:51 a.m.) Pisces has good advice about partnerships, contracts, and agreements. Legal and public relations interests are also in focus. You share well today, you cooperate, and as a result some important work can be put together. It's a day when two heads are much better than one. Orange is your color; your lucky number is 5.

Tuesday, April 25 (Moon in Pisces) Sign contracts, enter into new agreements. Joint endeavors, especially those with your mate, can go forward under existing aspects. Conversation, interviews, and conferences will go well. Always consider the alternative to the plan you want to adopt. Your lucky color is ivory. Hot combination numbers: 7 and 34.

Wednesday, April 26 (Moon in Pisces to Aries 9:41 a.m.) A Scorpio and a Cancer can be helpful, but it is up to you to solicit their assistance. A spouse or partner will have the glue to put joint efforts together. In-laws can have an amazing idea or plan for you. Your winning colors are purple and sky blue. Lucky lottery numbers: 9, 18, 27, 36, 45, 6.

Thursday, April 27 (Moon in Aries) Aries will get things started. You could feel that you are being pushed and pressured a little. Talk about recent financial gains, savings, and investments appeal more to you than to the others. The changes that others are trying to impose upon you are rather overwhelming. Hot combination numbers: 2 and 20.

Friday, April 28 (Moon in Aries to Taurus 7:53 p.m.) As the month winds down, check your bank balance and reconsider an investment that isn't doing very well. Talks with banker and broker may be just what you need. There is considerable worry over new taxes you consider dreadfully unfair. The bridge between senior citizens and aggressive youth has fallen. Your lucky number is 4.

Saturday, April 29 (Moon in Taurus) The solar eclipse can pressure what you have going for yourself at a distance. Information may not arrive on time. There is a buildup of accident-producing potential with long-distance travel. It's not a good day for forcing changes upon yourself or others.

Taurus and another Virgo are in the picture. Lucky lottery numbers: 6, 15, 24, 33, 42, 29.

Sunday, April 30 (Moon in Taurus)   Keep to the status quo; avoid making changes in any of your schedules. Organization work may not be going just right. There can be some unexpected tardiness. Money could be lost and wasted, because the eclipse patterns still prevail. Make that long-distance phone call now. Your lucky number is 8.

MAY 1995

Monday, May 1 (Moon in Taurus to Gemini 7:53 a.m.)   You can make splendid progress in your career, especially where you felt held up earlier in the year. This is a day for telling all on the job and getting new projects under way. Listen to those in authority and don't delegate any work to a questionable underling. Mocha is your color; your lucky number is 1.

Tuesday, May 2 (Moon in Gemini)   Gemini has winning ideas in all work impacting your career. You can cash in on past victories and achievements. There are improvements in atmosphere and environment that can bring higher effort. You can't do better than improving lighting and comfort on the job. Hot combination numbers: 3 and 30.

Wednesday, May 3 (Moon in Gemini to Cancer 8:45 p.m.)   Your career picks up steam. Professional attitudes are favored. Talk things over with your immediate supervisor and don't give anybody the feeling that you have gone over their head. Expertise is your middle name and what you set in motion on the job today will endure. Lucky lottery numbers: 5, 14, 23, 32, 41, 50.

Thursday, May 4 (Moon in Cancer)   Be friendly on and off the job. Church and club membership and participation can top your agenda. You'll want to be with kindred spirits, with people who share your views on important issues. You dislike extremism generally, but never more than at this time. Hot combination numbers: 7 and 25.

Friday, May 5 (Moon in Cancer)   Work won't get all your attention on a day that is ideal for enjoying people, friendships, group activities, and church/club membership and participation. You are in a witty, humorous, especially friendly and cheerful mood. You can win others over to your point of view. A Pisces and a Cancer are helpful. Cherry is your color; your lucky number is 9.

Saturday, May 6 (Moon in Cancer to Leo 8:55 a.m.)   This is a wonderful day for taking off like a big bird and enjoying a trek through park or woods. You want to trace the advance of spring, spend time in the great outdoors, and enjoy friendly chats with those who accompany you and those you meet on your trek. Lucky lottery numbers: 2, 11, 20, 29, 38, 47.

Sunday, May 7 (Moon in Leo)   Leo makes a dramatic entrance and appeal. You are looking ahead to changes, improvements, and corrections and want to finish up any chores and tasks that might get in the way. Good trends exist for window shopping, studying sales catalogues, and helping neighbors plant their gardens. Your lucky number is 4.

Monday, May 8 (Moon in Leo to Virgo 6:33 p.m.)   This is a splendid day for completions, ridding yourself of no-win projects and attitudes, dealing with big organizations and institutions, and coming to grips with what might be going on behind the scenes. An Aries and a Sagittarius have key roles. Strawberry and lime are winning colors; your lucky number is 8.

Tuesday, May 9 (Moon in Virgo)   Today and tomorrow you are in your lunar high cycle, where your talents are multiplied and where you can put your logic, reason, practicality, and persistence to amazing use. You're the winner and can challenge others quietly and efficiently. Soft blues and golds go well. Hot combination numbers: 1 and 10.

Wednesday, May 10 (Moon in Virgo)   Go for the prizes! You have everything going for you now—determination, endurance, and an ability to complement the skills of others. Push hard now and take advantage of emerging opportunities at once. Your winning colors are taupe and orchid. Lucky lottery numbers: 3, 12, 21, 30, 39, 48.

Thursday, May 11 (Moon in Virgo to Libra 12:30 a.m.)
Push wealth production on this financially beneficial day. Your earning power is rising and you can promote an increase in income. It's a fine day for putting your many tools and skills to use in a secondary source of capital. Emerald is your color; your lucky number is 5.

Friday, May 12 (Moon in Libra)   A Gemini and an Aquarius should be invited to participate. There are lots of opportunities there for you to pick up and run with. Sales, advertising, and bargain hunting get the green lights. For more cash on hand, dispose of items you no longer need. Hot combination numbers: 7 and 25.

Saturday, May 13 (Moon in Libra to Scorpio 2:53 a.m.)
Scorpio is interested in how you are doing the job. The accent is on love of locality, of the familiar and the traditional. Lessons are learned easily now, so keep your eyes and ears wide open. Communicate, moving about your neighborhood. Lilac and mauve are your colors. Lucky lottery numbers: 9, 18, 27, 36, 45 and 3.

Sunday, May 14 (Moon in Scorpio)   The full moon illuminates local, immediate, and pressing matters. Transportation and communications get green lights and high marks. If you are entertaining, invite neighbors as well as relatives and friends. A good neighbor is worth more than ten faraway relatives and friends. Your lucky number is 2.

Monday, May 15 (Moon in Scorpio to Sagittarius 2:58 a.m.)   Sagittarius and Aries figure prominently. Family, residential, real estate, mortgages, and leases have top billing. Ownership and property won't let you forget them. You will feel part of your community now, for better or for worse. Support local merchants where you can. Your lucky number is 6.

Tuesday, May 16 (Moon in Sagittarius)   Socialize with members of your family. Discuss their future with teenagers and younger children. You could hear that someone you like is moving away. Your community economy seems to be on the front burner. Try to banish any gloom and doom that others bring to you. Primrose is your color; your lucky number is 8.

Wednesday, May 17 (Moon in Sagittarius to Capricorn 2:36 a.m.)   Information arrives; the cat is out of the bag. A Taurus and a Capricorn have front seats. It would be a shame to let this day slip past without flying off to ecstasy with your lover. You can have the feeling that you are now learning things you should have mastered long ago. Tan is your color. Lucky lottery numbers: 1, 10, 19, 28, 37, 46.

Thursday, May 18 (Moon in Capricorn)   Your practicality is appreciated by loved ones, even if they may chafe at the bit now and then. Determination in socializing, entertaining, and in dealing with your adored one is the best ingredient for a day like this. Another Virgo has the right ideas. Hot combination numbers: 3 and 21.

Friday, May 19 (Moon in Capricorn to Aquarius 3:39 a.m.)   Aquarius and Leo are aboard. Happiness is therapeutic. Try to avoid difficult people and jobs for best results under these aspects. Be cautious in dining out; kitchens are not being inspected very well. See if your own youngsters wash their hands before dining. Hot combination numbers: 5 and 14.

Saturday, May 20 (Moon in Aquarius)   Spring cleaning that was put off earlier can be tackled successfully now. There are probably many youngsters who would like to help, most likely for a little money. Ask questions of those who are trying to be more mysterious than they have any right to be. Baby blue is your color. Lucky lottery numbers: 7, 16, 25, 34, 43, 10.

Sunday, May 21 (Moon in Aquarius to Pisces 8:40 a.m.)   Pisces is represented. Your marriage or other marital state is high on the agenda, along with other partnerships, joint endeavors, and investments of time, energy, and money. You could be wondering about a legal involvement. How the world sees you is a question crossing your mind. Your lucky number is 9.

Monday, May 22 (Moon in Pisces)   A Scorpio and a Cancer have parts to play. Sharing, cooperating, and showing proper consideration for the other guy are points of pressure. There can be a strong sense of frustration if you have to work closely with a lazy assistant. Winning colors are ecru and beige; your lucky number is 4.

Tuesday, May 23 (Moon in Pisces to Aries 3:13 p.m.)   You could find partners or others edgy and irritable, and this could only make you want to isolate yourself. However, it may be difficult to find a truly peaceful environment under existing aspects. There are some financial worries making the rounds, or at least the illusion of upcoming insecurity. Violet and mauve are your colors. Pick five: 6, 15, 24, 33, 42.

Wednesday, May 24 (Moon in Aries)   Gemini and Aries have key roles. Your career can slow down and seem sluggish. Authority is questioned—you can hardly call that a professional attitude. Even so, impressive changes can be made, including corrections and improvements. Beige and canary are winning colors. Lucky lottery numbers: 8, 17, 26, 35, 44 and 50.

Thursday, May 25 (Moon in Aries)   Push savings; investments; and time-, labor-, and money-saving devices and technologies. Search for new tax shelters, as the taxes on everything everywhere are rising. There is a strong desire to make changes that bring back yesterday. Lucky colors are amber and turquoise; your lucky number is 1.

Friday, May 26 (Moon in Aries to Taurus 1:47 a.m.)   The desire to get away from it all is strong. You are sick of the usual, familiar, and boring, and would like to fly off with your beloved. Perhaps this can be worked out in some way for a few memorable days. You cling, holding things close to your breast. Neutral colors like flesh may do it; your lucky number is 3.

Saturday, May 27 (Moon in Taurus)   Taurus wants to travel, and the invitation may come to you. Try to do something different today, such as dining out in a newly opened restaurant, or visiting an art gallery, museum, or local place of historic interest. Phone somebody you haven't heard from since December. Lucky lottery numbers: 5, 14, 23, 32, 41, 48.

Sunday, May 28 (Moon in Taurus to Gemini 2:07 p.m.)   Today is excellent for recycling last summer's vacation by talking about it, remembering the laughs and the surprises, and studying all the photographs and other souvenirs. Phone somebody you met casually while traveling and swore you would keep in touch with. Azure blue is your color; your lucky number is 7.

Monday, May 29 (Moon in Gemini)   The new moon illuminates your career, your sense of responsibility, and the right way to exercise authority. Talks with those in charge will clear the air of suspicions and false conclusions. Gemini and Aquarius are on stage, with much to say about what is going on. Beige is your color; your lucky number is 2.

Tuesday, May 30 (Moon in Gemini)   It would be wrong to neglect any duties, obligations, and responsibilities that top your daily agenda. Studies will demand their share of time. You also learn much from discussions with unusual types. A peaceful atmosphere at work is the real foundation block to outstanding success. Your lucky number is 4.

Wednesday, May 31 (Moon in Gemini to Cancer 2:59 a.m.)   A Pisces and a Cancer come aboard. Socialize to your heart's content now. Group activities, time well spent with kindred spirits, and all church and club membership and participation matters are accented. Old friendships mean most to you, but new relationships can be formed. Lucky lottery numbers: 6, 15, 24, 33, 42 and 31.

Thursday, June 1 (Moon in Cancer) You want to get out of yourself, so to speak, and to participate in what seems like important organizations and movements. You can be strongly conscious of the passing time now and want to make your mark, do your part, and encourage magnificent victories and achievements. A Scorpio and a Cancer are in your corner. Your color is strawberry; your lucky number is 5.

Friday, June 2 (Moon in Cancer to Leo 3:17 p.m.) A friendly approach will win for you. Be personable, interested in the sacred cows of associates, jovial, and willing to listen to some boring remarks by nice people. You want to fit in, but you could find some talkative types are pressuring you and the discussion you have started. Okra green is your color; your lucky number is 7.

Saturday, June 3 (Moon in Leo) Leo and Aries will take over and dramatize the events. There are fine trends for completing jobs begun earlier around the grounds of your home. See your friendly hardware store clerk for lawn and yard problems. Today is fine for sprucing up the appearance of your porch, patio, or breezeway. Emerald is your color. Lucky lottery numbers: 9, 18, 27, 36, 45 and 3.

Sunday, June 4 (Moon in Leo) What has been held back can be released today. Write letters to utility companies you have a bone to pick with. You do well when you take on large organizations and institutions. Mistakes have become a part of the American way and you are not one to let them continue. Auburn is your color; your lucky number is 2.

Monday, June 5 (Moon in Leo to Virgo 1:46 a.m.) This is your day to breeze ahead of the competition; to make good impressions; to spruce up your personal appearance, and to really go for it socially, financially, and careerwise. Hold the initiative, take the lead, speak out in your own behalf and demonstrate self-confidence. Your lucky number is 6.

Tuesday, June 6 (Moon in Virgo)   Still in your lunar-cycle high, you can have what you want today. The opposition is overwhelmed by your personality assets—determination, practicality, and reasonable behavior. Another Virgo can be helpful. You excel at giving service to others and you appreciate anything done for you. Pick five: 8, 19, 26, 35, 44.

Wednesday, June 7 (Moon in Virgo to Libra 9:13 a.m.)   You can take on City Hall today. You have the facts and they tend to serve your wishes and aspirations. Let the world see you at your best and stake claims to rights, privileges, and money you feel is yours. Taurus and Capricorn will reply. Your winning colors are tawny and blond. Lucky lottery numbers: 1, 10, 19, 28, 37, 46.

Thursday, June 8 (Moon in Libra)   Push wealth production. Your earning power can rise and your income can be increased under existing aspects. Sales, advertising, self-promotion, and self-realization are strongly featured. A Libra and an Aquarius come aboard with good advice. Look for a new source of income. Your lucky number is 3.

Friday, June 9 (Moon in Libra to Scorpio 1:03 p.m.)   Be cautious in spending. It's not that you aren't earning enough, but are you too self-indulgent or is there a beloved drain on your income? There can be gains from special sales, wiser and more careful shopping, and from such assists as using coupons and buying lower-priced generic products. Strawberry is your color; your lucky number is 5.

Saturday, June 10 (Moon in Scorpio)   Scorpio makes you feel at home wherever you happen to be. Fine trends exist in neighborhood matters, talks with siblings, and handling all pressing and immediate matters. It's a day for learning by doing and listening. You gain from sticking to the task at hand and concentrating on doing a good job. Marigold is your color. Lucky lottery numbers; 7, 16, 25, 34, 43, 1.

Sunday, June 11 (Moon in Scorpio to Sagittarius 1:50 p.m.)   A Pisces and a Cancer have key roles. Narrow your sights so that emerging opportunities don't escape your attention. Communications and transportation matters get top billing. What is right under your nose, so to speak, is more important than the big guns and bright lights at a distance. Your lucky number is 9.

Monday, June 12 (Moon in Sagittarius)   Domestic interests push everything else out of the way. What you own, used to own, and want to own are on the table. Property matters and the upkeep of your home can occupy some of your attention. Family members have their gripes and it would be well to listen to them. Wear pastels. Your lucky number is 4.

Tuesday, June 13 (Moon in Sagittarius to Capricorn 1:05 p.m.)   The full moon illuminates family and residential matters, the property you own and the property you would like to own. You could learn some information about your community that is a little upsetting. Relatives may seem to be in conflict with each other and it could be up to you to play peacemaker. Your color is purple. Hot combination numbers: 6 and 33.

Wednesday, June 14 (Moon in Capricorn)   Capricorn can bring compliments and favors. Your love life is strongly stimulated and you and your beloved would enjoy a memorable trip to ecstasy. You are creative, original, investigative, flexible, and versatile in everything under prevailing aspects. Parties and entertainments are recommended. Lucky lottery numbers: 8, 17, 26, 35, 44, 50.

Thursday, June 15 (Moon in Capricorn to Aquarius 12:52 p.m.)   You see the romance and the adventure where others see only what's wrong. So it's up to you to encourage, guide, guard, invite, reassure, entertain, and make others happy. Be one with your beloved; togetherness will pay off, especially where you are bent on giving pleasure. Fuchsia is your color; your lucky number is 1.

Friday, June 16 (Moon in Aquarius)   Emphasized are your work, the services you give others, and the services you receive. Take care of your health and be sure that the kitchens from which your food comes are clean and sanitary. Unfortunately, our current slipshod ways are tampering with overall physical well-being. Your lucky number is 3.

Saturday, June 17 (Moon in Aquarius to Pisces 3:13 p.m.) Leo and Gemini and the matters ruled by these signs are vital. Peace of mind and of soul are therapeutic. The work you do today should be significant, and your assistants should be cheerful, talkative types. It's a day for finding out how rare a June day can be. Red is your color. Lucky lottery numbers: 5, 14, 23, 32, 41 and 50.

Sunday, June 18 (Moon in Pisces) Pisces comes on deck. Sharing, working in harmony with a partner, and reviewing upcoming contracts and agreements are all featured. Check all important moves out with spouse and business partners for best results. Joint investments can be figured out under these trends. Pastels are in. Your lucky number is 7.

Monday, June 19 (Moon in Pisces to Aries 9:29 p.m.) Marriage, legal, and public relations interests get green lights. Talks, instead of arguments and long harangues, can achieve. But nobody really wants to be commanded, ordered, or threatened under existing aspects. Somebody may think you are too uppity. Pinks and lemons do well; your lucky number is 2.

Tuesday, June 20 (Moon in Aries) Push savings of money, time, and labor. Study the new technologies in your own immediate field of work. Investments may be showing more than you had anticipated. Organization work is inviting, because your boss and coworkers are well disposed toward you. Claret red and cherry are your colors; your lucky number is 4.

Wednesday, June 21 (Moon in Aries) Changes, improvements, and corrections are favored. Talks with your banker, broker, or other money adviser are going to produce plenty. A former spouse and former in-laws can make waves. Custodial matters are uncertain and there can be some mischief-making around these issues. Lucky lottery numbers: 6, 15, 24, 33, 42, 3.

Thursday, June 22 (Moon in Aries to Taurus 7:35 a.m.)   It's a wonderful day for getting away from the grind. Taurus and another Virgo will make marvelous companions. You want new experiences and new scenes, so sightseeing warms your heart. Visit relatives at a distance for some new advantages. Chartreuse is your color; your lucky number is 8.

Friday, June 23 (Moon in Taurus)   Keep on the go. Dine in unusual restaurants. Take the guided tours and accept the fact that time is going to rush when you are this happy. You feel very earthy and physical, and you want to be with kindred spirits. There can be a meeting with somebody you'd love to know better, but ships do pass each other by. Your lucky number is 1.

Saturday, June 24 (Moon in Taurus to Gemini 8:02 p.m.)   The more active you are today, the better you can savor these experiences. Things happen fast. Your feet are itchy and all might-have-beens should be banished with a smile. Is this some sort of delayed spring fever? Oh, how happy Capricorn can make you! Lucky lottery numbers: 3, 12, 21, 30, 39, 48.

Sunday, June 25 (Moon in Gemini)   Gemini says it very well and you can pick up the threads of projects abandoned earlier. Fabulous progress can be made in your career from now until the end of June. Show some enthusiasm for the sacred cows of supervisors and coworkers. People want your undivided attention. Your lucky number is 5.

Monday, June 26 (Moon in Gemini)   There are things that have to be said today, even if you don't feel like saying them. You see people on the wrong track. Fast tracks lead to failure under these trends. Headquarters tends to ask silly questions and come up with ridiculous solutions to problems. Your lucky number is 9.

Tuesday, June 27 (Moon in Gemini to Cancer 8:56 a.m.) It's important that you consider the other side of the matter or situation. Alternatives can be better. Keep your options open until the last minute. Libra and Aquarius may be able to pacify the opposition. It's difficult to accept certain challenges now. Hot combination numbers: 2 and 20.

Wednesday, June 28 (Moon in Cancer) The new moon illuminates social situations, church and club involvements, friendships, group activities, what can and can't be accomplished via the social side of your job and hobbies. A Pisces and a Cancer figure prominently. There are new ways to please friends. Lucky lottery numbers: 4, 13, 22, 31, 40, 7.

Thursday, June 29 (Moon in Cancer to Leo 9:02 p.m.) Listen to what another Virgo and a Cancer have to suggest or merely imply. Some information may be revealed unintentionally. Friendships can make the day and you will enjoy looking back with someone who has known you a long time. You can improve your public image now. Hot combination numbers: 6 and 33.

Friday, June 30 (Moon in Leo) Leo has pointers on how to finish up odd chores more quickly. Fine trends exist for looking back over the month and figuring out what you have learned, what you have achieved, and where you may have failed. Be sure you are taking full advantage of past experiences. Lavender and white are your colors; your lucky number is 8.

JULY 1995

Saturday, July 1 (Moon in Leo) Prepare, dealing in prefaces and prologues. Take care of the finishing details in work that should be gotten out of the way by the end of July. Aries and Sagittarius are in your corner. What is transpiring behind the scenes will impact your life in the days ahead. Lucky lottery numbers: 8, 17, 26, 35, 44, 01.

Sunday, July 2 (Moon in Leo to Virgo 7:35 a.m.) Now you are in your lunar-cycle high and can begin new projects. Hold the initiative and zero in on split-second opportunities that may be unanticipated. Be ready to march to the tune of those in charge. Let the world know your ambitions. Violet is your color; your lucky number is 1.

Monday, July 3 (Moon in Virgo)   Be strong, sure, and take the lead. Your powers of persuasion are unbeatable. Agreements can be secured. Your determination, patience, and endurance will all pay handsome dividends today. Another Virgo is supportive. Stand tall in any confrontation, for you can win through Virgo-type persistence. Your lucky number is 5.

Tuesday, July 4 (Moon in Virgo to Libra 3:55 p.m.)   Taurus and Capricorn are ready to help you. Spruce up your personal appearance. Arise early and organize your time well, so you can make these hours count for much in personal advancement. Master and finish the chores that you are good at and that others find boring. Off-white is your color; your lucky number is 7.

Wednesday, July 5 (Moon in Libra)   You can increase your financial take under existing aspects. New sources of capital can be run to earth. You may figure out ways of earning money through special sales, good advertising, and by putting tools and skills you own to use in a leisure-time second occupation. Lucky lottery numbers: 9, 18, 27, 36, 45, 19.

Thursday, July 6 (Moon in Libra to Scorpio 9:19 p.m.)   Self-disciplined ways are required in marriage and other business partnerships as Saturn assumes retrograde movement in your seventh house. Lunar trends favor your earning power and income. The encouragement you offer to assistants will work to your ultimate advantage. Raspberry is your color; your lucky number is 2.

Friday, July 7 (Moon in Scorpio)   Scorpio and Taurus have key roles. The localized matters offer new scope. Studies, hobbies, siblings, and neighbors are all aboard. You do well when you concentrate on immediate and pressing matters. Steer clear of impossible goals and systems. Failures are merely prefaces to gains. Your lucky number is 4.

Saturday, July 8 (Moon in Scorpio to Sagittarius 11:38 p.m.) There are a thousand chores and tasks around your house and its grounds and, as a result, you may wish you could just ignore them. But great progress can be made, if you tackle them in an organized and systematic way, putting the youngsters to work, too. Marigold is your color. Lucky lottery numbers: 6, 15, 24, 33, 42, 3.

Sunday, July 9 (Moon in Sagittarius) Sagittarius can be a popular relative, operating on the level of very old and also of very young listeners. It's the family that wants your attention, advice, and affection under these aspects. The grounds of your home require special attention also. Cinnamon and white are your colors; your lucky number is 8.

Monday, July 10 (Moon in Sagittarius to Capricorn 11:44 p.m.) Get estimates on work you hope to have done on your home. Do what you can to save the trees on your property. The local ecology can be of some concern. Aries and Leo have key roles in decisions that have to be made. Talk at work can be about invisibles and illusions. Your lucky number is 3.

Tuesday, July 11 (Moon in Capricorn) Capricorn comes aboard. Your love department gets first-rate stimulation. You know instinctively how to please your beloved, and together you fly off to ecstasy. Try to get away from chattering youngsters. A little privacy can add plenty of spice to the act. Your lucky number is 5.

Wednesday, July 12 (Moon in Capricorn to Aquarius 11:21 p.m.) The full moon illuminates new ways to please your lover. You see the romance and the adventure that are connected with lovemaking. Courtship gets high marks. Socialize in spontaneous ways for best results. You get along well now with the very old and the very young. Auburn is your color. Lucky lottery numbers: 7, 16, 25, 34, 43, 11.

Thursday, July 12 (Moon in Aquarius)   Aquarius and Gemini figure prominently. Eating certain rich foods can be related to upset stomachs. There is a trend that suggests resistance of hard work due to flippant attitudes of others. There can be some discomfort from tight clothing, and from riding in cluttered cars. Lemon is your color; your lucky number is 9.

Friday, July 14 (Moon in Aquariusus)   There are incompletions, goals only halfway met, and misinterpreted instructions and directions. Duties, responsibilities, and obligations are overlooked quite easily under these aspects. Libra would help, if asked, so that these conditions could be improved. Fuchsia is your color; your lucky number is 2.

Saturday, July 15 (Moon in Aquarius to Pisces 12:37 a.m.) Pisces and a Scorpio have vital roles. In unity, there is greater strength. Work that has been resisting you can be done well now. Share, amend, make promises, and forgive those who tend to get in the way, while thinking that they are helping. Marriage, contracts, and agreements are favored. Lucky lottery numbers: 4, 13, 22, 31, 40, 49.

Sunday, July 16 (Moon in Pisces)   Avoid anything that could result in a trying lawsuit. Keep your wits about you when pressured by tiresome people. Teamwork will succeed where lone operations can fail. Discussions with your mate and others you have known a long time can be helpful. The maternal instinct is strong. Your lucky number is 6.

Monday, July 17 (Moon in Pisces to Aries 5:23 a.m.)   The financial side of the month improves and you can make headway in savings, budgeting, investing wisely, and warring on waste. Aries and Leo are in your corner. The cost of living is inching up but you do well in revising your shopping attitudes. Your lucky number is 1.

Tuesday, July 18 (Moon in Aries)   Pay dues, collect what is due you, work on business files and allied papers. Much can be learned from reading a book on the economy or certain financial pages in magazines and newspapers. Today is fine for dealing in changes, improvements, and corrections. Your colors are taupe and mauve—Your lucky number is 3.

Wednesday, July 19 (Moon in Aries to Taurus 2:20 p.m.) Sagittarius will explain it all. Push for new money gains. Talk things over with your banker and broker. Listen to advice of former neighbors and coworkers on how to make ends meet. Maneuver the budget a bit, if you are planning your vacation trip. Lucky lottery numbers: 5, 14, 23, 32, 41, 50.

Thursday, July 20 (Moon in Taurus) Today is excellent for taking a breather, getting in a bit of travel, visiting relatives within the 300-mile radius, or beginning a longer vacation. Winning colors are ecru and eggshell; Your lucky number is 7.

Friday, July 21 (Moon in Taurus) Today favors travel, possessions, and the acquisition of new belongings, and gives you an earthy feeling about life. Another Virgo and a Capricorn will influence your thinking and doing. Long-range and long-distance interests get top billing. Your winning colors are azure blue and nutmeg; your lucky number is 9.

Saturday, July 22 (Moon in Taurus to Gemini 2:23 a.m.) Career duties, responsibilities and obligations can spill over into the weekend. Gemini pushes you into required actions. You may have to exercise your authority with teenagers, even when you fear their resentment and anger a bit. It's one of those days when you feel the weight of problems of these times. Pastels are right to wear. Lucky lottery numbers: 2, 11, 20, 29, 38, 47.

Sunday, July 23 (Moon in Gemini) Talks with coworkers can give your morale a boost. Steer clear of unfounded rumors about the security of your job. Libra tries to smooth things over. There can be some mischief making connected with jealousy or a need to punish you for something you did or didn't do. Your lucky number is 4.

Monday, July 24 (Moon in Gemini to Cancer 3:16 p.m.) Aquarius may not take things as seriously as you would want. Career requirements take top billing. Professional attitudes are necessary, Use authority in a quiet way that doesn't stir up any hornet's nest of opposition. You could find those in authority rather edgy. Your lucky number is 8.

Tuesday, July 25 (Moon in Cancer)   A Pisces and a Cancer come aboard. Friendships can make this an enjoyable day. Group activities, church and club involvements, and the social side of your job are all paths to delight and joy. Older women have much to give in the way of advice and new directions. Pistachio green and lime are your colors; your lucky number is 1.

Wednesday, July 26 (Moon in Cancer)   There is a strong desire to finish certain chores before the month ends. You are strongly conscious of the passing of the month and of summer. But there are many pleasant distractions coming at you from all directions and less work gets done than you anticipated. Pinks and blues are right. Lucky lottery numbers: 3, 12, 21, 30, 39, 48.

Thursday, July 27 (Moon in Cancer to Leo 3:07 a.m.)   The new moon illuminates the past and it's just possible that you can extract something additional from matters you ordinarily would consider finished and closed out. Fine rays exist for completions, mailing things off, presenting projects to a higher authority, and seeking approval. Ivory and old rose are your colors; your lucky number is 5.

Friday, July 28 (Moon in Leo)   There is enlightenment operating now that is based on past experiences, including past defeats and failures. This is a good learning day and you gain from mulling events over in your mind. Leo makes a dramatic entrance and exit. Primrose and beige are your colors. Pick five: 7, 16, 25, 34, 43.

Saturday, July 29 (Moon in Leo to Virgo 1:12 a.m.) Prepare, dealing in prologues and prefaces, not only depending on lessons learned in the past but using them to make these closing days of July pay off more handsomely. As the day rushes along, spruce up your personal appearance and be ready for major opportunities. Wear pastels. Lucky lottery numbers: 9, 18, 27, 36, 45, 48.

Sunday, July 30 (Moon in Virgo) Now in your high lunar cycle, you can work miracles in your own life. Seize and hold the initiative upon awakening, and air your aspirations. Speak up in your own behalf and know that what you want is within your scope. You can accept challenges courageously. Amber is your color; your lucky number 2

Monday, July 31 (Moon in Virgo to Libra 9:23 p.m.) Another Virgo and a Capricorn have key roles. Today is excellent for pushing your highly personalized aims. Be where the action is today. Let the world know that you are on the scene and ready for star goodies. Your determination, methodical ways, and ability to stick with a boring task are going to pay off well. Plum is your color; your lucky number is 6.

AUGUST 1995

Tuesday, August 1 (Moon in Libra) Push for higher income and greater earning power. Under prevailing aspects, you can improve your value to the job and to your employers. Financial transactions, sales, and unanticipated purchases are all favored. Libra and Gemini have key roles. Money due you for some time can materialize. Hot combination numbers: 5 and 41.

Wednesday, August 2 (Moon in Libra) You can't do better than pleasing those in authority and eventually realizing the benefits of such a harmonious relationship. Striving and fending off interruptions will produce high caliber work. Stick to proved systems. Winning colors are mauve and beige. Lucky lottery numbers: 7, 16, 25, 34, 43, 2.

Thursday, August 3 (Moon in Libra to Scorpio 3:29 a.m.) Scorpio comes aboard, bringing passion, confidence, and engineering abilities to the work that must be done today. You deal well with the local scene. Communications and transportation matters are favored, along with studies, learning processes, and hobbies. Hot combination numbers: 9 and 27.

Friday, August 4 (Moon in Scorpio)   A Pisces and a Cancer have front seats, as you stick to the work that will produce the most profit. Know what you can do now to make yourself stand out on the job. Victories and achievements are carrying a big dollar sign. Lavender and white are your winning colors; your lucky number is 2.

Saturday, August 5 (Moon in Scorpio to Sagittarius 7:14 a.m.)   Sagittarius takes over. Family, residential, ownership, and property matters are accented. The day should be planned early with your mate and children in mind. There are things children want to do in the summer and this is a fine day for extracting quality time. Cherry is your color. Lucky lottery numbers: 4, 13, 22, 31, 40, 49.

Sunday, August 6 (Moon in Scorpio)   Today is fine for inspecting newly built homes, driving out into the country to see land that is available for a weekend retreat, and considering ways of making your home seem larger and more comfortable. See exhibits connected with home improvement tasks, some of which you could do yourself. Your lucky number is 6.

Monday, August 7 (Moon in Sagittarius to Capricorn 8:52 a.m.)   Get estimates from those who can make improvements on your home and its grounds. The urge to beautify is strong. It's a day when you could switch from home improvements to making your lawn and backyard become more a part of your living arrangements. Decks, breezeways, patio, and outbuildings are favored. Your lucky number is 1.

Tuesday, August 8 (Moon in Capricorn)   Capricorn brings affection, approval, and appreciation. It would be a shame to not use these hours to draw more closely to your beloved. There is romance and adventure in the air, which you could transfer to your personal and marital agenda. Dialogue never was more important. Pick five: 3, 12, 21, 30, 39.

Wednesday, August 9 (Moon in Capricorn to Aquarius 9:29 a.m.) It's an excellent day for parties, entertainments, or a picnic wherever children excitedly suggest. It's a romantic cycle, full of adventure potential; it's fine for beach and water activities and other summer experiences. This evening is even more romantic if you are with your own contemporaries. All the colors of the rainbow are yours. Lucky lottery numbers: 5, 14, 23, 32, 41, 50.

Thursday, August 10 (Moon in Aquarius) Aquarius and Leo have key roles. You could get a lot of boring detail work done under these trends. The job, rather than your career, is in focus. You could hear some summer complaints in much younger folk. Avoid superlarge meals and go in for simple dishes. Beige and taupe are your colors; your lucky number is 7.

Friday, August 11 (Moon in Aquarius to Pisces 10:46 a.m.) Gemini and Libra figure prominently. Today is fine for organizing a pleasurable weekend, baking a fruit cobbler, and making a lot of ice cream. Coworkers and supervisors would love an invitation to your patio or to a local swimming pool. People want to shout that it's summer. Pick five: 9, 18, 27, 36, 45.

Saturday, August 12 (Moon in Pisces) Today is fine for new bonding with your mate and in-laws. You want to share, to cooperate, to please, and to show respect. The more you can relax off the job, the better you will be under existing aspects. Being with loved ones is therapeutic for you. Stick to foods that spell joy, delight, and pleasure. Lucky lottery numbers: 2, 11, 20, 29, 38, 47.

Sunday, August 13 (Moon in Pisces to Aries 2:41 p.m.) Today is excellent for head-to-head meaningful conversations with your beloved. Avoid legal involvements under prevailing aspects and don't expect much in the way of public relations. There are critics all over the place. People rebel against the familiar and the usual. Winning colors are yellow and strawberry; your lucky number is 4.

Monday, August 14 (Moon in Aries)   Aries enters the picture and can't be ignored. Push security matters, changes that can result in more security, all savings, investments, and both cost and standard of living interests. you can do quite well by working on a new budget for your household. Silver and pink are going to do it for you; your lucky number is 8.

Tuesday, August 15 (Moon in Aries to Taurus 10:25 p.m.)   Today is excellent for improving situations and conditions. The changes you inaugurate today are apt to show endurance. A Leo and a Sagittarius have key roles. Avoid fiery exchanges with younger people and with those who seem to never grow up. The unwrinkled can be testy. Cerulean blue is your color. Pick five: 1, 10, 19, 28, 37.

Wednesday, August 16 (Moon in Taurus)   This day is fine for beginning a trip, working on long-range and long-distance matters, making important phone calls, and writing business letters that speak well for you. Taurus and another Virgo are in the picture. Matters of the higher mind are taking over. Purple is your color. Lucky lottery numbers: 3, 12, 21, 30, 39, 48.

Thursday, August 17 (Moon in Taurus)   Sightseeing, dining in an unusual waterside restaurant, or preparing a gourmet seafood dinner for your companions are all well aspected. Visiting places of special historical or local interest are in the picture. Winning colors are magenta, indigo, and champagne. Hot combination numbers: 5 and 14.

Friday, August 18 (Moon in Taurus to Gemini 9:40 a.m.) Today is fine for driving in beautiful rural areas. Shopping in country stores and by the side of the road will give a pleasurable surprise. Phone, write postcards, buy souvenirs, and, on the way home, buy baskets of fruit in season for possible canning. Olive and emerald are winning colors; your lucky number is 7.

Saturday, August 19 (Moon in Gemini)   Gemini has a lot to tell you. What has been transpiring in your career and very possibly in a secret, behind-the-scenes way will now be revealed. You are told things you would rather not hear. Be professional in all responses, and don't tell more than you want to. Purple and blue are your colors. Lucky lottery numbers: 9, 18, 27, 36, 45, 33.

Sunday, August 20 (Moon in Gemini to Cancer 10:24 p.m.)   Listen to Aquarius for good results. Fine trends exist for preparing for the work week ahead and for warming up to what you have to do tomorrow. You can cash in on your proved reputation, prestige, and status, but not in a blow-hard way. Pale gold and canary yellow are your colors. Keep abreast of the economic news. Your lucky number is 2.

Monday, August 21 (Moon in Cancer)   The Cancer sign and all that it rules will impact your day—friendship, group activities, the social side of your job and of your hobbies, and all church and club membership and participation matters. Your winning colors are beige and pale gold. Dress more formally tonight. Your lucky number is 6.

Tuesday, August 22 (Moon in Cancer)   You are in a good cycle for enjoying the summer scene. A Scorpio has something interesting to say to you. Your heart could be stirred by what you hear and witness today. Even if your club has suspended operations for the summer, it would be good idea to keep in touch with dear clubmates. Your lucky number is 8.

Wednesday, August 23 (Moon in Cancer to Leo 10:13 a.m.) Trust what Pisces says today. Celebrations, parties, and family get-togethers are all favored. You want to enjoy quality time with your closest friends, with the people who know how to boost your morale when it flags. Your public image can be improved under prevailing aspects. Brown is your color. Lucky lottery numbers: 1, 10, 19, 28, 37, 46.

Thursday, August 24 (Moon in Leo)   Leo will help you complete projects you want out of the way before the end of August. Fine trends exist for dealing with large organizations and with people you seldom see. Your suspicions about what is happening behind the scenes are quite accurate. Raspberry is your color. Pick five: 3, 12, 21, 30, 39.

Friday, August 25 (Moon in Leo to Virgo 7:50 p.m.) The past is very much in focus and you can extract new gains from matters you ordinarily would consider finished and closed. How about looking up former neighbors, in-laws, and old school chums? You want to reminisce under these aspects. Winning colors are salmon and umber. Hot combination numbers: 5 and 14.

Saturday, August 26 (Moon in Virgo) This is one of your great and promising days. The new moon is illuminating all that you can do now that you are in your August lunar-cycle high. There is enlightenment as to where you should steer your personal plans. Be yourself—practical, hardworking, determined, and enduring. Lucky lottery numbers: 7, 16, 25, 34, 43, 10.

Sunday, August 27 (Moon in Virgo) Don't let these hours of high personal potential get away from you. Arise early and get going, take the lead, and air your long-range aspirations and hopes for the future. Don't let anybody budge you from your perch, when you know you are right. Persuade, convince. Your lucky number is 9.

Monday, August 28 (Moon in Virgo to Libra 3:15 a.m.) This is a good money day with new funds in focus. Your earning power and income get high marks. You can dispose of what you no longer need at a good profit. Buying, selling, advertising, and handling money are all well aspected. Your winning colors are ruby and champagne; your lucky number is 4.

Tuesday, August 29 (Moon in Libra) You can depend on the financial advice you receive from a Libra. Fine trends exist in wealth production and can make this a red-letter day. Push earning power, hold special sales, subscribe to a money magazine or report. There is a lot of usable financial information around today. apricot is your color; your lucky number is 6.

Wednesday, August 30 (Moon in Libra to Scorpio 8:12 p.m.) Push for financial gains. Talk things over with your accountant or broker. Know what you have been failing to do to increase your income. A Gemini and an Aquarius have creative ideas, full of imagination, and some of these can be applicable to what you want to do. Red is your color. Lucky lottery numbers: 8, 17, 26, 35, 44, 30.

Thursday, August 31 (Moon in Scorpio) Scorpio makes the scene full of strength, power, and passion. Push local, here-and-now, immediate, and pressing matters, and show the courage of your convictions in front of others. Studies, hobbies, communications, and movement within the 300-mile radius are favored. Pinks and blues will do it. Hot combination numbers: 1 and 10.

SEPTEMBER 1995

Friday, September 1 (Moon in Scorpio to Sagittarius 12:57 p.m.) Trust Scorpio to get it right. Push communications and transportation matters. Pounce upon opportunities as soon as they announce themselves. Remember to take advantage of everything you have going for yourself today, including what you have learned from life's difficult hours. Amber is your color; your lucky number is 9.

Saturday, September 2 (Moon in Sagittarius) Sagittarius and Gemini will disagree and give onlookers the impression that they are not unhappy about this. Domestic interests can top your agenda. Summer is fading and there are many annual chores to be done around the grounds of your home. Your lucky colors are apricot and primrose. Lucky lottery numbers: 2, 11, 20, 29, 38, 47.

Sunday, September 3 (Moon in Sagittarius to Capricorn 3:45 p.m.) Entertain people you met for the first time this past summer. Real estate, ownership, and all property matters are in focus. You will feel that your social circle and your world are both expanding. People seem much more important to you than places. Peach and canary yellow are winning colors, your lucky number is 4.

Monday, September 4 (Moon in Capricorn)   Capricorn is more affectionate than he or she wants to project. This is a good day for making love and experiencing ecstasy. You want to be with people, to promote your offspring, and to make your parents happy. You are the bridge across which the older and younger generations will travel. Your lucky number is 8.

Tuesday, September 5 (Moon in Capricorn to Aquarius 5:47 p.m.)   Capricorn brings a sense of passionate desire, of deep earthiness, and of physical attraction. Parties and entertainments also are represented. Affairs of your own children and other young people are impulsive and compulsive. You do well when you bring the generations together. Pick five: 1, 10, 19, 28, 37.

Wednesday, September 6 (Moon in Aquarius)   Aquarius has his or her own family values, but they allow more latitude to others than most solar groups. The family has its own work projects, however, some members don't feel like making much of a contribution. Indian Summer can make for sluggish conditions. Violet and lavender are your colors. Lucky lottery numbers: 3, 12, 21, 30, 39, 48.

Thursday, September 7 (Moon in Aquarius to Pisces 8:08 p.m.)   Protect your health by watching what you eat and being careful when climbing and descending. Games can bring certain injuries under these trends. Know where children are and what they are doing. Truly, the devil finds work for idle little hands. Peace of mind is your evening goal. Okra green and russet are your colors; your lucky number is 5.

Friday, September 8 (Moon in Pisces)   Pisces cooperates with you and the end results can be impressive. Marriage and other partnerships, as well as legal and public relation matters, get top billing. A strong sense of unity underlies the day, but partners do not always understand your determination. Orchid is your color; your lucky number is 7.

Saturday, September 9 (Moon in Pisces)   The full moon illuminates marriage, business partnerships, sharing, joint endeavors, and joint investments. Contracts and agreements receive new enlightenment. A Pisces can be exceptionally helpful. Saffron yellow is your winning color. Lucky lottery numbers: 9, 18, 27, 36, 45, 3.

Sunday, September 10 (Moon in Pisces to Aries 12:14 a.m.)   Aries comes across. Push for dialogue about the national economy, especially if an authoritative person happens to be present. Savings, investments, and improved budgeting are in the picture. You'll want to know more about economic trends at a time when financial matters seem confusing. Your lucky number is 2.

Monday, September 11 (Moon in Aries)   You can dislodge any logjam in wealth production under these aspects and find ways to save a little on groceries, your car, and anything wasteful in your life. Leo and Sagittarius can be helpful. Russet and pinecone green are your colors; your lucky number is 6.

Tuesday, September 12 (Moon in Aries to Taurus 7:21 a.m.)   Taurus brings good news. Travel, what's perking for you at a distance, and people from or at a distance are all well aspected. You reach out, you extend your thinking, you are interested in the long-range view and potential of things. Security matters are high on your agenda. Your lucky number is 8.

Wednesday, September 13 (Moon in Taurus)   Travel, getting away from it all for a few days, and dealing in both long-range and long-distance matters are favored. If you can't get away, then change the way you travel to and from work, drop in at a popular restaurant, and retire early to dream of faraway places. Scorpio and Capricorn get high marks. Lucky lottery numbers: 1, 10, 19, 28, 37, 46.

Thursday, September 14 (Moon in Taurus to Gemini 5:48 p.m.)   Good news is perking for you at a distance. Taking in some new sights, writing letters, and phoning a relative long distance are all good possibilities. Another Virgo will join you in conversation concerning matters of the higher mind. Titian gold is your color; your lucky number is 3.

Friday, September 15 (Moon in Gemini)   Gemini may surprise you. This is a fine day for taking a great leap forward in your career. The more professional you are, the more your words and deeds will be appreciated. Dress a little more formally than the others. High and lofty ideas become you. Fuchsia is your color; your lucky number is 5.

Saturday, September 16 (Moon in Gemini)   Libra will help you appreciate your lot in life. Weekday work can spill over into today and keep you from doing what you want to do. If you run into a coworker at the mall or elsewhere, avoid discussing what is taking place at the plant or office. Lucky lottery numbers: 7, 16, 25, 34, 43, 1.

Sunday, September 17 (Moon in Gemini to Cancer 6:16 a.m.)   Talk social matters over with a Cancer and a Pisces. What has been escaping your attention can be brought up. You are going to learn things about friends and members of your club. Group activities bring the least pleasure. Reading gets high grades. Emerald is your color; your lucky number is 9.

Monday, September 18 (Moon in Cancer)   The social side of things takes precedence over business. There is much gossip making the rounds. You could encounter a person who tires you out by his or her mere presence. Older women intend to win, no matter what else is lost. Be cautious in your dealings with them. Azure blue is your color; your lucky number is 4.

Tuesday, September 19 (Moon in Cancer to Leo 6:19 p.m.)   There are many distractions and it would be well to ward off those that interfere with finishing your work on time. People tend to bring their private lives and social situations into work. Why do some people want to tell all about their most personal situations? Canary yellow is your color? Pick five: 6, 15, 24, 33, 42.

Wednesday, September 20 (Moon in Leo)   Leo makes a dramatic entrance and exit. You do well now where you are finishing up work that should be finished now, before you enter your lunar high cycle on the 22nd. You encounter people with superegos. It may be difficult to change the subject. Tawny beige and saffron yellow are your colors. Lucky lottery numbers: 8, 17, 26, 35, 44, 50.

Thursday, September 21 (Moon in Leo)   You can take on big organizations and institutions today. You could feel you have been overcharged. There is annoyance at the way everything seems to be increasing in price, yet quality doesn't seem to be as good as it used to be. Much is taking place behind the scenes. Your color is bay green; your lucky number is 1.

Friday, September 22 (Moon in Leo to Virgo 4:01 a.m.)   You are now in the most dynamic cycle of the month. Today, tomorrow, and the next day you can maneuver, shift, and change the direction of your goals. You can take over in any crisis. You can zero in on deteriorating circumstances and situations and improve the outlook. Your lucky number is 3.

Saturday, September 23 (Moon in Virgo)   Seize and hold the initiative. Lead, command, explain, investigate, and persuade. You'll have your own way if you are self-confident and self-reliant. Accent your natural persistence, endurance, patience and perseverence. Tell just enough, not too much. Lucky lottery numbers: 5, 14, 23, 32, 41, 8.

Sunday, September 24 (Moon in Virgo to Libra 10:50 a.m.)   The new moon illuminates your potential earning power and your overall wealth production. Your property is increasing in value, but be sure you aren't being cheated at the cash registers. The economy is a good topic of conversation, if you are in the presence of serious people. Your lucky number is 7.

Monday, September 25 (Moon in Libra)   You can increase your earnings under prevailing aspects, especially if you put your mind to it. Where the bargains are lurking is where you should be. It may be time to switch your shopping from one food market to another. Taurus is a good penny pincher and can tell you all about it. Your lucky number is 2.

Tuesday, September 26 (Moon in Libra to Scorpio 3:20 p.m.)   A talk with the big boss could provide you with some elusive information. You have to get all the facts before making a hard-and-fast decision about your employment and money generally. Is it time to take a few courses in order to keep up there with those who are better educated? Your lucky number is 4.

Wednesday, September 27 (Moon in Scorpio)   You can extract new gains from the local scene, from your own learning processes, and from those immediate and pressing obligations that you are meeting. Siblings and neighbors are in the know and will prove willing to help if you ask them direct questions. Black and white are your colors. Lucky lottery numbers: 6, 15, 24, 33, 42, 51.

Thursday, September 28 (Moon in Scorpio to Sagittarius 6:30 p.m.)   Scorpio and a Cancer have front seats. Narrow your sights and go for the dot in your employment target. Where you concentrate under this sky spectacle, you are not going to fall short of aspirations and desires. Your learning processes are activated. Wheat and pale gold are your colors; your lucky number is 8.

Friday, September 29 (Moon in Sagittarius)   Trust Sagittarius on a day like this. The family and its desires top your agenda. It's a good day for lawn and yard maintenance, and for attention to matters related to property, ownership, rents, mortgages, and leases. A community improvement plan could be organized well. Chartreuse is your color; your lucky number is 1.

Saturday, September 30 (Moon in Sagittarius to Capricorn 9:10 p.m.)   An Aries and a Leo figure prominently. Continue cleanup work that says good-bye to summer. Spectacular reddish-browns are your winning colors. Spend quality time with your children, instructing them in home and property maintenance matters. You will bond even more tightly with loved ones. Lucky lottery numbers: 3, 12, 21, 30, 39, 48.

OCTOBER 1995

Sunday, October 1 (Moon in Capricorn)   The day is ideal for you, bringing out your affectionate nature. You are pleased with those who have shown up. You see romance and adventure potential in your own surroundings. October's bright blue shades are going to win approval. Your lucky number is 3.

Monday, October 2 (Moon in Capricorn to Aquarius 11:59 p.m.)   Another Virgo is supportive, as you indulge yourself and compete where necessary. You know you can win under these aspects, so speak up in behalf of yourself. Your self-confidence is running interference for you in business, financial, and social matters. Old rose and browns are your colors; your lucky number is 7.

Tuesday, October 3 (Moon in Aquarius)   Aquarius adds to your pleasure. Work that others are shying away from may be just what you enjoy doing. There is a good payoff for preventive-medicine routines and for sticking with jobs that the boss wants finished. Watch your intake of unusual foods and liquids. Pistaschio green is your color; your lucky number is 9.

Wednesday, October 4 (Moon in Aquarius)   Stay in touch with shy, quiet, and self-effacing seniors, who may need a little attention from you. Know when your teenagers are pushing themselves too much. These are strange times in which people seek to prove themselves by putting their bodies to tests. Auburn is your color. Lucky lottery numbers: 2, 11, 20, 29, 38, 47.

Thursday, October 5 (Moon in Aquarius to Pisces 3:35 a.m.)   Pisces and a Cancer have key roles. More is gained through willing cooperation and a sense of sharing burdens than by any independent actions. The laws, conventions, and standards of behavior apply rigorously today. Beware of pity, for it can lead you into trouble. Pick five: 4, 13, 22, 31, 40.

Friday, October 6 (Moon in Pisces)   Duties, responsibilities, and obligations should be discussed and shared. Put feelers out about what possible reception your ideas will receive before actually pushing them on a partner. Questions, letter writing, and phone calls are all part of the developing picture. Apricot and plum are your colors; your lucky number is 6.

Saturday, October 7 (Moon in Pisces to Aries 8:41 a.m.) Discuss; be quiet and dignified while advancing ideas; and be willing to cooperate and consider alternatives. Teamwork requires compromise under these aspects. There are good trends for extracting quality time for you and your beloved from a rather busy day. Pinecone green is your color. Lucky lottery numbers: 8, 17, 26, 35, 44, 2.

Sunday, October 8 (Moon in Aries)   The full moon illuminates savings, investments, budgeting, and both the cost and the standard of living. Read business and sales pages of your newspaper. Is it time for you to use more coupons than is generally the case? There is enlightenment on new ways of saving cash. Whites and off-whites are right; your lucky number is 1.

Monday, October 9 (Moon in Aries to Taurus 4:05 p.m.)   Talks with your banker and broker may be in order. You are involved in savings, investments, overall security matters, and the progressive changes you can implement. The accent is on improvements and corrections all along the line of endeavor. Pumpkin is your color; your lucky number is 5.

Tuesday, October 10 (Moon in Taurus)   It's always a good idea to get away from the grind for a few days. You could take off now with a lot of self-confidence. Changing your scene gives a new sense of purpose and you will see your way around bottlenecks. Take the long-range view of everything. Emerald is your color; your lucky number is 7.

Wednesday, October 11 (Moon in Taurus)   Today is fine for seeing people at a distance, taking care of what is on the back burner, and extending your efforts in the interest of next month and next year. Another Virgo and a Capricorn can give you strong support. Your lucky colors are ecru and turquoise. Lucky lottery numbers: 9, 18, 27, 36, 45, 6.

Thursday, October 12 (Moon in Taurus to Gemini 2:10 a.m.)   Count Gemini in. You can make good headway in your career and use authority well, so that it rebounds to your benefit. Professional, status, and prestige matters get high marks. Talk things over with your supervisor and don't step on the toes of touchy coworkers. Your lucky number is 2.

Friday, October 13 (Moon in Gemini)   Gemini will tell you all about the old traditional superstitions connected with a Friday the thirteenth. In the Orient, it's ten-ten day, or October 10th, that gets the attention. You can advance in your career if you keep your nose to the grindstone. Plum is your color; your lucky number is 4.

Saturday, October 14 (Moon in Gemini to Cancer 2:20 p.m.)   Libra and Aquarius have front seats. Cash in on your good reputation and your earned status and prestige under these aspects. Work done much earlier in life may suddenly seem important again. Assistance isn't all it should be today. Lucky lottery numbers: 6, 15, 24, 33, 42, 9.

Sunday, October 15 (Moon in Cancer)   A Cancer and a Scorpio are especially friendly. You want to spend part of the day with kindred spirits. Church and club involvements can encroach on your leisure time. Phone friends who have been coping with difficulties. Your winning colors are dove gray and white; your lucky number is 8.

Monday, October 16 (Moon in Cancer)   You could find some coworkers who are trying to be too friendly. There are some nosy types who want to know more about you and what you do away from work. You can become annoyed because you respect your own privacy so much. Is it time to leave one group or clique and make your way into a new one? Your lucky number is 3.

Tuesday, October 17 (Moon in Cancer to Leo 2:46 a.m.) Trust Leo to add it all up accurately. You are empowered to extract more gains from past experiences and situations. Former neighbors may wish you would phone and arrange a meeting. That old chestnut about what goes around coming around again is in the picture. Reddish browns are your colors; your lucky number is 5.

Wednesday, October 18 (Moon in Leo) An Aquarius and an Aries may have the information and the explanations. Today is fine for settling old debts and finishing up odd chores, which are generally overlooked and delayed. Try to recall what this day should mean to you. It would be easy to overlook a birthday or other special day under these aspects. Lucky lottery numbers: 7, 16, 25, 34, 43, 40.

Thursday, October 19 (Moon in Leo to Virgo 11:11 a.m.) Take care of all usual and everyday tasks and be out from under them before the eclipse patterns of the 24th. Know what is going on in the lives of your siblings; you may be able to help them in some sort of emergency. A Sagittarius is the one in question. Acorn brown is your color; your lucky number is 9.

Friday, October 20 (Moon in Virgo) Today and tomorrow constitute your lunar-cycle high, when you can force things your way. You are persuasive, silver-tongued, and offer a trustworthy sense of comfort that appeals to others. People want peace of mind, and you are able to produce this for them. Mocha is your color; your lucky number is 2.

Saturday, October 21 (Moon in Virgo to Libra 8:15 p.m.) Step lively so that you can get a lot of things done today. Encourage and guide assistants and double your production. This is a fine day for letting the world see you at your best. Speak up in your own behalf. If you look rich and royal, fate will make you that way. Lucky lottery numbers: 4, 13, 22, 31, 40, 47.

Sunday, October 22 (Moon in Libra)   You come up with good ideas to apply your basic earning power. The financial pages of your newspaper hold some special and pertinent information for you. Libra comes front and center and you want just what is your due, no more and no less. Your colors are eggshell and peach; your lucky number is 6.

Monday, October 23 (Moon in Libra)   Today is not good for travel or for forcing your opinions and ideas on others. There are no changes right now, with a total solar eclipse coming up tomorrow. Be especially careful what you say in front of children. The neighborhood gossip is out and in action. Yellow and auburn are winning colors; your lucky number is 1.

Tuesday, October 24 (Moon in Libra to Scorpio 12:07 a.m.)   A total solar eclipse can pressure travel, communications, learning processes, and relations with siblings and neighbors. The local scene is confusing. Studies, hobbies, and immediate and pressing matters are blacked out. Make no changes today. Chocolate and white are your colors; your lucky number is 3.

Wednesday, October 25 (Moon in Scorpio)   This is not a day for passion, wierd sexual practices, or real understanding between the genders or races. All local travel is pressured in the wake of the eclipse. It would be easy to become involved with the wrong people, including strangers. Plumbing, flooding, and other water troubles are possible. Lucky lottery numbers: 5, 14, 23, 32, 41, 11.

Thursday, October 26 (Moon in Scorpio to Sagittarius 1:56 a.m.)   Sagittarius tends to clear the atmosphere of misunderstandings and recriminations. Travel is still under a warning light. The family expects you to give total attention, even when your job also is demanding. Be as cheerful and diplomatic as possible. Cherry and deep pink are your colors; your lucky number is 7.

Friday, October 27 (Moon in Sagittarius)   Home is where your heart is today. Spend as much quality time as possible with your beloved and other members of your immediate family. All that you have put into your home in the past year is paying handsome dividends in comfort and pleasure. Purple and rust are winning colors; your lucky number is 9.

Saturday, October 28 (Moon in Sagittarius to Capricorn 3:15 a.m.) Everything is right in your world now and Capricorn and another Virgo will assure you of this. Today is fine for rewarding sex, for attaining magnificent ecstasy, and for seeing the romance and adventure potential of the day and weekend. Be imaginative, original, flexible, and willing. Lucky lottery numbers: 2, 11, 20, 29, 38, 47.

Sunday, October 29 (Moon in Capricorn; Daylight Saving Time Ends) Speak up, let those present know what you believe and want. Push your personal public relations and advertising. Spruce up your appearance so that you stand out. Champagne and canary yellow are winning colors. You are loving and loved under the existing trends. The romance of autumn excites you. Your lucky number is 4.

Monday, October 30 (Moon in Capricorn to Aquarius 4:23 a.m.) Aquarius and Libra are interested in your opinion. It's an excellent day to help loved ones and those people you want to impress with your special skills and talents. Buy special clothing for winter sports and travel needs. Don't disappoint those in charge. Your lucky number is 8.

Tuesday, October 31 (Moon in Aquarius) If work has been piling up, this is a good cycle for tackling it. Arise early to be on the job before the others. Stick with tasks until the very end. You can improve your image in the workplace now. A future increase in salary could be conceived today. Your lucky number is 1.

NOVEMBER 1995

Wednesday, November 1 (Moon in Aquarius to Pisces 8:17 a.m.) Stick to usual preventive-medicine routines. Work can be piling up and you may conclude that your help is not worth much. There is a silent cry coming your way for more freedom of expression. Someone may see you as too set in your ways and apt to overlook alternatives. Lucky lottery numbers: 9, 18, 27, 36, 45, 1.

Thursday, November 2 (Moon in Pisces) Pisces and Cancer are in the picture. You blend and meld. You identify with your beloved. This is a fine day for honoring all contracts, agreements, obligations, and responsibilities. Marriage, as well as business sharing and cooperating, get high grades. Legal and public relations matters are favored. Your lucky number is 2.

Friday, November 3 (Moon in Pisces to Aries 2:21 p.m.) You are warming up to household, lawn, and yard tasks. Aries has some good ideas about how to tear down and then rebuild around your place. But new ways presented to you may not be to your liking, since traditional views are now most important to you. Pumpkin is your color. Pick five: 4, 13, 22, 31, 40.

Saturday, November 4 (Moon in Aries) Push savings, investments, financial improvements and corrections. Leo and Sagittarius have key roles. Make changes in routines that are more in line with fall than summer. Today is fine for giving bushes, shrubbery, and trees a good once-over. Buy seasonal bargains. Lucky lottery numbers: 6, 15, 24, 33, 42, 4.

Sunday, November 5 (Moon in Aries to Taurus 10:35 p.m.) Work on kitchen and business-hour budgets. The desire to save a little more is particularly strong. Investments may be ripe for some changes. Your urge to have more cash at the end of each month was never stronger. Members of the family must be encouraged to cooperate on the cost of living. Your lucky number is 8.

Monday, November 6 (Moon in Taurus) Travel, a brief respite from the job, and a sense of escape are dominant trends. Taurus and another Virgo are in the picture. Excellent trends exist where you are on the go, doing a little sightseeing, changing your scene and your attitude. It's not a bad idea to be alone for a while. Old rose is your color; Your lucky number is 3.

Tuesday, November 7 (Moon in Taurus)   The full moon illuminates the travel you are doing and the travel you want to do. Study travel folders. View the movies a friend brought back from a trip earlier in the year. Long-range and long-distance matters will empower you to reach out for more joy and delight. Pick five: 5, 14, 23, 32, 41.

Wednesday, November 8 (Moon in Taurus to Gemini 8:55 a.m.)   You tend to be rather possessive of what you know and of what you have just learned. Some may say you are closemouthed. Even so, you are probably saving the feelings of some older people. Phone, write letters, but don't let off steam when things slow down. Lucky lottery numbers: 7, 16, 25, 34, 43, 17.

Thursday, November 9 (Moon in Gemini)   Give Gemini and Libra all the latitude they need and they will work miracles in your favor. Talk things over rather than merely finding fault. Past studies and hobby interests are coming back in focus and can help you solve some problems. Sky blue and baby pink are winning colors; your lucky number is 9.

Friday, November 10 (Moon in Gemini to Cancer 8:57 p.m.)   Aquarius is in your corner. You can take a great leap forward in your career and, as a result, be given more responsibility on the job. It would be easy for you to please your employer now, when your hard work and remarkable endurance are in evidence. Violet is your color; your lucky number is 2.

Saturday, November 11 (Moon in Cancer)   You are in a remarkable period when friendship brings joy, delight, and plenty of approval, affection, and appreciation. You enjoy being with kindred spirits, but even with new acquaintances you feel very much at home. You want to please, to be noticed, to be loved. Lucky lottery numbers: 4, 13, 22, 31, 40, 7.

Sunday, November 12 (Moon in Cancer)   See people who boost your morale. Phone and ask some dear friends to come over and perhaps bring one of their friends you haven't met. You feel very much a part of life, or the clique, and want to spread sunshine and good cheer. Your welcome mat is golden. Your lucky number is 6.

Monday, November 13 (Moon in Cancer to Leo 9:37 a.m.)   It's a good day for talking things over rather than pushing ahead alone. Friendships are like money in the bank at a time like this. Keep in touch with water-sign people (Cancer, Scorpio, and Pisces) who have been helpful before. Stay out in front for best results. Your lucky number is 1.

Tuesday, November 14 (Moon in Leo)   Leo has something to tell you. There are projects that should be completed today even if you let other things go. Old doors must be closed before new ones can be opened. The angry reds are your colors. You deal well today with large organizations and people with big egos. Your lucky number is 3.

Wednesday, November 15 (Moon in Leo to Virgo 9:02 p.m.)   Deal in completions and epilogues, but at the same time keep in mind that after finales come new beginnings. An Aries and a Sagittarius are in your corner. What is going on behind the scenes is going to influence your day more than you realized. Apricot is your color. Lucky lottery numbers: 5, 14, 23, 32, 41, 11.

Thursday, November 16 (Moon in Virgo)   Today and tomorrow constitute your lunar high cycle when you serve all of November's upcoming interests in a first-class way. Others will defer to your good sense and your reasonable requests and suggestions. Be outgoing, cheerful, and self-reliant. Hot combination numbers: 7 and 25.

Friday, November 17 (Moon in Virgo)   Let those around you know about your ambitions and aspirations. Lead, organize, reorganize, doing what you are sure will keep you in the lead. There is a strong feeling, really intuitive, of what must be done and of what can be postponed.

Don't fail your friends. Red is your color; your lucky number is 9.

Saturday, November 18 (Moon in Virgo to Libra 5:18 a.m.) Libra has the financial information. Push your earning power; run down new sources of capital; and make sure you are using your skills, tools, appliances, and knowledge to the fullest, perhaps in a secondary source of income. Your colors are ecru and russet. Lucky lottery numbers: 2, 11, 20, 29, 38, 47.

Sunday, November 19 (Moon in Libra) You can come to pretty accurate financial conclusions now. What can you sell that will bring in a little cash for the upcoming holidays? Sales, advertising, talking financial matters over with a Gemini are all good possibilities. Justice must be your guiding sentinel. Your lucky number is 4.

Monday, November 20 (Moon in Libra to Scorpio 9:40 a.m.) Financial conferences, seminars, and on-the-job training are favored. You can increase your take in a project that is just getting under way. The more organized you are now, the more money you are going to acquire. Write business letters, phone for information. Your lucky number is 8.

Tuesday, November 21 (Moon in Scorpio) Scorpio comes on deck. Everyday interests, the usual, the familiar, your learning processes, siblings, and neighbors are all in focus. Information is there for you to pick up by listening and observing. Studies and hobbies will pay off. Your colors are lavender and beige; your lucky number is 1.

Wednesday, November 22 (Moon in Scorpio to Sagittarius 10:56 a.m.) The new moon illuminates the local scene, as well as all immediate and pressing matters. You know where to go and how to get there today. A Pisces and a Cancer are on your side. Communicate cautiously so that you will not be misinterpreted or misquoted. Mischief is the word. Lucky lottery numbers: 3, 12, 21, 30, 39, 48.

Thursday, November 23 (Moon in Sagittarius)   It's a definite Sagittarius day, when you can share outdoor interests with your loved ones. Weather permitting, light a fire in your fireplace for that auld lang syne family feeling. Invite relatives, long-term friends, and good old neighbors to your warmth. Your lucky number is 5.

Friday, November 24 (Moon in Sagittarius to Capricorn 10:48 a.m.)   Home maintenance matters are favored. Get estimates of any work that has to be done. The community may be having too much to say about its revival and rehabilitation—call in the experts. There is a trend of good luck where you are dealing with vitally important matters. Lapis blue is your color; your lucky number is 7.

Saturday, November 25 (Moon in Capricorn)   Capricorn and another Virgo have the inside track. This is a perfect day to make love. There is a lot of romance and a spirit of adventure in the air. Entertain spontaneously and invite the most exciting types you know. Talks with your parents and children will go well. Lucky lottery numbers: 9, 18, 27, 36, 45, 13.

Sunday, November 26 (Moon in Capricorn to Aquarius 11:15 a.m.)   Relax with your beloved. Your children may have special questions to ask you. Parties, entertainments, spontaneity are in the picture. You want to spend time with those who give you approval, appreciation, respect, and affection. Keep your doors open to sentimental types. Your lucky number is 2.

Monday, November 27 (Moon in Aquarius)   Aquarius is in the picture. Push for improvements in your overall well-being. Avoid the overadvertised and high-blown diets. If you want to lose a few pounds, walk a few more miles a day and decrease your intake of food at each meal. People can get on your nerves at work. Your lucky number is 6.

Tuesday, November 28 (Moon in Aquarius to Pisces 1:59 p.m.)   You can catch up on any work that has been neglected or postponed, but ward off the pleasant distractions that can come your way this afternoon. Read health, medical, and nutritional literature. You could find yourself buttonholed by a boring person. Pick five: 8, 17, 26, 35, 44.

Wednesday, November 29 (Moon in Pisces)   Pisces has your good at heart, but may be slow to point this out. Marriage, business partnerships, your public image, and all legal and public relations matters are illuminated. You can make spectacular progress if you relate to another and work in harmony with partners. Lucky lottery numbers: 1, 10, 19, 28, 37, 46.

Thursday, November 30 (Moon in Pisces to Aries 7:51 p.m.   Share, cooperate, consider the feelings of your beloved. Kindness and courtesy will pay handsome dividends under existing aspects. Heart-to-heart and pillow-to-pillow talks will produce the desired ends. A Scorpio and a Cancer have key roles. You advance because of the help you receive. Your lucky number is 3.

DECEMBER 1995

Friday, December 1 (Moon in Aries)   Figure out just how much money you have to spend on the upcoming holidays. Work on household, seasonal, and holiday budgets. Resolve to learn where the bargains are. You have good opportunities to bring about changes that will make for a sense of unity later on in the month. Cinnamon is your color; your lucky number is 3.

Saturday, December 2 (Moon in Aries)   You can make good headway on household chores and holiday decorations under prevailing aspects. Work from lists and begin addressing holiday greeting cards. Discuss the personal wishes of relatives, and try to leave some slack in your arrangements to meet unanticipated changes. Lucky lottery numbers: 5, 14, 23, 32, 41, 2.

Sunday, December 3 (Moon in Aries to Taurus 4:40 a.m.) Taurus and another Virgo will prove helpful. Mail cards that have to travel a long way. Shop for presents for people at a distance. Phone, write letters, with the high aim of letting others know that you care. Start seasonal jobs that can be returned to again and again. Beet red is your color; your lucky number is 7.

Monday, December 4 (Moon in Taurus)   Mail gifts that have to travel a considerable distance. Long-range matters also get the green light. Capricorn is interested in your opinions about mutual friends. Information and special news can arrive. Somebody may come across to you as overly critical. Your lucky number is 2.

Tuesday, December 5 (Moon in Taurus to Gemini 3:35 p.m.)   You could give others the impression that you are overly possessive of what you own and of what you know. News from a distance can arrive and change your view of things. Plan your month ahead under these favorable aspects but leave room for changes around the 20th. Hot combination numbers: 4 and 31.

Wednesday, December 6 (Moon in Gemini)   Gemini has the creative ideas. You tend to say and do the right things, which holds you in good stead with the air signs (Aquarius, Libra, and Gemini.) Your winning colors are turquoise and blue. Lucky lottery numbers: 6, 15, 24, 33, 42, 12.

Thursday, December 7 (Moon in Gemini)   The full moon illuminates career matters and gives you ideas about coping with problems on the job and dealing with higher-ups. You can take a bird's-eye view of your career potential this afternoon. You can build high on your earned reputation. Hot combination numbers: 8 and 35.

Friday, December 8 (Moon in Gemini to Cancer 3:44 a.m.)   A Cancer and a Scorpio have a good opinion of your efforts. It's an excellent day for advancing in your career via the social side of your job. Your employer appreciates all that you do to develop teamwork. Socializing on the grand scale would go well this evening. Hot combination numbers 1 and 10.

Saturday, December 9 (Moon in Cancer)   Talk things over with a Scorpio and a Cancer. This is a fine day for immersing yourself in the holiday—putting up your tree and your outdoor and indoor lights, mailing gifts and greeting cards, and, if there is still time, doing a little shopping. Friends would love to meet you at the mall. Angry reds are in. Lucky lottery numbers: 3, 12, 21, 30, 39, 48.

Sunday, December 10 (Moon in Cancer to Leo 4:24 p.m.)   Today is fine for church and club and other organizational affairs. Annual charitable events, special committee meetings, and doing your humanitarian bit in line with seasonal trends. Buy gifts for coworkers. Your lucky number is 5. Gemini and Aquarius have key roles.

Monday, December 11 (Moon in Leo)   Invite a Leo to help you finish some plans that involve many people including some who aren't present. What you owe certain older people, younger people, handicapped and homeless folk, and all that can be done for them behind the scenes is favored. Amber and canary are your colors; your lucky number is 9.

Tuesday, December 12 (Moon in Leo)   Capricorn has something to tell you. It's an excellent day to deal with large organizations and institutions and to learn what is happening behind the scenes. Quietude reigns and you can do some really helpful and meaningful thinking. Close old doors so that new ones can be opened. Your lucky number is 2.

Wednesday, December 13 (Moon in Leo to Virgo 4:26 a.m.) Today, tomorrow, and the next day are among your most meaningful days this month. You are in your lunar-cycle high when you can catch up, breeze ahead, get all important shows on the road, and successfully bring pressure on the malingerers and laggards. Wear a little gray. Lucky lottery numbers: 4, 13, 22, 31, 40, 10.

Thursday, December 14 (Moon in Virgo)   Arise early, hold the initiative, and take the lead. Others will get out of your way. It will be easy to win people over to your view point. Push your natural Virgo assets for all they are worth—your practicality, determination, and persistence. Hot combination numbers: 6 and 15.

Friday, December 15 *(Moon in Virgo to Libra 2:09 p.m.)*   Stand tall, airing your aspirations with confidence and self-reliance. Stick up for what you believe. Earn the respect of the opposition by refusing to be quiet when you spot waste in government and elsewhere. Let those in Washington know that you are counting the lies and broken promises. Hot combination numbers: 8 and 35.

Saturday, December 16 *(Moon in Libra)*   You can make some extra money today via a special sale, successful advertising, taking on a few hours extra work, and putting your special skills, tools, and financial ideas to work. What you own is increasing in value. Some pre-holiday sales should be honored. Lucky lottery numbers: 1, 10, 19, 28, 37, 46.

Sunday, December 17 *(Moon in Libra to Scorpio 8:07 p.m.)*   This is a good money day and a fine series of hours when you experience nonfinancial payoffs. Good work done in the distant past can be honored today. You can extract some gains based on the goodwill you've been spreading. Libra and Gemini have key roles. Magenta and red are your colors; your lucky number is 3.

Monday, December 18 *(Moon in Scorpio)*   Take care of small, miniscule, detail matters. Studies, hobbies, transportation, and communications get their due. Siblings and neighbors have the conversation potential you are looking for. A Scorpio and a Cancer figure prominently. What you seek is under your nose and at your elbow. Indigo and red are your colors; your lucky number is 7.

Tuesday, December 19 *(Moon in Scorpio to Sagittarius 10:13 p.m.)*   Good trends exist in learning processes, working on arts and crafts for children, taking part in a children's story hour, and generally bringing the holiday spirit down to earth for the little folk. Students, schools, and faculty are hoping to be remembered by you. Ecru and snow are winners; your lucky number is 9.

Wednesday, December 20 (Moon in Sagittarius)   Sagittarius comes forward. Family, home, special cooking, baking, and preserving are represented. You could hear from an almost-forgotten source. The great outdoors beckons and you will enjoy driving about and seeing all the holiday lights. Cherry and claret red are winning colors. Lucky lottery numbers: 2, 11, 20, 29, 38, 47.

Thursday, December 21 (Moon in Sagittarius to Capricorn 9:46 p.m.)   Real estate, property, and ownership matters dominate. Amid all the glamour, some point of deterioration may be observed in the physical plant of your home. Plan home maintenance work for the spring of 1996. Know what the members of your immediate family want from your Christmas tree. Your lucky number is 4.

Friday, December 22 (Moon in Capricorn)   The new moon illuminates family, home, community, property, ownership, and ancestral matters. You're of the clan, the tribe, and you sense links to distant past and future. Universal rules and laws must be honored. You feel very much a part of present-day society. Red, white, and blue are your colors; your lucky number is 6.

Saturday, December 23 (Moon in Capricorn to Aquarius 8:52 p.m.)   Immersed in the holiday spirit, you love and are loved. The romance of all the old traditions are warming your heart. The children's sense of adventure catches you. Somehow, having Christmas Eve on Sunday seems to make everything easier for you. Make love this evening. Flesh and coral are your colors. Lucky lottery numbers: 8, 17, 26, 35, 44, 20.

Sunday, December 24 (Moon in Aquarius)   A perfect Eve of Christmas when you can relax and avoid the crowds of strangers. You'll want to remain with your family and dearest friends at this time. Though Aquarius is all for a party, don't permit any part of the day to involve more work. Stay free, outgoing, cheerful. Your lucky number is 1.

Monday, December 25 (Moon in Aquarius to Pisces 9:45 p.m.)   One of the gifts on your tree is a new flair for

279

independence. You want to spend more time with kindred spirits who really understand you and less with the critics and whiners. The day offers you opportunities for your Virgo skills, but do so only where they promote inner joy. Your lucky number is 5.

Tuesday, December 26 (Moon in Pisces) Pisces deserves your assistance, understanding, and special consideration. Marriage, other types of teamwork, legal and public relations interests get the green lights. Write thank-you notes but avoid the big mad sales. Peace of mind is what you are searching for and you can find it. Off white is your color. Hot combination numbers: 7 and 34.

Wednesday, December 27 (Moon in Pisces) Maroon and scarlet are inviting colors. A Scorpio and a Cancer offer true understanding. Invite an easygoing, but enchanting friend to meet you at a special type of restaurant, perhaps one specializing in grand fish casseroles. You want to relax and just talk. Lucky lottery numbers: 9, 18, 27, 36, 45, 15.

Thursday, December 28 (Moon in Pisces to Aries 2:06 a.m.) Aries and Leo want to see you. There are some good trends related to savings and ways in which you can increase your holdings during the year ahead. Investments come in for a review and a chat with your broker won't go amiss. The cost and standard of living seem up for grabs. Titian gold is your color; your lucky number is 2.

Friday, December 29 (Moon in Aries) Some real savings can be realized under prevailing star trends. You can please others by warring on waste and setting the pace for wider living. What changes have you in mind for the year ahead? Write them down now and try to figure out ways to make them more promising and more realistic. Hot combination numbers: 4 and 22.

Saturday, December 30 (Moon in Aries to Taurus 10:21 a.m.) Persistence and patience will pay off in any confrontation with an aggressive person. Let critics and challengers scream and rage. A quiet mien and quiet words will turn away all wrath. You gain because you bring knowledge and proved facts to the table. You can end the year on strong achievement. Lucky lottery numbers: 6, 15, 24, 33, 42, 30.

Sunday, December 31 (Moon in Taurus)   Your thoughts can wander and be far away as the year ends. You can possess strongly the promise of 1996, but changes made at a distance can impact your earning power and belongings. Taurus and Capricorn are strongly persuasive; and you feel much as they do about a very earthy New Year's Eve. Your lucky number is 8.

ABOUT THIS SERIES

This is one of a series of
twelve Day-by-Day Astrological Guides
for the signs in 1995
by Sydney Omarr

ABOUT THE AUTHOR

Born on August 5, 1926, in Philadelphia, Omarr was the only person ever given full-time duty in the U.S. Army as an astrologer. He also is regarded as the most erudite astrologer of our time and the best known, through his syndicated column (300 newspapers) and his radio and television programs (he is Merv Griffin's "resident astrologer"). Omarr has been called the most "knowledgeable astrologer since Evangeline Adams." His forecasts of Nixon's downfall, the end of World War II in mid-August of 1945, the assassination of John F. Kennedy, Roosevelt's election to the fourth term and his death in office ... these and many others are on record and quoted enough to be considered "legendary."

The Most Important Money/Power/Romantic-Love Discovery Since The Industrial Revolution © 1994

Receive Free — The valuable, 8000-word Neo-Tech Information Package

An entire new field of knowledge has been discovered by Dr. Frank R. Wallace, a former Senior Research Chemist for E.I. du Pont de Nemours & Co. For over a decade, Dr. Wallace researched Psychuous Advantages to uncover a powerful array of new knowledge called Neo-Tech. That new knowledge allows any person to prosper monetarily, personally, romantically, and financially anywhere in the world, even during personal or financial hard times, inflation, boom times, recession, depression, war.

Neo-Tech is a new, scientific method for capturing major financial and personal advantages everywhere. Neo-Tech is a new knowledge that has nothing to do with positive thinking, religion, or anything mystical. Once a person is exposed to Neo-Tech, he can quietly profit from anyone — anywhere, anytime. He can prosper almost anywhere on earth and succeed under almost any economic or political condition. Combined with Psychuous Advantages, Neo-Tech applies to all money and power gathering techniques — to all situations involving the transfer of money, power, or love.

Neo-Tech has its roots in the constant financial pressures and incentives to develop the easiest, most profitable methods of gaining advantages. Over the decades, all successful salesmen, businessmen, politicians, writers, lawyers, entrepreneurs, investors, speculators, gamers and Casanovas have secretly searched for shortcuts that require little skill yet contain the invisible effectiveness of the most advanced techniques. Dr. Wallace identified those shortcuts and honed them into practical formats called Neo-Tech. Those never-before-known formats transfer money, power, and prestige from the uninformed to the informed. Those informed can automatically take control of most situations involving money and power.

Who is The Neo-Tech Man?

He is a man of quiet power — a man who cannot lose. He can extract money at will. He can control anyone unknowledgeable about Neo-Tech — man or woman.

The Neo-Tech man has the power to render others helpless, even wipe them out, but he wisely chooses to use just enough of his power to give himself unbeatable casino-like advantages in all his endeavors for maximum long-range profits. His Neo-Tech maneuvers are so subtle that they can be executed with casual confidence. His hidden techniques let him win consistently and comfortably — year after year, decade after decade. Eventually, Neo-Tech men and women will quietly rule everywhere.

The Neo-Tech man can easily and safely beat any opponent. He can quickly impoverish anyone he chooses. He can immediately and consistently acquire large amounts of money. He has the power to make more money in a week than most people without Neo-Tech make in a full year. He commands profits and respect. He controls business deals and emotional situations to acquire money and power...and to command love. He can regain lost love. He can subjugate a business or personal adversary. He wins any lover at will. He can predict stock prices — even gold and silver prices. He quietly rules all.

Within a week, an ordinary person can become a professional Neo-Tech practitioner. As people gain this knowledge, they will immediately begin using its techniques because they are irresistibly easy and overwhelmingly potent. Within days after gaining this knowledge, a person can safely bankrupt opponents — or slowly profit from them, week after week. He can benefit from business and investment endeavors — from dealing with the boss to the biggest oil deal. He can also benefit from any relationship — from gaining the respect of peers to inducing love from a partner or regaining lost love from an ex-partner. He will gain easy money and power in business, investments, the professions, politics, and personal life.

Indeed, with Neo-Tech, a person not only captures unbeatable advantages over others, but commands shortcuts to profits, power, and romance. The ordinary person can quickly become a Clark Kent — a quiet superman — taking command of all. He can financially and emotionally control whomever he deals with. He becomes the man-on-the-hill, now. He is armed with an unbeatable weapon. All will yield to the new-breed Neo-Tech man, the no-limit man. ...All except the Neo-Tech man will die unfulfilled...without ever knowing wealth, power, and romantic love.

ARE YOU DESTINED FOR TRUE LOVE?
ASK ME ABOUT LOVE FAME FORTUNE
"I CAN TELL YOU WHAT THE FUTURE HOLDS"
DISCOVER YOUR SECRET DESTINY!
CALL NOW!
Talk LIVE with America's leading professional Psychics and Astrologers.
1-800-693-SEER
(7337)
Call anytime. Open 24 hours! $3.99 per minute.
Must be 18+. For entertainment purposes only.

AMAZING PSYCHIC PREDICTIONS

*Now you too can experience the **Astonishing Accuracy** of the world's most gifted psychics!*

Discover *YOUR* Destiny! Ask About
LOVE • SUCCESS • MONEY
LIVE ANSWERS TO ALL YOUR QUESTIONS!

1-800-510-TELL
(8 3 5 5)